Methods of Money Laundering

Methods of Money Laundering

Circumventing Anti-Money Laundering Mechanisms

Fabian Teichmann

Wolters Kluwer

Published by:
Kluwer Law International B.V.
PO Box 316
2400 AH Alphen aan den Rijn
The Netherlands
E-mail: international-sales@wolterskluwer.com
Website: lrus.wolterskluwer.com

Sold and distributed by:
Wolters Kluwer Legal & Regulatory U.S.
7201 McKinney Circle
Frederick, MD 21704
United States of America
E-mail: customer.service@wolterskluwer.com

ISBN 978-94-035-3723-8

e-Book: ISBN 978-94-035-3743-6
web-PDF: ISBN 978-94-035-3764-1

'Methoden der Geldwäscherei 2. Auflage' is published by Schulthess Juristische Medien AG, Zurich - Basel - Geneva 2021

ISBN 978-3-7255-8285-3
www.schulthess.com

Table of Contents

About the Author

Fabian M. Teichmann is a lawyer and notary public in Switzerland. After obtaining a Bachelor of Science in Economics and Finance from Bocconi University in Italy, he obtained Master's in Management (Harvard University, USA), Law and Accounting and Finance (University of St Gallen, Switzerland). He also holds Doctorates in Law from the University of Zurich (Switzerland) and in Economics and Social Sciences from the University of Kassel (Germany). Dr Teichmann obtained his LLM from King's College London (UK). In addition to his work as a lawyer and notary, he teaches courses on compliance issues, corruption, money laundering and terrorist financing at various universities in Germany and abroad. He is also the author of several monographs and more than hundred academic articles.

Preface and Acknowledgements

This is the slightly expanded and updated edition of my dissertation published in 2016 entitled *Umgehungsmöglichkeiten der Geldwäschereipräventionsmassnahmen.* This revised edition is published under a new title because, unlike the dissertation, it is no longer primarily aimed at academics but at practitioners, which the additions take into account. Nevertheless, care was taken not to compromise the scientific nature of the work.

By way of introduction, I would like to thank Prof. Dr Dr h.c. Hans-Heiner Kühne, who has significantly shaped and promoted my academic career. I would also like to thank numerous colleagues, academics, practitioners and students who have encouraged me to write this book. Countless expert discussions have provided valuable suggestions for this expanded new edition.

I would also like to express my special thanks to Prof. Dr Dr h.c. Martin Killias, who spontaneously encouraged me to write my dissertation on possibilities of circumventing money laundering prevention measures and subsequently supervised my work with extraordinary commitment as my first supervisor. I would also like to thank Prof. Dr Daniel Jositsch, who, despite his myriad commitments as a member of the Council of States, agreed to be my second supervisor. I would also like to take this opportunity to thank Dr Giangly Isenring, Anastasiia Lukash and Lorenz Biberstein for their active support in implementing the empirical study.

Furthermore, I would like to emphasize that the present work would not have been possible without the expert and keen support of the interview partners. For reasons of discretion, I am not allowed to mention the interview partners by name. However, I look forward to embracing further opportunities for cooperation and exchanges of ideas.

I would also like to thank the Swiss Association of Compliance Officers and its honorary president, Urs Bigger, as well as another anonymous partner for their support, as they enabled access to a large number of compliance experts for the quantitative study. This significantly increased the validity of this study.

Finally, I would like to thank my research assistant, Marie-Christin Falker, and Urs Watter from Schulthess Juristische Medien AG. Marie-Christin Falker provided me with significant support in updating and expanding the book. Urs Watter has enthusiastically and consistently pushed the new edition forward from the publishing side.

The present edition is also dedicated to my family, who made it possible for me to study abroad and subsequently complete a doctorate. It should be mentioned in particular that my great-grandparents and grandparents sacrificed a large part of their lives to ensure that this opportunity would be available to me and to future generations. This book is therefore dedicated to Max Zeiller and my other ancestors.

Fabian Teichmann
St Gallen/Zurich, February 2021

CHAPTER 1

Introduction

The media prophesy the end of the letterbox company and consider this a decisive step in the fight against money laundering. New registers are to make the ownership structures of companies and foundations more transparent.[1] According to the Fourth Anti-money Laundering Directive of the European Union, authorities with a legitimate interest should be able to inspect these registers.[2] Nevertheless, according to media reports, money laundering remains a serious problem in Switzerland. Banks in particular are facing criticism.[3] A linking of national registers at the level of the European Union is planned and should help to fight not only money laundering but also tax fraud.[4] However, it is questionable whether these registers are actually suitable for combating money laundering. Through the use of frontmen,[5] beneficial owners' true identities can still be concealed.[6] Furthermore, it should be noted that many companies suitable for money laundering do not appear suspicious at first glance; thus, inclusion in a register would not pose a problem for some of them. It should also be explicitly mentioned here that money launderers are not necessarily dependent on letterbox companies and foundations. Therefore, it can be assumed that these registers could at most lead money laundering to shift into other areas.[7] The Fifth Anti-money Laundering Directive now deals with the provision of services involving digital currencies in order to counteract this shift.[8]

However, at least the reports made to the Swiss Money Laundering Reporting Office (MLRO) are often considered effective in the fight against money laundering.

1. Tagesschau, 2015.
2. Neue Zürcher Zeitung, 2014.
3. Finews, 2021; Schumacher & Bossard, 2021.
4. Reuters, 2015.
5. In this book, the generic masculine is used for better readability. Female and other gender identities are explicitly included as far as it is necessary for the statement.
6. Teichmann, 2016b; Teichmann, 2016c; *see also* Salmen, 2021; Teichmann & Falker, 2020f; Teichmann, 2020d; Teichmann & Camprubi, 2019.
7. Teichmann, 2017h.
8. Jourová, 2018.

The number of reports has increased significantly in recent years.[9] However, this should also be put into perspective, considering various sectors are not subject to reporting requirements.[10] For example, the art trade is characterized by non-transparent pricing and a lack of identification obligations.[11] Thus, an increase in reports does not mean that money laundering is impossible in Switzerland. On the contrary, it can be assumed that financial intermediaries are increasingly becoming more conscientious in fulfilling their reporting obligations. This could be due, among other things, to the sometimes-draconian penalties for money laundering offences. However, it still seems to be possible to engage in money laundering through supposedly reputable financial intermediaries abroad. European financial intermediaries operating in Eastern Europe, in particular, seem to be popular with money launderers. While it is true that individual states are taking stronger actions against money laundering, ultimately, money is very mobile.[12]

It should also be mentioned that many industries are not sufficiently regulated to make money laundering significantly more difficult. For example, the real estate market in London seems to be a ‘paradise’ for money laundering.[13] The same is probably true for cities in Spain and South Africa.[14] This is often due to the fact that money launderers evade the existing rules and look for new fields of activity. Even new regulations can only remedy this to a limited extent, as money launderers are usually not bound by parliamentary decision-making processes and can thus react much more quickly and flexibly than governments. In the worst case, money launderers would be forced to move abroad because of new legislative measures. Therefore, the logic behind stricter anti-money laundering regulations and their costly implementation can be critically questioned. Ultimately, money laundering can be made more difficult but not entirely prevented.[15]

The aim of this book is to show how easily existing money laundering prevention mechanisms can be circumvented. On the one hand, the aim is to anticipate the behaviour of educated and intelligent money launderers so that legislative measures can be taken to respond to these approaches. On the other hand, however, it is precisely these legislative measures that are to be questioned. The legislator’s response to the methods of money laundering of the future does not necessarily have to be a tightening of the laws. Rather, one should query the raison d’être behind money laundering offences.

The literature currently focuses predominantly on the fact that money is being laundered. High sums are often mentioned but rarely sufficiently substantiated. Moreover, the well-known triad of ‘placement, layering, and integration’ is described as the standard procedure behind money laundering, and stricter measures to combat money laundering are called for. However, while the literature assumes that money *is*

9. Meldestelle für Geldwäscherei, 2019.
10. Teichmann, 2019b.
11. Dagirmanjian, 2019; Buomberger, 2015.
12. Lord et al., 2019; Bartz, 2015; Spiegel Online, 2015; Teichmann & Falker, 2020a; Focus, 2015.
13. Theurer, 2015; Teichmann, 2017e; Teichmann, 2018b; Teichmann & Falker, 2020c.
14. Boles, 2017; Müller, 2015.
15. Teichmann & Hürlimann, 2019.

laundered, it neglects to consider *how* money is laundered in the first place. In order to combat money laundering effectively, one must first understand how intelligent money launderers operate – only then can one ultimately develop targeted and meaningful measures to combat money laundering. This book aims to contribute to the further development of understanding the modus operandi of intelligent money launderers.

The offence of money laundering, in the sense of Article 305bis of the Swiss Criminal Code (SCC), was introduced in Switzerland and in various other countries because receiving stolen goods was already prohibited, and it was believed that 'receiving money' should not go unpunished. It was hoped that this would provide a means of punishing intelligent criminals who operate in the shadows and are rarely identified but benefit financially from drug trafficking, arms trafficking and human trafficking. The offence of money laundering originated in the United States of America, where the principle of immediacy is more important than it is in Europe, and it was hoped that the new offence would facilitate the presentation of evidence. This was especially true with regard to the 'War on Drugs'. Unfortunately, this strategy's anticipated results have not yet materialized.[16]

If one assumes that criminals are in principle clumsy, uneducated and not very intelligent, then there is no need to resort to the offence of money laundering since the predicate offence should have already resulted in these criminals having been caught. The offence of money laundering is therefore also particularly aimed at punishing intelligent offenders. Assuming that at least some of the criminals are intelligent and educated, one can also assume that clever methods of money laundering are developed and used. This raises the question of whether there is a need for the further tightening of money laundering legislation or whether undertaking other ways of combating crime might be more sensible. It should also be taken into account that criminals are mobile in an increasingly globalized world and can also launder their money abroad if necessary.[17]

In order to be able to assess whether there are actually numerous possibilities to circumvent the existing money laundering prevention measures, an empirical study was conducted. The following questions were asked.

Research question: What are the possibilities to circumvent the existing money laundering prevention measures?

Sub-question 1: What is the specific procedure for laundering money?

Sub-question 2: What risks arise from the circumvention methods presented?

In order to answer these questions satisfactorily, informal interviews were first conducted with money launderers and their accomplices as part of a preliminary study. Subsequently, seventeen interviews were conducted with money laundering prevention experts. These interviews were transcribed and analysed using a text-reduction procedure.[18] Finally, the findings obtained in the qualitative content analysis were verified in a quantitative study. In particular, the study examined whether compliance experts themselves believe in the effectiveness of the money laundering prevention

16. Killias, 2015.
17. Teichmann & Falker, 2020d.
18. Mayring, 2010.

measures in place and whether they are aware of how these prevention measures can be circumvented.

Ultimately, this chapter argues that money laundering prevention is not a panacea against (organized) crime. In order to effectively fight corruption, for example, legislators should rather focus on administrative reforms than on creating additional control mechanisms.[19] Currently, additional control mechanisms are being established in many areas, further weakening the efficiency of public administration and encouraging corruption. To a large extent, attempts are being made to counter this problem by making it impossible to use the incriminated bribes. Although taking this approach seems obvious at first glance, experience has shown that it is not particularly effective. The methods of circumventing money laundering prevention measures presented in this book intend to show that money can still be easily laundered despite the numerous steps that have been taken to combat money laundering. Therefore, existing approaches to combat money laundering will be critically questioned.

Scrutinizing money laundering prevention measures should also focus on increasing bureaucratic control efforts in particular. Currently, there is a threat of extending the predicate offences of money laundering to include tax offences, but no one seems to be bothered by the fact that the strategy of combating crime through money laundering offences has largely failed thus far.[20] In order to show how nonsensical the current implementation of money laundering prevention measures is, the author will demonstrate the basic steps that can be taken to circumvent these measures. This leads to two possibilities: either the existing measures of prevention are drastically tightened and extended to almost all branches of the economy or the financial sector is relieved of the burden it bears and alternative ways of fighting this type of crime are sought instead.

19. Alomari, 2020; Killias, 2011; Teichmann, 2017a; Teichmann, 2017i; Teichmann et al., 2020; Killias, 2011; Teichmann, 2016a; Teichmann, 2019a.
20. Killias, 2015.

CHAPTER 2

Definition of Money Laundering, Legal Basis and Literature Analysis

2.1 DEFINITION OF MONEY LAUNDERING AND ITS LEGAL BASIS

The starting point for this book is Swiss criminal law. In Switzerland, the offence of money laundering is regulated in a single provision of the Special Part of the Criminal Code (SCC), namely Article 305bis.[21] It states the following:

> Money laundering
> (1) Any person who commits an act likely to frustrate the tracing, tracing or confiscation of property which he knows or must assume to be derived from a crime shall be liable to a custodial sentence not exceeding three years or to a monetary penalty.
> (2) In serious cases, the penalty is imprisonment for up to five years or a fine. The custodial sentence shall be combined with a fine of up to 500 daily penalty units. A serious case exists in particular if the offender:
> a. acts as a member of a criminal organisation;
> b. acts as a member of a gang that has come together for the purpose of continuing to engage in money laundering;
> c. achieves a large turnover or a substantial profit through commercial money laundering.
> (3) The offender shall also be punished if the principal offence was committed abroad and this is also punishable at the place of commission.[22]

The definition of money laundering in Article 305bis SCC also applies to this book. The decision to apply the definition of Article 305bis SCC to this book not only is based on the fact that it seems to make sense for a book to be oriented towards the SCC but also takes into account that Article 305bis covers all relevant elements of the offence that also play a role abroad. It should be noted that Article 305bis is only applicable if

21. Killias, 2009.
22. SCC, 2015.

the money laundered derived from the commission of a crime.[23] Arguably, this also includes any criminal proceeds.[24] This is due to the fact that the offence of money laundering is systematically classified as an offence against the administration of justice and is thus not related to the predicate offence.[25] Jurisprudence of the Federal Supreme Court has thus assumed genuine competition with the predicate offence in Federal Court Ruling 122 IV 211, among others.[26]

The restriction of the applicability of Article 305bis to crimes as predicate offences is not seen as an obstacle in the context of this book exploring appropriate money laundering methods because it is irrelevant whether the assets originate from a crime or a less serious predicate offence. Rather, it is assumed that incriminated funds exist and need to be laundered. Thus, the use of a national standard does not significantly limit comparability at the international level.

Although this book uses the definition of Article 305bis of the SCC, we will briefly look at examples of how the offence of money laundering has been defined abroad. For this purpose, excerpts from foreign penal codes will be examined and briefly commented on where appropriate. In Germany, section 261(1) of the German Criminal Code (GCC) states: '(1) Any person who conceals an object resulting from an unlawful act referred to in sentence 2, conceals its origin or frustrates or endangers the tracing, finding, forfeiture, confiscation or seizure of such an object shall be liable to a custodial sentence of three months to five years.'[27]

This is followed in the GCC by a list of predicate offences. The list of possible predicate offences in the GCC is considerably more extensive than in the SCC. In addition to felonies, it also includes numerous misdemeanours as well as commercial or gang tax evasion. Interestingly, the definition of the offences suitable for money laundering in the GCC hardly differs from Article 305bis SCC. Only forfeiture is not explicitly mentioned in the SCC.

In Austria, the definition of the offence of money laundering is much more complicated but ultimately similar to its Swiss equivalent. Thus, section 165 of the Austrian Criminal Code (ACC) describes it as the following:

> (1) Any person who commits property arising from a felony, an offence against the property of another punishable by imprisonment for more than one year, an offence under sections 223, 224, 225, 229, 230, 269, 278, 288, 289, 293, 295 or 304 to 309, an offence against the provisions of intellectual property law committed on a commercial basis or a financial offence of smuggling or evasion of import or export duties falling within the jurisdiction of the courts, conceals or disguises their origin, in particular by making false statements in legal transactions about the origin or true nature of these property items, the ownership or other rights to them, the authority to dispose of them, their transfer or where they are located, shall be punished by imprisonment for not more than three years.[28]

23. Killias, 2009.
24. Killias, 2009.
25. Killias, 2009.
26. Killias, 2009.
27. GCC, 2015.
28. ACC, 2015.

Subsequently, the Austrian legislator uses four further paragraphs in a somewhat cumbersome manner to supplement this rather incomplete definition. Paragraph 2 deals specifically with intentional safekeeping, custody, investment, administration, conversion, realization and transfer to third parties. Paragraph 3 extends the elements of the offence listed in paragraph 2 to the assets of criminal organizations and terrorist groups. Paragraph 4 provides for an aggravation of the penalty for offences above EUR 50,000 or as a member of a criminal organization. Paragraph 5 also states that the criminal's wages are also to be considered incriminated money. In conclusion, it can be said that although the Austrian definition is more detailed than the variant contained in Article 305bis of the SCC, the contents are ultimately very similar. Only the extension of the offence of money laundering to terrorist financing is noteworthy. This should be viewed critically, however, since terrorism financing is a similar offence but not exactly the same.

The various definitions of money laundering touched upon in this chapter could ultimately be further expounded and elaborated on in a book of their own. However, that is not the purpose of this book. Instead, the empirical results are placed in the foreground. The author only takes the liberty of stating that the definition of money laundering contained in Article 305bis of the SCC encompasses all the essential elements of the offence at the international level concisely and clearly. Only the list of predicate offences varies in comparison with the regulations of other legislatures. However, since this book is primarily concerned with the methods of money laundering and not with the origins of incriminated funds, this limitation is not considered a significant disadvantage.

In most countries, parallel to the criminal offence of money laundering is a series of regulations on the prevention of money laundering. In Switzerland, this takes the form of the Money Laundering Act (AMLA) of 10 October 1997. Article 1 of the AMLA states: 'This Act regulates the combating of money laundering within the meaning of Article 305bis of the Criminal Code (SCC), the combating of terrorist financing within the meaning of Article 260^{quinquies} paragraph 1 SCC and the ensuring of due diligence in financial transactions'.[29]

Article 2 defines the financial intermediaries subject to the AMLA. Article 3 specifies that the parties must be identified. Articles 4 and 5 specify that the beneficial owner must be identified. Article 6 sets out duties of clarification, and Article 7 deals with documentation duties. There are exceptions according to Article 7a for assets of low value. Article 8 specifies the organizational measures to be taken. Article 9 mentions reporting obligations, and Article 10 defines the preconditions for freezing assets. Article 10a defines information prohibitions. The rest of the system concerns the day-to-day duties of financial intermediaries to an extent and can be taken from the law, as they are of limited importance to this book.

At the international level, the UN Convention against Illicit Traffic in Narcotic Drugs (1988), the UN Convention on the Suppression of the Financing of Terrorism (2002) and the UN Convention against Transnational Organized Crime (2003), as well

29. AMLA, 2015.

as the UN Convention against Corruption (2005) are particularly relevant.[30] Furthermore, the Council of Europe Convention on Laundering, Search, Seizure and Confiscation of the Proceeds from Crime (1990) and the Council of Europe Convention on Laundering, Search, Seizure and Confiscation of the Proceeds from Crime and on the Financing of Terrorism (2005) play an important role in the fight against money laundering.[31] However, these conventions will not be discussed in detail since the focus of this book is on Article 305bis of the SCC and the question of how money can be laundered in Switzerland in particular.

2.2 LITERATURE ANALYSIS

The brief overview of the state of research in the field of money laundering that follows reflects the prevailing doctrine and not necessarily the views of the author of this book. In particular, the author is of the opinion that all estimates of the extent of money laundering should be viewed especially critically because a serious assessment of the economic extent of this phenomenon is extremely difficult to achieve. Furthermore, while the proposed measures to be taken according to the literature are all laudable, they should also be put into perspective with regard to the empirical results of this book.[32]

In the context of this literature analysis, the focus is on establishing an academic view of money laundering. The discussion of the empirical results, on the other hand, is supplemented by sources from practice and the press in order not to compromise its relevance to reality by providing overly theoretical explanations.

Money laundering has probably existed since the invention of money.[33] It is considered a by-product of criminal activity.[34] Before 1986, however, money laundering was not a criminal offence anywhere in the world.[35] However, as early as 1985, calls for the introduction of a money laundering offence were growing louder in Switzerland as part of the revision of the criminal law on property.[36] At that time, however, money laundering was rather the continuation of commercial activities by illegal means. Now, money laundering is regularly presented as a threat to public security. In this context, it is repeatedly emphasized that money laundering primarily serves organized crime in order to smuggle ill-gotten gains into the legal economic cycle. Originally, the fight against money laundering served primarily to combat the international drug trade. Today, it is sometimes part of the basic responsibility of banks to fight money laundering and terrorist financing.[37] With the money laundering

30. United Nations Office on Drugs and Crime, 2015.
31. International Monetary Fund, 2015.
32. Levi et al., 2017.
33. Müller et al., 2007.
34. Argentiniero et al., 2008.
35. Sharman, 2008.
36. Stratenwerth, 1984; Williams, 2001; Hunter, 2015.
37. Kruisbergen et al., 2019; Mitsch, 2015; Weber & Kruisbergen, 2019. Amicelle, 2017; Pieth, 2015; Pieth & Ivory, 2011; Teichmann, 2018a.

offence, criminal law is de facto downgraded to a substitute for financial supervision law.[38]

Because the international community cannot agree on what counts as a predicate offence, nations differ in how they define money laundering.[39] While US companies often have to apply heightened standards of due diligence, as is evident with regard to trade with companies in Iran, for example, other countries are much more tolerant.[40] At the same time, some nations – particularly in the former Soviet Union – are virtually renowned for their shadow economies that favour money laundering and tax evasion.[41] Furthermore, countries' self-reports can also be manipulated.[42] Therefore, the comparability of money laundering in different countries is limited.[43]

Nevertheless, international cooperation in the fight against money laundering is of fundamental importance.[44] This is due, among other things, to the fact that predicate offences such as burglary, receiving stolen goods and car theft have become increasingly international since the collapse of the former Eastern Bloc.[45] Furthermore, the number of international bank transfers is steadily increasing.[46] The transnational nature of money laundering[47] thus poses a great challenge for many domestic law enforcement agencies, which usually act nationally.[48] For this reason, legislators have been trying to combat money laundering for some time through international agreements.[49] However, it should not be forgotten that it was or is partly in the interest of certain states to tolerate money laundering. In the past, the G7 actually received massive criticism for exerting pressure on offshore centres, although doing so eventually raised global standards in the fight against money laundering.[50]

Money laundering often involves the allocation of assets around the world, thereby circumventing national legislation. Almost all definitions of the offence include references to hiding, moving or investing incriminated assets.[51] Normally, incriminated assets are provided with a supposedly legal paper trail.[52] The main aim of money laundering is to ensure that the assets can no longer be attributed to their illegal source. All proceeds of the predicate offence are considered incriminated assets.[53] On the one hand, money laundering is about hiding assets, but on the other hand, it is also about

38. Dietzi, 1992.
39. Van Fossen, 2003.
40. Unger & Busuioc, 2007; Teichmann, 2017b; Yeoh, 2019.
41. Stack, 2015.
42. Deleanu, 2017.
43. Schneider, 2010.
44. Hughes, 1991; Steblianko et al., 2020; Teichmann & Falker, 2020b; Van Duyne et al., 2018; Verhage, 2016.
45. Killias, 2011; Kobryn, 2017.
46. Breslow et al., 2017.
47. *See also* Ferwerda et al., 2020.
48. Richards, 1998.
49. Schmidt, 2015.
50. Hinterseer, 2002; Hartmann, 2000.
51. Buchanan, 2004; Morris-Cotterill, 2001.
52. Van Duyne, 2003; *see also* Teichmann & Falker, 2020e; Teichmann & Park, 2018a, b, c; Teichmann & Köb, 2018.
53. Johnson & Desmond, 2003; Stessens, 2000.

converting the assets into non-suspicious objects or investments.[54] The allocation of incriminated assets is not primarily about the expected return but rather about the avoidance of controls.[55]

Money laundering is often associated with drug trafficking[56] but now also includes the proceeds of a variety of other crimes.[57] The focus here is primarily on organized crime.[58] However, it is also often argued that the proceeds of economic crimes are laundered.[59] In this context, the interplay of money laundering and corruption is often mentioned.[60] Money laundering is sometimes even described as one of the biggest economic cost factors of corruption.[61] Furthermore, arms trafficking and prostitution, for example, are now considered predicate offences in many countries.[62] Tax evasion is also frequently considered a predicate offence.[63] In this context, it should be pointed out that contrary to general assumptions, countries with favourable tax regimes are not necessarily suitable locations for money laundering.[64]

Since the passing of the Patriot Act of 2001 in the USA, money laundering has repeatedly been associated with terrorist financing. This is due to the recognition that terrorist organizations usually need money to finance their activities.[65] In the wake of the attacks of 11 September 2001, the US government put money laundering on a par with terrorist financing.[66] At this point, it is worth remembering that this is a new, reverse form of money laundering, whereby funds are primarily collected to finance future crimes.[67] With regard to the fight against terrorist financing, it already seems clear to many actors that banks are dependent on the support of the government, and the close cooperation between banks and investigative authorities is also indispensable in the fight against money laundering. However, this book deals exclusively with money laundering and does not deal with terrorist financing in detail. Nonetheless, it is mentioned occasionally in passing because of its known connection to money laundering.[68]

Money laundering is normally considered an autonomous criminal offence, the purpose of which is to convert illegal assets into (apparently) legal assets.[69] In the past, it has often been argued that the offence of money laundering is misused to impose an

54. Welling, 1989; *see also* Teichmann & Falker, 2020g, i.
55. Alldridge, 2003.
56. Barone et al., 2017; Farfán-Méndez, 2019.
57. Levi, 2002.
58. Gaetke & Welling, 1992; Levi & Soudijn, 2020; Teichmann & Falker, 2020k.
59. Wohlers & Kundlich, 2010.
60. Armney & Melese, 2017; Chaikin & Sharman, 2009; Clarke, 2020; Jansics, 2018; Rose-Ackerman, 2016; Teichmann, 2020b; Zali & Maulidi, 2018.
61. Lacey & George, 2002.
62. Lilley, 2003.
63. Hampton & Levi, 1999; Lutz & Kern, 2017; Suter et al., 2019.
64. Mitchell, 2004.
65. Gouvin, 2003; Ozkan, 2016; Koh, 2006.
66. Johnson, 2003.
67. Casella, 2003; Lowe, 2017; Naheem, 2020; Teichmann, 2017g, d; Zagaris, 2004.
68. Schroeder, 2001.
69. Masciandaro, 1999.

additional sanction on less serious offences; it is therefore important that the courts follow the original intention of the legislator.[70]

In view of the frequent connections between money and crime, it seems obvious at first glance to use anti-money laundering efforts as a means of fighting crime.[71] After all, concealing the origins of bribes is a fundamental element of a successful corruption operation.[72] Furthermore, it is often argued that the financial system needs to be protected from the negative consequences of incriminated funds.[73] The current international regulatory system has been heavily rocked by scandal.[74]

The Financial Action Task Force (FATF) seems to concentrate primarily on shaping national legal systems and their implementation.[75] In the past, it largely focused on financial service providers.[76] The International Monetary Fund has supported these efforts, particularly since 2000 with regard to offshore banking centres. The FATF was initially an association of a few states but membership is becoming increasingly popular as it coordinates and evaluates international efforts to combat money laundering.[77] To this end, Member States must regularly conduct national risk analyses and report to the FATF.[78] One problem here is that there is no standard for these analyses, so the data are difficult to compare.[79] A lack of compliance can in turn lead to the jurisdiction concerned being blacklisted.[80] Since 2001, the FATF has also been officially combating terrorist financing.[81]

However, the FATF's proposed measures often come into conflict with fundamental rights.[82] Furthermore, the fight against money laundering often conflicts with banking secrecy.[83] This is due to the fact that banking secrecy is often an obstacle in the context of law enforcement[84] or is even seen as a facilitating factor for money laundering.[85] In addition, not all countries have sufficient resources to combat money laundering effectively.[86] This is certainly a serious problem in view of the FATF's quest for global rules and standards.[87] Ultimately, the FATF also repeatedly hits its limits due to informal networks promoting the circumvention of its standards.[88]

70. Adams, 2000; Sittlington & Harvey, 2018; Gurulé, 1994.
71. Cuellar, 2003; Rusanov & Pudovochkin, 2020.
72. Jositsch, 2004.
73. Gilmore, 1992.
74. Levi & Reuter, 2006.
75. Levi & Gilmore, 2002; Murrar & Barakat, 2020.
76. Alexander, 2001; Tsingou, 2018.
77. Holder, 2003; Hülsse & Kerwer, 2007; Doyle, 2011; Mekpor, 2019; Mekpor et al., 2018.
78. *See*, e.g., Kordik & Kurilovska, 2017.
79. Ferwerda & Reuter, 2018.
80. Ferwerda et al., 2019.
81. Kersten, 2002.
82. Mitsilegas & Gilmore, 2007.
83. Nguyen, 2018; Plombeck, 1988.
84. Hernandez, 1992.
85. Carlin & Lokanan, 2018.
86. Sultzer, 1995.
87. Hülsse, 2007.
88. Perkel, 2004.

The economic impact of money laundering is often described as negative because it can damage the reputation of certain industries or nations, such as Russia.[89] It is repeatedly argued that money laundering harms legitimate private sector activities, undermines the financial system, represents a loss of control over economic policy and leads to economic instability.[90] Furthermore, money laundering is regularly associated with tax evasion in the USA and Germany. Moreover, it is often claimed that money laundering contributes to the growth of illegal markets.[91] To make matters worse, so-called sterile investments in antiques, jewellery or other tangible assets do not contribute to economic growth.[92] However, critics have argued that money laundering is the price to be paid for capital mobility.[93]

On the other hand, the fight against money laundering is often associated with a more stable financial system, less crime and a strengthening of economic development.[94] In particular, the fight against money laundering is said to be suitable for fighting corruption.[95] Nevertheless, the public seems to be less interested in money laundering than in other crimes, such as drug trafficking.[96] Furthermore, it can be noted that the offence of money laundering has been misused in the press in the past to justify new legal measures for other offences.[97]

The Federal Bureau of Investigation estimated the volume of money laundering in 2001 to be worth USD 1,500 billion.[98] It is believed that the volume of money laundering more than doubled between 1995 and 2006 in the twenty most developed Organisation for Economic Co-operation and Development (OECD) countries. Some have argued that up to 19% of the gross domestic product of the EU-fifteen countries comes from money laundering. However, the availability of data to measure the extent of global money laundering is extremely limited. It is questionable to what extent so-called rational supplements can compensate for this weak data situation. Finally, it should be borne in mind that generally little is known about the economic dimensions of the shadow economy.[99] In conclusion, it can nevertheless be said that the empirical data on the extent of money laundering are not particularly convincing.[100]

It is undisputed that data on crime have improved significantly over the last twenty years. More recently, it has even been argued that data could also be measured in real time.[101] However, it should be emphasized that these measurements are only considered for banking and logistics transactions and should be viewed critically there as well.

89. Dobrowolski & Sulkowski, 2019; Lyeonov et al., 2019; Quirk, 1997a.
90. McDowell, 2001.
91. Reuter, 2004; Masciandaro, 1998.
92. Bartlett, 2002.
93. Tsingou, 2010.
94. Schott, 2006.
95. Sharman & Chaikin, 2009.
96. Unger et al., 2006.
97. Nichols, 1997.
98. Takáts, 2007; Schneider, 2008.
99. Bagella et al., 2009; Walker, 1999; Van Duyne, 1994.
100. Harvey, 2005.
101. Walker & Unger, 2009; Zdanowicz, 2004.

The analysis of cash transactions has been considered promising since the 1990s.[102] However, this model quickly reaches its limits. This is especially true if the money launderer refrains from bringing the cash into contact with banks and instead places it in cash-intensive industries. Only the transaction analyses introduced by banks, in which the customer influences the matrix with his behaviour, are considered helpful in identifying unusual transactions.[103] These models are sometimes extremely complex and require innovative approaches to data management.[104]

Money launderers often rely on accountants for help.[105] At the same time, auditing plays a major role in detecting money laundering offences.[106] However, there are also much simpler methods that can be used to launder money, such as by making hawala transactions, which do not require any special expertise. These include, for example, hundi and black-market peso exchange systems.[107] These underground banks are in fact in clear competition with the financial institutions required by most legislators.[108]

Other common methods of money laundering are the subversion of thresholds (so-called smurfing), the invoicing of services not rendered or goods not delivered (so-called misinvoicing), the exchange of stolen valuables (so-called bartering), trading in derivatives and simple bank transfers.[109] Offshore companies and casinos are also considered good places to launder money.[110] However, the acquisition of luxury goods and the granting of loans also seem to play an important role.[111] Furthermore, real estate is also considered extremely attractive for money launderers.[112] It is always true that the money laundering devices that imitate real business transactions as closely as possible are the most successful.[113] For smaller amounts, safe-deposit boxes or bonded warehouses can also be used. It can therefore be stated that there are both simple and complex methods of money laundering.[114]

It is possible to distinguish between three stages in the process of money laundering. In the first, 'placement', the money is placed. This is supposedly the most important and at the same time the most difficult step in money laundering because the incriminated assets are freed from the coarsest negative traces in this step.[115] This is followed by the second stage, 'layering', whereby the money is given a plausible backstory. In the course of the third stage, 'integration', the money finds its way into the legal economic cycle. Bank accounts in different jurisdictions are often used for layering. This is followed by transfers through various accounts to make traceability

102. Senator et al., 1995; *see also* Riccardi & Levi, 2018.
103. *See,* e.g., Teichmann & Falker, 2020h; Teichmann, 2017f; Kingdon, 2004.
104. Zhang, 2003.
105. Mitchell et al., 1998; Ravenda et al., 2017; Ravenda et al., 2018.
106. Amara et al., 2020; Cindori, 2018; Norton, 2018.
107. Jost & Sandhu, 2003; Passas, 2003.
108. McCusker, 2005.
109. Quirk, 1997b.
110. Ferwerda & Kleemans, 2019; Robinson, 1996.
111. Alldridge, 2008.
112. Schneider, 2004.
113. Blum et al., 1998.
114. Nagel, 2020; Hey, 2010.
115. Graber, 2009.

difficult and to undermine thresholds. In the course of integration, it should already no longer be possible to prove the illegal origins of the funds.[116] However, variations in these three steps can also be applied, for example, if the funds are already available in an electronic form.[117]

The liberalization of the economy in Eastern Europe and Asia has made combating money laundering much more difficult.[118] The further development of the Internet has also significantly complicated the prevention of money laundering with regard to the anonymity it offers.[119] One thinks here, for example, of gambling on the Internet.[120] In this context, credit cards are becoming a major risk factor. Electronic currencies also represent a new obstacle for law enforcement authorities.[121] At this point, cryptocurrencies, such as Bitcoin, should be mentioned in particular, which have already attracted massive attention from researchers as well as legislators and regulators due to their suitability for money laundering.[122] The mobility of incriminated assets poses a major challenge to combating money laundering. The increasing globalization of financial markets should also not be underestimated.[123]

Private and public actors work together on the international and national level to combat money laundering.[124] Financial institutions are considered important partners of governments in the fight against money laundering.[125] Since 1 January 2020, the regulatory framework for financial institutions has been newly defined based on the Swiss Federal Act on Financial Institutions of 15 June 2018. The law regulates asset managers, trustees, managers of collective assets, fund management companies and securities firms to varying degrees of severity. Banks, on the other hand, remain subject to the Banking Act.[126]

While banks have become accustomed to increasing regulation, they continue to complain about the associated obligations.[127] At the same time, cultural, regulatory or other factors sometimes make compliance with due diligence obligations more difficult.[128] It is true that an increasing acceptance of reporting obligations has been observed since the 1990s.[129] However, the associated costs are enormous. For example,

116. Schneider & Windischbauer, 2008; Arzt et al., 2009; Trechsel, 1997; Madinger, 2011; Grosse, 2001; Gao & Xu, 2009.
117. Cassella, 2018.
118. Savona, 2000.
119. Mugarura & Ssali, 2020; Philippson, 2001.
120. Schopper, 2002.
121. Hugel & Kelly, 2003; Straub, 2001.
122. *See*, e.g., Albrecht et al., 2019; Barone & Masciandaro, 2018; Bryans, 2014; Campbell-Verduyn, 2018; Crawford & Guan, 2020; Custers et al., 2020; Danwerth, 2018; Dupuis & Gleason, 2020; Dynru & Dykyl, 2018; Fletcher et al., 2021; Florea & Nitu, 2020; Flühmann & Bahar, 2019; Flühmann et al., 2017; Forgang, 2019; Frick, 2019; Godinho Silva, 2019; Haffke et al., 2020; Hameed, 2019; Mabunda, 2018; Molo & Drzalic, 2019; Müller et al., 2018, Naheem, 2018; Peyer & Winter, 2019; Ronc & Schuppli, 2018; Trautmann & Kissler, 2020.
123. Harmon, 1988; Simmons, 2000.
124. Verhage, 2009.
125. De Koker, 2006.
126. Bahar, 2019; De Vos Burchart, 2017.
127. Geiger & Wuensch, 2007.
128. *See*, e.g., ElYacoubi, 2020.
129. Hall, 1995.

new staff must be recruited and trained, new computer programs must be purchased and internal processes must be revised.[130] In particular, technical tools, such as artificial intelligence, machine learning, software tools and automation, are currently gaining importance in the fight against money laundering (so-called RegTech).[131] Ultimately, a well-trained compliance team and the correct implementation of measures are of the utmost importance.[132] Furthermore, numerous banking business models had to be changed or abolished as part of the fight against money laundering.[133]

Therefore, it has often been suggested that anti-money laundering laws should be designed to create incentives for banks to collect as much information as possible, particularly because the negative impact of money laundering on banks is limited.[134] At the same time, regulation should always be proportionate to the risk being mitigated.[135] A risk-based approach to money laundering is thus needed.[136] An insecurity-based approach would also be conceivable.[137] Furthermore, the literature also deals with economic approaches to money laundering prevention.[138] Self-regulation by the private sector also plays an important role.[139] Ultimately, legal and societal interests must be aligned.[140]

The costs of imposing additional compliance obligations must also be in reasonable proportion to their potential benefits.[141] It should also be borne in mind that while banks should know their clients and the origins of their clients' funds, they were not created to engage in investigative activities. Furthermore, organizational and personal obstacles – such as good or bad relationships and the commercial interests of bankers – should not be underestimated. The goodwill of bankers is ultimately a critical factor for the success of money laundering prevention measures.[142]

The literature recognizes that combating terrorist financing primarily means new challenges for financial institutions and that its value in the fight against terrorism is not all that great. Therefore, legislators should not simply follow the guidelines of the FATF with regard to combating money laundering but critically question the sense and purpose of their measures.[143] Among other things, it should be borne in mind that money launderers prefer areas where the probability of being caught is low. Furthermore, the inertia of the legislator should not be disregarded. Many legislative measures require further regulations in order to constitute real obstacles for money launderers

130. Favarel-Garrigues et al., 2008.
131. Badal-Valero et al., 2018; Canhoto, 2020; Demetis, 2018; Eifrem, 2019; Freij, 2020; Klimova et al., 2020; Kurum, 2020; Leonov et al., 2019; Salehi et al., 2017; Shaikh & Nazir, 2018; Sobreira Leite et al., 2019.
132. Isa et al., 2015; Krambia-Kapardis et al., 2019; Stacchezzini et al., 2020.
133. Zagaris & Castilla, 1993.
134. Lawlor-Forsyth & Gallant, 2018; Masciandaro & Filotto, 2001.
135. Gill & Tayler, 2004.
136. Ai & Tang, 2011; Ross & Hannan, 2007; Savona & Riccardi, 2019; Simonova, 2011.
137. Bello & Harvey, 2017.
138. *See,* e.g., Imanpour et al., 2019; Loayza et al., 2019.
139. De Koker, 2003; Friedrich & Quick, 2019; Schleiffer & von Riedmatten, 2019.
140. Van Duyne et al., 2003.
141. Harvey, 2004.
142. Alford, 1993; Levi, 1991; Moser, 1995.
143. Lyden, 2003; Teichmann, 2017c; Van Duyne, 1998.

and therefore only have a deterrent effect in the medium or long term.[144] Furthermore, it should be admitted that anti-money laundering laws have failed to achieve their original goal of effectively combating drug trafficking.[145] The general effectiveness of the current anti-money laundering measures is often questioned and examined in the literature.[146]

However, placing a new focus on the risk profiles of specific countries and sectors could be helpful.[147] Europe has already followed the USA in applying a risk-based approach. These risk profiles could be used to further develop the software used by financial service providers. In developing these risk profiles, it should be borne in mind that, among other things, both firms and individuals develop and use alternative methods of money laundering when legislative measures focus exclusively on financial institutions.[148] These new findings could be used for the further development of transaction analyses.[149]

Furthermore, the introduction of an international financial intelligence unit (FIU) would be worth considering in order to unite individual national efforts.[150] Furthermore, national as well as international cooperation could also be intensified with regard to extradition and information exchange.[151] The same applies to the exchange of information between banks.[152] However, care should be taken to ensure that law enforcement agencies cannot abuse money laundering laws to confiscate disproportionate sums.[153] Another problem arises for defence lawyers, who, like banks, are on the frontlines of FATF compliance, since this can lead to conflicts with professional standards and ethical aspects of legal professional privilege.[154] Once clients have committed a predicate offence that has provided them with incriminated assets, the ultimate question is whether the defence lawyer may accept those assets as payment.[155] The Panama Papers have further proven that law firms may well be involved in large-scale money laundering.[156] The attempt to impose stricter due diligence requirements on defence lawyers has been met with different reactions in different jurisdictions, ranging from apparent rejection in the USA to the maximum use of self-regulation under EU directives in France.[157]

144. Force, 1999; Masciandaro, 2005.
145. Razzano, 1994.
146. *See*, e.g., Gambarov, 2018; Gara et al., 2019; Jayasekara, 2020; Kirschenbaum & Véron, 2018; Koster, 2020; Levi, 2020a; Pol, 2018, 2020; Verhage, 2016; Zolkaflil et al., 2019.
147. Zdanowicz, 2009; Unger, 2009.
148. Watkins, 2003; De Boyrie, 2005; Teichmann, 2020a.
149. Gao & Ye, 2007.
150. Thony, 1996.
151. Javasuriya, 2003; Passas, 2018; Pavlidis, 2020; Simanjuntak et al., 2019.
152. Cash, 2019; Vnukova et al., 2019.
153. Gordin, 1995.
154. Benson, 2018; Gichuki, 2020; Go & Benarkah, 2019; Levi, 2020b; Svedberg Helgesson & Mörth, 2018; Lutz & Kern, 2019; Svenonius & Mörth, 2020.
155. Wohlers, 2004.
156. Del Mundo, 2019.
157. Nougayrède, 2019.

In implementing all these measures, however, free trade and economic integration must not be unduly burdened.[158] Nor should it be forgotten with regard to surveillance measures that the state ultimately has to ensure both security and freedom and that excessive control in the context of combating money laundering at least significantly restricts the freedom of citizens.[159] Finally, it should be borne in mind that there is no panacea available to resolve the issue of money laundering and that different countries have to implement different measures in order to be successful.[160]

158. Zagaris & MacDonald, 1992.
159. Vlcek, 2008.
160. Vaithilingam & Nair, 2007, p. 364; Teichmann & Falker, 2020j.

CHAPTER 3

Empirical Investigation

3.1 RESEARCH METHODOLOGY

The methodological approach to this research can be divided into four parts. First, a preliminary study was conducted to determine how the topic of money laundering is viewed from the perspective of the perpetrators (i.e., the money launderers and their accomplices). In the main study, interviews were conducted with numerous experts on the topic of combating money laundering. The aim was to identify gaps in the system from the perspective of the prevention experts. Subsequently, the results of the preliminary and the main studies were reviewed in a quantitative study. Whether the participants' understanding of the system corresponds to that of the compliance officers was examined. In particular, the aim was to determine whether compliance officers are aware of the methods used to circumvent existing money laundering prevention provisions and whether these are perceived in the compliance officers' everyday work. In order to verify and further develop the findings of the original empirical study published in 2016, a follow-up study was conducted.

3.1.1 Preliminary Study

From January 2011 to March 2014, the author made contact with money launderers and persons close to them in order to develop an initial exploratory understanding of the topic of money laundering. The preliminary study was imperative to determine whether there was a significant research gap that could be addressed in the context of a book. If the preliminary study had shown that money launderers consider it almost impossible to 'launder' their assets in the sense of Article 305ter SCC, pursuing further research in this legal and criminological area would have been nonsensical. Furthermore, the preliminary study aimed to help shed light on the perspectives of money launderers themselves and develop a questionnaire for experts on the basis thereof.

Due to the potential criminal consequences of their actions, money launderers are generally not willing to be formally interviewed and recorded. Therefore, their perspectives can only be marginally considered in the main study. Thus, the author decided to conduct informal interviews with the money launderers, facilitators and their contact persons listed in Table 3.1. The author documented these conversations in the form of handwritten notes.

In order to develop as comprehensive an understanding of the money laundering process as possible, the author conducted interviews with people active as various links in the money laundering chain. Intermediaries ultimately play just as large a role as private bankers and money launderers. For obvious reasons, the interlocutors are anonymized.

Table 3.1 Pre-study Interview Partners

Number	*Function*	*Country of Residence*	*Interview Language*
1	Private banker	United Arab Emirates	English
2	Private banker	United Arab Emirates	German
3	Private banker	United Arab Emirates	English
4	Investment advisor	Switzerland	German
5	Mediator	Italy	Italian
6	Mediator	Italy	Italian
7	Money launderer	Russia	Russian
8	Money launderer	Russia	Russian
9	Mediator	Kazakhstan	Russian
10	Private banker	Austria	German

3.1.2 Main Study

Due to the explorative nature of this study, expert interviews asking open questions was considered as an appropriate approach to take. This was justified, among other things, by the early research phase, the focus on the Interview partner's perspective, the only roughly specified topic and the open response framework. The aim of the interviews was to gather as much information about the Interview partner's expertise as possible. In casu, the aim was to develop an understanding of money laundering methods that were considered as low risk as possible.[161]

The interviews were analysed using a qualitative content analysis following Mayring.[162] In the process, units of analysis were first defined and statements relevant

161. Froschauer & Lueger, 2003, p. 35; Bogner et al., 2014, p. 24.
162. Mayring, 2010.

to the content were assigned to specific categories. Subsequently, these statements were paraphrased and generalized. Paraphrases with similar content were deleted as part of the reduction process. Statements that were made only marginally are mentioned in the complete table of generalizations in the Appendix, but for reasons of relevance and clarity, they were excluded from Table 3.2.[163]

Within the framework of the main study, eighteen money laundering prevention experts from different countries were interviewed. When selecting the interview partners, particular attention was paid to who had the relevant information and who was willing to share it. This means that money launderers and their helpers were excluded from the outset because they were not prepared to either comment publicly on these issues or be recorded doing so. However, recording and transcription were necessary to ensure the research methods were valid.[164] At the same time, experts had to be called in unforeseen at times, as specialized knowledge was required for the further development of certain methods and it became apparent in the course of the interview series that money laundering experts do not have sufficient specialized knowledge on certain topics. Thus, to develop a deeper understanding of money laundering in the antiquities trade, for example, an interview with an Egyptologist was sought. A full list of interview partners is provided in Table 3.2.

Table 3.2 Interview Partners: Expert Interviews

Name	*Function*	*Country*	*Interview Language*
Interview partner 1	Fraud investigation and dispute services partner at a Big Four consulting firm	United Arab Emirates	English
Interview partner 2	Expert on money laundering at the Federal Office of Police	Switzerland	German
Interview partner 3	Professor of corporate law at a business university	Austria	German
Interview partner 4	Member of the Financial Market Working Group of an anti-corruption organization	Germany	German
Interview partner 5	Head of a bank's legal department	Germany	German

163. Mayring, 2010, p. 68.
164. Gläser & Laudel, 2009, pp. 117 ff.

Name	*Function*	*Country*	*Interview Language*
Interview partner 6	Egyptologist and expert in the art and antiquities trade at a university	Germany	German
Interview partner 7	Public prosecutor at a cantonal public prosecutor's office	Switzerland	German
Interview partner 8	Expert on money laundering and counter-terrorism at the Financial Market Authority	Austria	German
Interview partner 9	Fraud investigation & dispute services partner at a Big Four consulting firm	Switzerland	German
Interview partner 10	Former department president of the Federal Criminal Police Office	Germany	German
Interview partner 11	Expert in criminal matters of a tax department	Switzerland	German
Interview partner 12	Expert on money laundering at the Federal Ministry of the Interior	Austria	German
Interview partner 13	Expert on money laundering at the Federal Criminal Police Office	Austria	German
Interview partner 14	Money laundering officer at a bank	Austria	German
Interview partner 15	Expert on money laundering at the Financial Market Authority	Switzerland	German
Interview partner 16	FIU	Liechtenstein	German
Interview partner 17	Head of a leading compliance institute	Switzerland	German
Interview partner 18	Money laundering expert at the Federal Ministry of Finance	Austria	German

3.1.3 Quantitative Investigation

The quantitative survey reviewed the results of the qualitative survey. In particular, the aim was to: (1) determine whether compliance officers believe that money launderers will switch to less-regulated industries to circumvent the money laundering prevention measures of financial service providers and (2) examine the role that the methods of circumventing the existing money laundering prevention measures developed in the qualitative preliminary and main studies of this book play in the everyday life of compliance officers.

For this purpose, an online questionnaire was designed based on the results of the qualitative evaluation of the expert interviews. This was sent to 1,200 compliance officers in Germany, Austria, Switzerland and Liechtenstein between 15 August and 5 October 2015 using the online service fluidsurveys.com. The compliance officers had two weeks to answer the questions. In addition to multiple-choice questions, each questionnaire also contained an option at the end to provide further information on specific methods of money laundering.

The author assumed that compliance officers are well aware that money launderers will increasingly switch to less-regulated industries in order to evade the increasing controls found in the financial sector. At the same time, however, and based on the preliminary and main studies, the author also assumed that the methods uncovered in the qualitative research would only exceptionally attract the attention of compliance officers in their day-to-day business.

> *Hypothesis 1: Money launderers increasingly switch to less-regulated industries in order to escape the controls of the financial sector.*
> *Hypothesis 2: The forms of money laundering developed in this study occur in practice but rarely attract the attention of compliance officers.*

To test these two hypotheses, all that is needed is a descriptive presentation of the results of the quantitative study. A complex statistical evaluation, for example, through multivariate analyses, would be too far-reaching in this case due to the simplicity of the question and the focus of the work in the area of qualitative investigation and would not lead to further insights.

In the period from 15 August 2015 to 5 October 2015, a total of 181 people participated in the survey. A total of 136 questionnaires were completed in full, and 45 questionnaires were incomplete. The author examined the incomplete questionnaires individually for their relevance. Questionnaires that only contained information on the person but not on the topic of money laundering were removed from the data set. Incomplete questionnaires that had gaps but still contained information on money laundering were retained. The percentage evaluation provides that only actually existing answers were taken into account. If a participant did not answer a question, the missing answer has no effect on the percentage distribution of the results of the respective answer to this question. In the end, a total of 153 questionnaires were considered in the evaluation of this study.

3.1.4 Follow-Up Study

Due to the positive response to the first edition of this book, the author decided to review and further develop the empirical results previously collected for the updated edition by means of a follow-up study. For this purpose, thirty informal expert interviews were conducted, the contents of which were summarized. In this way, diverse, practical and relevant perspectives could be taken into account. In particular, the perspectives of people who would not have been willing to participate in a formal interview were taken into account. Due to the informal setting and the exposed nature of the Interview partners, no further information on their identities can be provided. As a result, four new, previously untreated methods of money laundering are analysed in sections 4.14–4.17.

The interlocutors each emphasized that the methods presented were of high practical relevance. The aim of the follow-up study was to offer practical recommendations for more effective money laundering prevention. Therefore, this updated edition is explicitly aimed at practitioners such as compliance officers, private bankers, asset managers, public prosecutors, defence lawyers and judges. Future studies could measure the prevalence of the circumscribed methods using quantitative methods.

3.2 RESULTS OF THE EMPIRICAL STUDY

3.2.1 Preliminary Study

The preliminary study found that the highly regulated banking sector in Switzerland tends to be unpopular with money launderers. Having to answer questions from well-trained compliance staff, which is perceived as annoying, is a hurdle for money launderers. Therefore, they switch either to foreign banks or to non-regulated sectors. The methods described by money launderers are briefly described in the following.

Gold seems to be very popular with money launderers. Compared to other assets, it has a decisive advantage: its anonymity can be massively increased by melting it down without it losing value. Gold bars usually have serial numbers. However, after melting one down, it is almost certainly no longer possible to trace from whom the money launderer acquired the gold. It therefore makes sense for money launderers to buy gold in cash occasionally and have it melted down. The money launderer can then either keep the gold as an investment or resell it. If he decides to sell it officially, he can claim that the gold came from an inheritance.

Jewellery also seems to be a well-suited vehicle for money laundering, and different models are used. The money launderer can use the purchase of jewellery at the placement level to exchange incriminated funds for material assets and thus make the traceability of the funds more difficult; however, this raises the problem of a possible loss of value in the course of a resale. Therefore, it makes sense for the money launderer to use the jewellery trade as a front. Since cash payments are common in the jewellery trade, the money launderer can bring incriminated funds into his official business by feigning fictitious transactions with independent third parties. There are no identification obligations in the jewellery trade in Switzerland for transactions below CHF 100,000. It would be hard to imagine jewellery shops on Zurich's Bahnhofstrasse asking for official identification when buying a high-value watch for CHF 30,000. Antique jewellery seems to be particularly suitable due to the lack of serial numbers and the limited traceability thereof.

The trade in rough diamonds is particularly attractive for money launderers with large amounts of capital and the corresponding requisite expertise. Rough diamonds offer the advantage of having difficult-to-trace origins. Moreover, they can be easily disguised. It should be mentioned at this point that diamonds can be cut and thus take on different shapes. Obtaining Kimberley certificates is not a big hurdle for money launderers to overcome. Even if they do not succeed in buying Kimberley certificates, money launderers could still sell the diamonds to jewellers who require cash payment from their customers and do not have to present certificates due to a tolerant or naive clientele. However, the preferred approach here also seems to be a mixture of legal and illegal assets. Rough diamonds are bought officially, and the official part of the actual purchase price is paid by bank transfer. Another unofficial part follows as a cash payment when the goods are handed over. Afterwards, the diamonds are processed and polished and sold on. The sale takes place officially for the actual value of the stones.

The antiques trade also seems to attract money launderers. This is based on the fact that the objective value of antiques is very difficult to establish. Although appraisals are regularly commissioned, there are no objective criteria for determining the market value of an item. It is often affected by supply and demand. Money launderers use this loophole to buy art objects officially and inexpensively. Part of the purchase price is paid by bank transfer and another part is paid in cash. Then the antiques are officially sold for the original purchase price. Of course, the original seller remains in possession of the cash. However, he can use it to make further purchases. With a wide circle of sellers and relatively small sums being exchanged, this procedure is unlikely to attract attention. Any straw men used to carry out the purchase serve to further conceal the illicit origins and illegal activities. Alternatively, the reserve price could be waived. In this case, the antiques would have to be declared as heirlooms and the sale price would officially be their actual market value. The purchase price would be settled by bank transfer.

Similar to their interest in the antiques trade, money launderers also seem to be attracted to the non-transparent pricing and the high anonymity of the art market. Moreover, it is not unusual for paintings to be paid for in cash. Since the monetary value of art is truly subjective, money launderers can launder money not only as clients but also as professional art dealers. As a client, the money launderer enjoys the opportunity to place his money without being questioned as to its origins. However, the problem of resale arises as a result since considerable losses have to be accepted as a potential consequence. However, as an art dealer with fictitious clients, the money launderer can buy his own paintings. In this way, he not only places funds but can also control the prices, since he sets the prices on both the buyer's and the seller's side.

Real estate purchases and renovations also seem to be very popular with money launderers. This usually involves mixing legal and illegal assets. First, money launderers look for a property in need of renovation in a country with tolerant notaries or very high taxes. This is to enable under-securitization. The official part of the actual purchase price is paid by bank transfer. Another part is paid in cash. Subsequently, the property is renovated. Here, the craftspeople are officially compensated for part of their services and materials by bank transfer. The remaining part of the costs is paid for in cash. In the event of an inspection by investigators, the money launderer has invoices for all the work and materials. Even if it is found that the invoices are extraordinarily low in value, the money launderer can invoke his negotiating skills. In case of doubt, an estimate could be made for a tax assessment on the money launderer and the workers could be audited. However, proving that illegal assets were used is likely to be difficult. Intelligent money launderers occasionally withdraw cash from their accounts in order to be able to provide support for any cash payments that they claim to have made. Subsequently, the renovated property can be either held or officially sold at the actual market value. In this case, the purchase price is usually demanded by bank transfer.

Consulting firms with foreign clients also seem to be suitable vehicles for money laundering. Whereas cash-intensive businesses, such as restaurants, cafes, ice cream parlours or clothing stores, require exerting a relatively high effort to maintain a physical presence, consultancy firms usually operate in the background. Payments for fictitious advisory services from foreign clients seem to be a good way for money launderers to give illicit assets validity. In this process, the money launderer sets up a consulting company and charges fictitious clients for fictitious consulting services. These services are paid for and then taxed. In this way, the money launderer succeeds in integrating incriminated funds into legal structures. Creating consulting companies in Switzerland catering to clients abroad seems to be particularly suitable for this method of money laundering. If a client is based in a country that is very reluctant to grant administrative or legal assistance to the Swiss authorities, it becomes difficult to check up on them. The money can easily be placed in Eastern Europe and then flow into Switzerland where it is invested under the Swiss consulting company's name.

Corporate restructuring also seems to enjoy certain popularity among money launderers as a vehicle for laundering incriminated funds. This is probably due to the fact that distressed companies are often desperately looking for a liquid saviour and rarely question the origins of the funds. After all, they would not want to risk alienating or even losing the rescuer. This method of money laundering is particularly interesting if banks have granted large loans to the distressed company since this puts the bank in a conflict of interest that should not be underestimated if the payments are processed through it. On the one hand, the bank has to verify the source of the incoming funds according to standard compliance regulations, but on the other hand, the company's rescuer may also save the bank from incurring considerable losses. If the bank rejects or even blocks funds arriving from abroad that appear dubious due to a suspicion of money laundering, this may result in massive losses for the bank that loaned the distressed company funds to begin with. This could be particularly relevant for small banks that do not have an overly diversified portfolio. Of course, the company to be restructured must have sufficient substance so that the money launderer does not have to accept too great a loss. Companies with value and liquidity problems seem to be ideal for this.

Banks in Dubai also seem to be popular with money launderers, mainly due to the fact that certain of them allegedly uphold very different standards of operation. While some banks have implemented compliance regulations in an exemplary manner, others are much more relaxed and transactions are handled much more loosely. Less reputable banks even encourage their customers to falsify receipts and present them with the incriminated cash to satisfy compliance departments. More reputable banks require complex proofs, but these can also be circumvented with relatively little skill or effort. For example, requiring the certification of foreign documents, such as withdrawal slips from banks, seems to be popular. Ideally, the authentication should be done by the United Arab Emirates (UAE) embassy in the document's country of origin. At first glance, this seems a very serious form of authentication. However, people tend to forget that the money launderer could present forged documents to the UAE embassy for authentication. In the end, the embassy has no way of verifying the authenticity of a withdrawal slip, as banks do not normally have to provide any information. Thus, the embassy ultimately only certifies that the copy of a document corresponds to the original. Reliable statements about the authenticity of the original cannot be made. However, the bank can argue that it has taken all organizational measures to prevent money laundering since it had a document certified by a government agency of the UAE presented to it before accepting the cash. This seems to benefit everyone involved. Another loophole in the system is clearly that an intelligent money launderer could present a genuine document to the UAE embassy. The resulting authentication would be undoubtedly watertight. However, nothing would prevent the money launderer from using it at several banks simultaneously or having the same document authenticated multiple times. Since banks do not exchange such compliance information among themselves, it would therefore be possible to use the same withdrawal slip at ten different banks.

In addition, safe-deposit boxes are suitable for hiding and safely storing incriminated assets. This can prevent the confiscation of assets originating from a crime. In the event of a house search, investigators are unlikely to discover the assets because cunning money launderers rent safe-deposit boxes that are stored outside of their homes and away from their business premises. Obviously, they do not only rely on safe-deposit boxes held by their regular banks since that is where investigators would first look. Instead, they rent safe-deposit boxes from banks and private providers in Switzerland and abroad with whom they maintain no other business relations, which helps hide their traces and ensures that the safe-deposit boxes cannot be connected back to them.

Money launderers also use the 'cash against cash' procedure to exchange foreign currency amongst themselves. In doing so, they operate within the sphere of activity of banks and exchange offices but outside of the regulated financial sector. At first glance, the idea that money launderers might exchange currency between them may not seem very realistic, but it is not so different from using bureaux de change or exchange offices to change the medium of exchange. Finding other money launderers with whom to exchange currency instead of using a bureau de change creates a mutually beneficial arrangement.

Currency exchange offices continue to be an interesting instrument used by money launderers. It is true that the large service providers are increasingly carrying out money laundering controls, but the reports they make to the MLRO come to nothing if a sufficiently heterogeneous group of straw men is used for the currency exchange. For example, Russian tourists who want to exchange euros for Swiss francs are unlikely to be noticed in conurbations such as Zurich or Geneva. If they do carry out suspicious transactions, a Russian passport is simply presented and the report is forwarded to the Russian authorities if necessary. The money launderer never comes to light. Alternatively, the money launderer can run small exchange offices himself and increase their turnover using his own foreign currency. The resulting profit is taxed and thus already has a paper trail.

3.2.2 Qualitative Investigation

3.2.2.1 Executive Summary of the Qualitative Study

First, the author would like to offer the reader a brief overview of the main results of the qualitative content analysis of the expert interviews. For this purpose, a tabular overview has been compiled in the form of an executive summary (Table 3.3). This should enable readers with little time to get an overview of the results of this book.

Table 3.3 Executive Summary of the Qualitative Content Analysis

Method	*General Suitability*	*Concrete Approach*	*Resources*	*Risks*
General statements	– Placement/Layering/ Integration – Primary aim: hide and seek – Secondary objective: interrupt detection	– Avoid the scope of application of the AMLA – Split larger amounts – Pool funds – Invest in tangible assets – Disguise the beneficial owner – Use straw men – Use existing structures – Establish plausibility – Form chains across multiple jurisdictions – Mix legal and illegal funds	– Alternative payment methods – Banks with weak/corrupt/tolerant compliance – Detailed contracts – Experts	– Attention of the banks – Attention of the authorities – Business risks – Fraud – Embezzlement
Gold	– Placement/layering – Change of the value carrier – Difficult to determine origin (after melting)	– Feign inheritance, taking into account the deceased's financial circumstances and tax declarations – Buy gold together and recast – Store in a bonded warehouse – Transfer ownership rights in the bonded warehouse	– Documentation of origins	– Fraud – Theft – Acquisition is registered, if applicable – Gold dealers are subject to Article 2, paragraph 3 AMLA – High volatility – Quantities easily traceable due to standardized prices – Weight and volume make transport difficult

Method	*General Suitability*	*Concrete Approach*	*Resources*	*Risks*
		– Take profits in the event of a positive price development – Transfer ownership rights in the bonded warehouse		
Jewellery	– Placement/layering – Anonymous – No fixed market prices – Value retention – Liquidity	– Establish actual activity in the jewellery trade – Fake customers – Distribute leaflets for jewellery purchase – Buy jewellery in holiday destinations – Declare as hereditary property and record in the estate register – Declare as a gift	– Expertise in processing and materials – Product with lack of comparability	– Estimation risks – Pawnshops already in the sights of the authorities
Rough diamonds	– Placement/layering/ Integration – Easy to transport – Good value retention – Origins difficult to trace	– Import in a briefcase or trouser pocket – Store in a bonded warehouse – Buy certificates of origin – Justify non-transparent pricing through cutting – Establish a company that trades in diamonds to ensure plausibility	– Diamond experts – Purchase documents (Kimberley certificate) – Gemstone cutter	– Lack of expertise – Dependence on professionals – Counterfeits – High comparability due to standardized evaluation criteria – High-risk industry creates buzz among banks – Kimberley Process

Antiques	– Antiques market not regulated – High turnover – Price formation influenced by collectors' prices – Value difficult to measure objectively	– Acquire expertise – Select unknown objects – Have false papers and expert reports issued by renowned archaeologists – Choose non-transparent markets – Mix legal with illegal goods – Make goods unrecognizable for transport and hide them in larger loads of modern art – Choose robust goods, such as clay vessels or jewellery made of semi-precious stones – Claim that the origins are the 'property of a private gentleman' – Auctions – Actively manage supply and demand – Set up shop with over-priced goods – Plausible sales – Declare cash as cash turnover – Observe threshold values	– Expertise – Restorers – Non-transparent markets – Volatile prices	– Increased attention from the authorities due to terrorist financing – Counterfeits – Traceability through serial numbers – Customs controls – Volatility of the antiques market

Method	*General Suitability*	*Concrete Approach*	*Resources*	*Risks*
Art	– Placement/layering/ integration – Art scene successfully defends itself against regulation and AMLA subordination – Lack of regulation – Value determination is non-transparent	– Cash payment – Auctions – Flea market as origin – Maintain a good relationship with the bank – Legal entities (domiciliary companies) as owners of the objects of art – Locating art dealers via Google – Seek private art lovers – Use duty-free warehouse for storage	– Professionals – Secure bearings – Cash – Small assets – Contacts with dubious art dealers – Civil law purchase contracts	– Counterfeits – Dishonest experts – Poor self-assessment – Notification by reputable art dealers – High volatility
Real estate	– Integration/layering – Lack of awareness in the real estate sector – Large disproportion between hazard potential and Suspicious Activity Reports (SARs) – International transactions also suitable for concealment	– Choose large cities with liquid real estate markets – Select problematic properties and properties in need of renovation – Acquire real estate through companies that have the acquisition and leasing of real estate as their corporate purpose – Use straw men – Incorporate offshore companies into the network	– Expertise – Restorers – Non-transparent markets – Volatile prices	– Increased attention from the authorities due to terrorist financing – Counterfeits – Traceability through serial numbers – Customs controls – Volatility of the antiques market

		– Have the wrong purchase price notarized – Appoint own notaries – Sell again at a loss if necessary – Ensure credible origin of the official purchase price – Avoid direct transfers from offshore destinations – Fake credits – Luxury refurbishment of properties in need of renovation – Payments under CHF 100,000 cash – Fake rental agreements – Control market value of properties via easement agreements		
Consulting companies	– Layering/integration – Legal and recognized entity – Hardly any controls, provided regulated areas are avoided – Non-transparent pricing	– Establish a public limited company in Switzerland – Establish subsidiaries abroad – Disguise beneficial owners – Offer services at home and abroad	– Placement possibilities (cash deposits) – Banks with correspondent banks – Offshore companies with bank accounts in Dubai – Advisor – Directors	– Administrative assistance/legal assistance – Lack of anonymity of the beneficial owner – Transaction analyses of the bank – Cash fees unusual

Method	*General Suitability*	*Concrete Approach*	*Resources*	*Risks*
	– Performance difficult to measure	– Set up a professional website – Set up a representative business address – Actually provide services in part – Involve existing societies – Relocate services abroad to destinations that make checks more difficult – Charge for market analyses – Invoice commission payments – Remittances from Russia and Latvia – Feign business expenses through acquisitions – Complex structures with multiple levels of obfuscation – Work with neighbouring countries and offshore centres – Accounts in different jurisdictions	– Good reputation	– Examination by police/prosecution – Audit by tax authorities – Attention in case of too-high fees or inactive companies

		– Pay attention to plausibility (especially relations of the totals, sector comparison). – Accept tax assessments consistently and pay taxes promptly		
Company renovations	– Placement/layering/integration – Paper trail – Non-transparent pricing	– Select companies in need of renovation – Disguise beneficial ownership by using small, foreign investors (business angels group) – Borrow – Check the plausibility of the origin of the equity capital – Use hidden reserves to justify profits – Assume a price fantasy	– Firms in need of investment, distressed firms with jobs at risk – Corrupt assessors – Company conglomerate	– Banks demand balance sheet – Tax authorities audit balance sheet – Business risks – Commercial register verifies information – Involvement of groups subject to reporting requirements
Banks in Dubai	– Placement/layering/integration – Cash-intensive city – Offshore banking centre – Recognized, not too exotic financial centre – Anti-money laundering standards in place – Free trade zones	– Establish a company in a free trade zone – Use straw men (domestic workers, professional secretaries) – Set up account with correspondent bank – Complex uses – Direct transfers	– Discreet, less cooperative banks – Incompetent or inattentive compliance departments – Unsuspicious environment – Restricted freedom of the press	– Transaction analyses of the financial intermediaries – Dependence on compliance officers – Unfamiliar legal system – Queries from the correspondent banks – Transport of cash

Method	*General Suitability*	*Concrete Approach*	*Resources*	*Risks*
		– Document processes and justify legal background – Avoid countries that give authorities access to financial transaction data		– Sale of information
Safe-deposit box	– Placement – Storage and concealment – Contents of the safe-deposit box are secret – High security – Unknown and inaccessible location – No integration into the economic cycle	– Visit private safe-deposit box providers without identification requirements – Transfer assets by handing over safe-deposit box (keys, codes), including contents	– Safe-deposit box provider who is not subject to the AMLA or comparable regulations	– Insufficient concealment – Loss of value due to inflation – Safe-deposit box can be searched
Cash against cash	– Placement preliminary stage – Difficult to detect – Organized crime – No integration of assets into economic cycle	– Involve (corrupt) central banks – Netting between criminals – Bogus invoices as a tool – Find other money launderers via app	– Financial intermediary with criminal intents – Corrupt government – Professional foreign exchange traders – Other money launderers – App to find exchange partners	– Counterfeit banknotes

Exchange offices	– Placement/layering – Anonymous mass activity – Currency unification as a disadvantage – Combination of virtual currencies and prepaid cards	– Establish a bureau de change – Use existing small businesses in the red-light district – Fake customers – Transactions between CHF 400 and CHF 800 – Show profits – Use prepaid cards for transporting foreign currencies – Use bills of exchange as a source of funds	– Fake passports or real passports of straw men – City with tourists – Physical business with credible official activity	– Exchange offices a recognized risk factor – Larger amounts attract attention – Exceeding limit values – Control mechanisms of the exchange offices lead to clarifications of origin – Smurfing made more difficult by monitoring – Transport of foreign currencies

3.2.3 Detailed Presentation of the Results with Citations of Evidence

The results of the qualitative study are presented in detail within the scope of this chapter. For the sake of clarity, the author has also opted for a tabular listing of the most important findings in this section, each with a supporting citation. It is explicitly pointed out that the findings contained in the column 'Generalization' are usually the result of a synthesis of several quotations. The citations given are merely exemplary in nature and are therefore not always congruent with the generalization.

It should also be emphasized here that the generalization should be considered within the context of its category in each case. For example, the summary in the subcategory 'Risks' focuses exclusively on the core content of the statement to be analysed with regard to risks and neglects other aspects. Thus, the generalization does not offer a mere summary but considers the core statement from the perspective of the respective category. The level of reduction, which merely summarizes the statement, was not presented due to its banality and in light of the space constraints.

Offering a banal summary would not have represented a particularly commendable intellectual achievement on the part of the author and would only have been of limited benefit to the reader. The author believes that presenting the original statement on the one hand and the category-related generalization on the other provides both maximum transparency and the greatest possible assistance to the reader when it comes to helping them draw conclusions. Since this approach is category based, only certain information was selected.

Table 3.4 Reduction with Citation

Generalization	*Representative Quote*	*Participant*
General statements – Concrete approach		
Avoid the scope of application of the AMLA	I think, um, there are certain areas in Switzerland that are not subject to the Money Laundering Act.	Interview partner 2
Split larger amounts of cash	A yes, so first and foremost, still the cash, because I can split it; I can divide it into small amounts, I can give it to different people, I can bring it together again and so on.	Interview partner 13
Pooling of funds with tangible assets	That would be a possibility, of course, but as soon as the source of funds can be somehow distributed in a credible way, it is also difficult. But I think this pooling of allegedly small turnovers, uh, is a, is a certain risk, and I think mobile material assets have a role or play a big role there.	Interview partner 11

Generalization	*Representative Quote*	*Participant*
Investment in tangible assets	I would always take refuge in tangible assets. So I would try to take refuge in tangible assets.	Interview partner 5
Disguise the beneficial owner	I would simply exhaust as many of the possibilities as possible in order to actually be sure that the, um, that the reference to me is veiled, so to speak, and that of course the reference before is also veiled there.	Interview partner 13
Use straw men	Or you use straw men, er straw, er straw men.	Interview partner 8
Use existing structures	It uses already existing structures.	Interview partner 16
Establish plausibility	If I were a money launderer, I would try to establish plausibility.	Interview partner 14
Form chains across multiple jurisdictions	Whether then different jurisdictions that have jurisdiction, companies log into offshore destination 1, there are executive offices under offshore destination 2, the account is in offshore destination 3. Very often, these offshore companies are another offshore company.	Interview partner 12
Mixing legal and illegal funds	In our country, at least, it has been the prevailing doctrine for years, as soon as it is mixed with legal assets and you can no longer prove exactly that the three euros are criminal money and the three euros are legally acquired money. That's when you get out.	Interview partner 13
General statements – Resources		
Alternative payment methods	With all the payment methods, technologies, rechargeable prepaid cards. So everything where the physical presence, I say, on one side of the pie is going down, on the other side where it's rechargeable.	Interview partner 12
Banks with weak/corrupt/tolerant compliance	Which bank is suitable here? A small bank that is under a lot of customer pressure might be suitable. Because here you might be more likely to Accept transactions without questioning them.	Interview partner 8

Generalization	*Representative Quote*	*Participant*
Detailed contracts	Yes, detailed contracts quite simply, perhaps even with product lists to go with them that don't even exist.	Interview partner 8
Experts	Then I would have to get people who have been doing this for many years and can tell me how I can plausibly present it to the bank official in a trial and who will take it off my hands.	Interview partner 14
General statements – Risks		
Screening of ownership structures by banks	With the areas where it's about trusts, about indirect ownership positions, because that has to be determined first. It has to be shareholder structure and so on. That is being done and it is being taken very seriously. At least at the banks I work for.	Interview partner 3
Queries from the banks	You have to expect that the bank will question where the money comes from and why this is being done. And a good money launderer is prepared for this situation.	Interview partner 16
Burden of proof of the authorities	The investigators' Achilles' heel is the burden of proof.	Interview partner 16
Business risks	Sure, so you always have to pay something for money laundering.	Interview partner 4
Fraud	Would be well advised to take a closer look at what it is and where it comes from. There is also a lot of fraud in the classical sense.	Interview partner 10
Embezzlement	Trustors have to be well paid. So if someone appears as an account holder and gets enough money for it, he has to think ten times about going against the trustor as long as he gets enough money for it every year.	Interview partner 16
Gold – Concrete approach		

Generalization	*Representative Quote*	*Participant*
Feigning inheritance while taking into account the deceased's financial circumstances and tax declarations	And of course, the wealthier someone is, the more there is in it, so to speak. I can come along with ten pictures, with, uh, 20 kilos of gold as a family inheritance, that's more credible than if I, as a simple wage earner, suddenly come along with 20 kilos, with 20 kilos of gold, which I supposedly inherited and, uh, which my relatives/If you look at the tax returns, that's actually, uh, that doesn't appear anywhere.	Interview partner 11
Buy gold together and recast	Of course, I can also buy gold and such together with my black money somewhere and then pour it over and sell it to a gold dealer, a licensed gold dealer, and say, yes, I bought this together as a family heirloom.	Interview partner 11
Storage in bonded warehouse	And I think the bonded warehouses are also a problem. And, uh, that, uh, because I think you could read a lot about that recently. It's also well known. Uh, there is already a, a big problem, that, uh, value, such mobile material assets are stored somewhere in an international area and never leave it. They leave, they change the owner maybe, maybe not even that, they stay there and nobody has any, really no knowledge about it. There, uh, is certainly a risk there. But here, I'm not sure how far the inventory obligation of the, uh, warehouse keepers goes. Whether they really know what, whether they have to record or know what exactly is in there.	Interview partner 11
Transfer ownership rights in the bonded warehouse	Um, they don't even have to move it; they can leave it in there and transfer the ownership there.	Interview partner 17
Profit-taking in the event of positive price development	Yes, you can see that as an investment, and when the price goes up, it's common to sell that again. Profit taking.	Interview partner 10
Gold – Resources		
Documentation of origin	Gold; I will have to document where I bought it.	Interview partner 12

Generalization	*Representative Quote*	*Participant*
Gold – Risks		
Fraud	We personally have big, um, frauds with gold, with gold bullion.	Interview partner 18
Theft	There is a danger that it will also get lost on the way.	Interview partner 17
Acquisition is registered if applicable	Gold has to be acquired somewhere, so it has to be registered again.	Interview partner 5
Gold dealers are subject to Article 2, paragraph 3 AMLA	Uh, and these businesses are, according to Art. 2, para. 3 Restriction of Competition Act; subject to the Money Laundering Act. Accordingly, we receive a few reports again and again from these gold traders, etc.	Interview partner 2
High volatility	The disadvantage is high volatility. Anyone who invested everything in gold as a money launderer three years ago has also lost quite a bit in the meantime.	Interview partner 16
Quantities easily traceable due to standardized prices	With gold, on the other hand, every buyer or seller wants to know the approximate price of gold at the moment. No, so if they bring 50,000 to the bank here on one day, because they say, I sold so-and-so many gold pieces, you know exactly, aha, it must have been so-and-so many goods or so-and-so many kilograms to generate that, and then the customer has to prove again, out of embarrassment, where did I get the others, where did I buy them? I would have to be able to produce receipts. So, that is difficult to manipulate, I think.	Interview partner 5
Weight and volume make transport difficult	But otherwise gold is of course, uh, yes, it already has a specific weight. So, a kilo of gold is a kilo of gold and, uh, yes, it's not so easy to transport.	Interview partner 17
Jewellery – Concrete approach		
Establish actual activity in the jewellery trade	If such jewellery purchases are faked in order to launder money, this also requires a certain actual activity.	Interview partner 11

Generalization	*Representative Quote*	*Participant*
Fake customers	And that's probably where people come and, uh, sell it, and of course you can/could pump up this business with black money. Who knows how much I really bought and sold this weekend?	Interview partner 11
Distribute leaflets for jewellery purchase	I have to perform somehow. But, uh, that's not, that's not great art, that's, uh, relatively easy, and, uh, without foisting something on someone, but you certainly know the flyers. Uh, next weekend, XY will be in the, somewhere in the shopping centre, and he'll buy your old jewellery.	Interview partner 11
Buy jewellery in holiday destinations	There are cases where people say why they buy so much jewellery in holiday destinations with cash and so on, because they want to avoid the paper trail. Officially, they say, well, the jewellery is from a friend.	Interview partner 18
Declare as hereditary property and record it in the estate register	Then it would have to have come up in – how do we say in our country? In probate proceedings.	Interview partner 14
Declare it as a gift	We have fifteen, er, ten, yes the 10,000 regulations cash control entry and exit, but for gifts, we don't have a single regulation on the source of funds.	Interview partner 18
Jewellery – Resources		
Expertise in processing and materials	There are various starting points for jewellery. On the one hand, it is of course good if you have mineralogical knowledge, i.e., if you can easily recognize what the original materials are … um, yes, if you can then also judge whether the production method, whether it looks antique or not.	Interview partner 6
Product with lack of comparability	As I said, with jewellery or antiques, a piece of jewellery can have any price. A piece of jewellery can cost 1,000 euros and you can sell it for 10,000. That already exists in the same way.	Interview partner 5

Generalization	*Representative Quote*	*Participant*
Jewellery – Risks		
Estimation risks	Yes, with antique jewellery, one might have a hard time estimating.	Interview partner 13
Pawnshops already in the sights of the authorities	We've heard about it through this working group, money laundering prevention, because pawnshops are on the radar.	Interview partner 4
Rough diamonds – Concrete approach		
Import in a briefcase or trouser pocket	It used to be common practice to import diamonds in a small suitcase or trouser pocket.	Interview partner 7
Storage in bonded warehouse	Of course, you can also smuggle things in there that are not obvious, I declare, I rent a compartment here in the bonded warehouse to store my antiques, and here is the list. I don't say that the Chinese vase is full of rough diamonds. And, uh, then, uh, I have the stuff in there. So it's like that, I can smuggle stuff, uh, goods in there that are not inventoried and maybe won't be discovered. That's also how it is here, uh, one part is officially public and something is floating behind it.	Interview partner 11
Buy certificates of origin	Certificates of origin, and I've also been to Africa on business a few times, and I know you can get anything for the money.	Interview partner 17
Justify non-transparent pricing through cutting	I can play with the price. I can say it's a much bigger cut and then worth more.	Interview partner 16
Rough diamonds – Resources		
Diamond experts	That's why it's always more difficult when I now have a rough diamond; do I have a glass bead or a rough diamond. That means I am always dependent on some expert.	Interview partner 18
Purchase documents (Kimberley certificate)	With gemstones, I will have to document where I bought it at some point.	Interview partner 12

Generalization	*Representative Quote*	*Participant*
Rough diamonds – risks		
Lack of expertise	This is an area where a lot of people don't really know.	Interview partner 12
Dependence on professionals	I personally would not do it. Being dependent on a specialist who can tell the difference between a glass bead and a rough diamond is something that I would involve some people with the knowledge to do, and this seems too risky to me.	Interview partner 18
Counterfeits	Perfect certificates for fraud. That is, where you have given a higher value than you actually sold your bling for.	Interview partner 12
High comparability due to standardized evaluation criteria	With diamonds, you have a fixed value again. If I had a high cash turnover, you would say, aha, he must have sold so-and-so many diamonds per day to launder the money like that.	Interview partner 5
High-risk industry creates buzz among banks	It's not our field of business. I would also not accept any company that is active in the rough diamond trade. I have already received several requests, but we refuse because/hm, hm, we don't know, we can't judge, we don't know how it works.	Interview partner 14
Kimberley Process	Yes, we have, that is part of the Kimberley Process.	Interview partner 17
Antiques – Concrete approach		
Select unknown objects	They should actually be things that come fresh from the earth, so to speak. In other words, things that are not yet known to science. If you were to find a life-size Roman bronze statue somewhere in the Mediterranean and put it on the market, it would be worth millions, um, of course, uh, people would immediately say that this is disreputable, it can't be right, it must have been collected illegally somehow.	Interview partner 6

Generalization	*Representative Quote*	*Participant*
Have false papers and expert reports issued by renowned archaeologists	This well-known axiologist had no reservations whatsoever and examined everything that was shown to him, published the things and through this, through publishing, one has a little bit of an entry point as a layperson to be able to judge whether the things are rare.	Interview partner 6
Choose non-transparent markets	You can sell Madonnas there, you can sell a painting there, and whether you then make a discount or a surcharge, no one can assess that.	Interview partner 5
Mixing legal with illegal goods	One can mix legal assets with illegal goods, making it even more difficult to determine what is illegal.	Interview partner 16
Making goods unrecognizable for transport and hiding them in larger loads of modern art	He smuggled things out of Egypt, for example, and made them very ugly beforehand. For example, he covered them with, uh, masses, uh, real sculpture with, uh, malleable mass and then painted them very garishly, colourfully, so that they looked like bazaar kitsch and every customs officer who looked at something like that immediately said, no, that's bazaar kitsch, that's terrible, and that's how he brought them to Great Britain.	Interview partner 6
Choose robust goods, such as clay vessels or jewellery made of semi-precious stones.	Other things, for example, clay vessels or even jewellery made from semi-precious stone, from this gemstone and so on, are a bit more robust.	Interview partner 6
Origin 'property of a private gentleman'	And, um, yes, X have, so since X has, the whole thing has, uh, [been] put on the market under the heading 'property of a private gentleman' in principle.	Interview partner 6
Auctions	Then offered them for sale at X in London.	Interview partner 6
Actively manage supply and demand	Of course, there is also supply and demand [laughs], which you can of course control.	Interview partner 12

Generalization	*Representative Quote*	*Participant*
Set up shop with overpriced goods	The tenant has his shop, and in this shop, they hang a few worthless pictures or put up a few figurines or a few chamber pots, the antique selections, and then, when you look in, you only see, aha, he's actually selling something.	Interview partner 5
Plausible sales	Yes, and if you check the plausibility of the turnover there.	Interview partner 7
Declare cash as cash turnover	So if we had an antique customer, we wouldn't find out how much he actually gets for his Madonna figures or pictures normally. And then I pay in a lot of money and then it's just not noticeable, a good deal has been made.	Interview partner 5
No upper limit	There is no upper limit on an amount above which it would become critical.	Interview partner 7
Antiques – Resources		
Expertise	And, uh, for that they would first have to, um, learn different languages, learn to read cuneiform. So different languages were simply written in cuneiform, so they would then have to, um, actually acquire specialist knowledge, which is what you actually do at university.	Interview partner 6
Restorers	So if they are very fragile things, let's say, metal objects are often very fragile, they are often already very corroded, for example through storage in the ground, and they would then actually have to be restored in order to be secured so that the corrosion process, for example, does not continue.	Interview partner 6
Non-transparent markets	But, of course, it is also a very intransparent market and everything that is intransparent is, of course, pleasing to the money launderer, because it becomes difficult again to recognize whether a transaction is plausible or no longer plausible.	Interview partner 17
Volatile prices	Between private companies, the prices are extremely volatile.	Interview partner 2

Generalization	*Representative Quote*	*Participant*
Antiques – Risks		
Increased attention from the authorities due to terrorist financing	One of the five or six ways of financing ISIS [the Islamic State] is effectively through antiquities. They destroy some things, but only things that they can't really sell … as far as antiquities are concerned, an important issue at the moment is of course the financing of ISIS the Islamic State, where Switzerland is relatively well positioned in terms of control mechanisms.	Interview partner 2
Counterfeits	And the risk that I get the wrong antique or (unintelligible) is huge.	Interview partner 18
Traceability through serial numbers	You have photos of things that have serial numbers, which were then taken up again.	Interview partner 6
Customs controls	Yes, that depends again, I would think, on how good these controls are and how well trained the customs officer is.	Interview partner 6
Volatility of the antiques market	Then there is the threat of a quasi-financial loss.	Interview partner 17
Art – Concrete approach		
Cash payment at auctions	Cash payments at auctions are historically accepted.	Interview partner 7
Flea market as origins	We have already seen cases where someone really bought a book at a flea market and then sold it on for 10 million because it was supposedly a rare work of art or a rare collector's item.	Interview partner 9
Maintain a good relationship with the bank	If we had a client whom we had known for a long time, whom we knew well, and who said that he had a work of art that he would sell, and we were not talking about sales in the millions, but about medium amounts, then that would probably be possible.	Interview partner 14

Generalization	*Representative Quote*	*Participant*
Legal entities (domiciliary companies) as owners of the objects of art	Especially when it is in the area of fine art, i.e. really paintings by great masters, etc., that is not done in cash; these art objects usually belong to legal entities, i.e. a separate domiciliary company is set up, which then owns the painting.	Interview partner 17
Locating art dealers via Google	Hm, yes, uh, I think I would actually, um, ask around, try to find out, um, if one then, so there are, uh, I think, um, about quite normal, I know Google search or so, the possibilities to just Google antiques dealers in the vicinity or be it in Switzerland for example and contact the people and say 'you know I have here, I would be interested in selling this, do you see possibilities there'?	Interview partner 6
Seek private art lovers	If there is a certain size of a market, I can also develop an activity as a free rider with people who also perhaps shy away from the spotlight. And then I can, uh, let this run alongside without actually entering this market.	Interview partner 11
Use duty-free warehouse for storage	Then there are these possibilities via duty-free warehouses to store the things for years.	Interview partner 2
Art – Resources		
Professionals	Again, I need a special, special professional. I need one; I have to buy their trust, otherwise, and – yes, and if it's really good-quality art, the vis-à-vis will probably be questioned more.	Interview partner 18
Secure bearings	But I think in Germany also somehow at the airport or something. These huge warehouses are relatively new. Where you can store things duty free in such a no-man's land. So works of art and whatever else, and I think even cars can be stored in these things.	Interview partner 10
Cash	It's easy to get in if you pay with cash.	Interview partner 17

Generalization	*Representative Quote*	*Participant*
Small assets	Well, if we say that it's now worth 4 million francs, that's a different story. There has to be something available right off the bat, but even with amounts of several 10,000 francs, you can move a lot of assets from A to B.	Interview partner 17
Contact with dubious art dealers	Well, I would first have to have contacts in the dubious art dealer circles.	Interview partner 6
Civil law purchase contracts	Often civil law contracts are sufficient.	Interview partner 9
Art – Risks		
Counterfeits	It is just insanely difficult to determine or have confirmed that the artwork is genuine or not.	Interview partner 17
Dishonest experts	Yes, because there are people who know much better or who pretend that it has some value.	Interview partner 17
Poor self-assessment	The fascinating thing about fine art is that many people don't want to admit that they don't understand anything about the subject and let themselves be blinded by it.	Interview partner 17
Reputable art dealers report suspicious activity	Art dealers who are reputable pay very close attention to who else is appearing on the market.	Interview partner 11
High volatility	Unlike gold or silver or jewellery, for example, where the precious metal has a market value, the value of art is always in the eye of the beholder and, ultimately, who is to say whether this painting by Picasso is really worth a million or 5 million?	Interview partner 9
Real estate – Concrete approach		
Choose large cities with liquid real estate markets	But in big cities, there are liquid real estate markets where you know exactly how much the property will still be worth in half a year.	Interview partner 16

Generalization	*Representative Quote*	*Participant*
Select problematic properties and properties in need of renovation	These are usually not the properties in the best locations, but I go to neighbourhoods with a high proportion of foreigners, uh, properties that are in need of renovation, um, I buy the whole property plus the building, renovate it or sell it again afterwards, uh, on a condominium basis, um, individually and make a nice profit.	Interview partner 17
Acquire real estate through companies that have the acquisition and leasing of real estate as their corporate purpose	Has the intention, must have it yes, to carry out the property acquisition or the intention to rent it out.	Interview partner 18
Use straw men	So in any case, with a name that doesn't stand out or with a business background that can be explained. The whole environment makes a decisive impression.	Interview partner 7
Incorporating offshore companies into the network	Let's say a company in Zug buys a property which is then paid for by its Cayman Islands subsidiary.	Interview partner 7
Have the wrong purchase price notarized	However, the residual risk remains, of course, as it is known that the amounts here are not all always declared as they should be and, uh, probably, uh, cash amounts also flow.	Interview partner 2
Use own notaries	If it is criminals who behave directly like this, there is a scene that also has its 'own notaries' who, of course, wouldn't do a damn thing to report anything then. There are notaries and lawyers involved for every purpose, also in the OK.	Interview partner 10
Sell again at a loss if necessary	Then you get the flat. Like this. Even though it might only be worth 500,000 or 480,000. Then you have a flat, and even if you sell it later at a loss, let's say 400,000 euros, you have at least laundered a large part of the money.	Interview partner 5

Generalization	*Representative Quote*	*Participant*
Ensure credible origin of the official purchase price	But it is of course, if I have the origin and the money is not incriminated, then I lack the foreshadowing, then the use per se is also relatively difficult to recognize as money laundering.	Interview partner 14
Avoid direct transfers from offshore destinations	Now the question is, where does the money come from? Maybe it was transferred for the purchase of real estate. The bank is satisfied with that because it is also plausible with the story that the client told me in Austria. The question is, where does the money come from beforehand? If it keeps coming from the Cayman Islands, I would question that again.	Interview partner 8
Fake credits	He financed himself, so to speak, with a fictitious loan. Then he bought the property, apparently without his own money, perhaps from the origin. Provided that the external financing is accepted, that's fine.	Interview partner 10
Luxury refurbishment of properties in need of renovation	If, on the other hand, I have an existing property and simply renovate it in luxury with a lot of money, then it looks a bit different, even if the, um, if the companies all invoice properly and account for it and book it with themselves. But they are not obliged to report anything.	Interview partner 11
Payments under CHF 100,000 in cash	So you never pay for real estate in cash. The most you can do is make a down payment in cash, and the money laundering law restricts payments for use to 100,000, so it has to be processed through a financial intermediary.	Interview partner 15
Fake rental agreements	And then you can also fake rental contracts. Produce rental income that then turns illegal assets into legal assets, so to speak. Because rental inflows come in that were not there in reality.	Interview partner 10

Generalization	*Representative Quote*	*Participant*
Control market value of properties via easement agreements	So before certain encumbrances flow in or encumbrance and sale prohibitions, rights of use that are registered, whether the right is there or not, that of course has an effect on the market value. And accordingly, I think I can also control it.	Interview partner 12
Real estate – Resources		
Liquid real estate market	If I have a reasonably liquid real estate market where I know I can buy and sell and don't have to accept a big drop in value, then of course I can take advantage of that by bringing large funds into circulation.	Interview partner 16
Good faith, inattentive lawyers, notaries and brokers	If I now make such a purchase, then both the notary and the broker would have to register and record this purchase price and the brokerage contract accordingly. Now an idiot comes along with good German who overpays and there you would have a trace of the money launderer again.	Interview partner 5
Cash-enthusiastic sellers	First, you still have to find someone who will sell you a property for cash.	Interview partner 7
Real estate – Risks		
Media attention	The media love it when you say, especially in the real estate business, 'Ah, the daughter of a Central Asian ruler has bought a villa for 75 million in the Lake Geneva area'.	Interview partner 17
Attention of law enforcement authorities	Um, because if you stand out, then there are always people from the law enforcement scene, police officers and maybe even public prosecutors, who take a look at something.	Interview partner 17
Attention of banks drawn to unusual transactions	The bank would have to ask where the money came from, and if the estate agent says he got it from a house sale, then he would have to say 'Aha, who gave you that in cash?'	Interview partner 4
Attention of the tax authorities in case of too low real estate transfer tax	That the real estate sector is certainly problematic, that the monitoring is there, that both the tax authorities are not very cooperative.	Interview partner 4

Generalization	*Representative Quote*	*Participant*
Suspicion of lawyers or notaries	Then we usually have lawyers and notaries who are responsible for signing the contracts. And I believe that there is also a bit of a safety net. So if a situation were really totally suspicious, I believe that one of the people involved would report it.	Interview partner 13
Comprehensive traceability through documentation of property transactions within the scope of the land register application	That may not be as easy as one imagines or because the real estate market is relatively highly regulated with the land registry and notarized contract and so on.	Interview partner 17
Business risks due to fluctuations in value	There is an economic risk, but I think people are happy to accept that.	Interview partner 17
Queries regarding the source of funds	Of course, especially with real estate, I have to ask myself where the money comes from.	Interview partner 14
Consulting companies – Concrete approach		
Establish a public limited company in Switzerland	What also happens, an example: Someone from Latvia has a million in cash. He deposits it in Latvia, transfers it to a trustee in Switzerland and instructs him to set up a Swiss limited company.	Interview partner 7
Establish subsidiaries abroad	You certainly have to have [laughing] sisters abroad.	Interview partner 7
Offer services at home and abroad	But, uh, it, on a very simplified structure, uh, then of course in Switzerland a company can officially offer services at home and abroad.	Interview partner 11
Set up a professional website	Well, then I would ask myself, well, okay, there is, so that's something, if I saw such a test case, then I would probably first Google the consultancy company and look at it, does it exist at all.	Interview partner 8
Set up a representative business address	I would also look at where I can buy additional services, such as representative business addresses, where I only have a forwarding order, address lists and so on. So that's how I would structure it.	Interview partner 12

Generalization	*Representative Quote*	*Participant*
Actually provide the service in part	It is important to ensure that if you make it so open or supposedly so open, that some part of it is actually provided.	Interview partner 11
Involve existing societies	So one, perhaps I would preferably buy on stock, which was founded years ago. Of course, that can also document a certain history, that this company has been around for a while.	Interview partner 12
Relocate service abroad to destinations that make checks more difficult	And that is already the case, foreign services abroad, for which a fee is then earned in Switzerland, is, uh, would be feasible, if the service cannot be verified, right.	Interview partner 11
Charge for market analyses	In terms of sales tax, they invoice other services or market analyses and so on, in order to raise money from a neighbouring country, and then pass it on to offshore areas, and these offshore areas then have a bank account in Switzerland, Vienna and Lake Zurich, and so on.	Interview partner 18
Invoice commission payments	The classic example of corruption, Mr Teichmann, is commission. Somebody is told that you are entitled to a commission, and he also invoices you, not just an advisor, so somehow the commission taker invoices you and then gets at least part of the money. Or he is part of a money laundering chain and passes on part of it. So the commission still exists, that's really factual knowledge now, in foreign corruption.	Interview partner 10
Transfers from Latvia	And the capital was transferred from Latvia to Switzerland.	Interview partner 7
Feigning business expenses through acquisitions	With a correspondingly huge turnover, yes, you need a certain percentage to reduce operating expenses, invest them or transfer them abroad.	Interview partner 12

Generalization	*Representative Quote*	*Participant*
Complex structures with multiple levels of obfuscation	So the more complex the matter becomes, the more financial centres are involved and the more complex the structures are, be they social structures or whatever, the more suitable the whole thing is, of course.	Interview partner 2
Involve neighbouring countries and offshore centres	These are the many companies that are interconnected and that quickly go abroad and have other companies there.	Interview partner 7
Accounts in different jurisdictions	Because the company is an offshore company and the account is somewhere else.	Interview partner 12
Pay attention to plausibility (especially relations of the totals, sector comparison)	I'm convinced that you can also make industry comparisons and say, okay, for a clothing boutique, this order of magnitude, for this location, for this product, uh, are our empirical values that the daily turnover is in this range.	Interview partner 17
Accept tax assessments consistently and pay taxes promptly	So even if I reduce the tax burden, of course I will accept the payments I have to make.	Interview partner 12
Consulting companies – Resources		
Placement possibilities (cash deposits)	But the cash has to enter the cycle somewhere.	Interview partner 5
Banks with correspondent banks	You just have to find institutions where you will eventually work as a correspondent bank or where/with whom you now work with the financial institution.	Interview partner 9
Offshore companies with bank accounts in Dubai	Letterbox companies in Dubai, they have bank accounts in Dubai, and that is just really difficult.	Interview partner 7

Generalization	*Representative Quote*	*Participant*
Advisor	But the Russian didn't know that you don't need the whole million and simply told the trustee to find him a joint-stock company, who took the whole million as share capital and then it was formally bound in the company. The Russian was of the opinion that he had the money at his disposal and could easily take it out of the company again. He was not aware that share capital cannot be reduced so easily. Of course, the Russian almost didn't get his money back this way.	Interview partner 7
Directors	There is the possibility to use directors, so that I really have an offer.	Interview partner 16
Good reputation	A good name and familiarity with the local conditions always helps. Let's say a trustee you know.	Interview partner 7
Consulting companies – Risks		
Administrative assistance/legal assistance	There anyway, so within the framework of administrative assistance. In the EU and with double tax agreements and so on, we pass on bank data, bank information to EU countries and third countries. And for/and the next step now is, if the tax authorities check Austrian entrepreneurs, then the/then Austrian banking secrecy no longer applies, and then they have to disclose more or less all accounts, bank details, in general.	Interview partner 18
Lack of anonymity of the beneficial owner	You must state who the beneficial owner is, at least at the bank.	Interview partner 7
Transaction analyses of the bank	And yes, and this company then handles the turnover that is later deposited with the bank, and if the bank didn't have the brightest head at the top, it wouldn't notice that the turnover of this company is much too high.	Interview partner 5

Generalization	*Representative Quote*	*Participant*
Cash fees unusual	Even if they can be documented with an invoice, I find that cash payments for consultancies are not standard at all.	Interview partner 17
Examination by the public prosecutor's office	If anyone, be it the tax authorities or the public prosecutor's office, wants to check a company, it stops very quickly at the border.	Interview partner 11
Audit by tax authorities	And if anyone gets the idea to check my books and sees that I actually/yes, to whom I, to whom I bill, and where that comes from. There is also the question, how credible is that? If I am active in Switzerland and abroad, at least the Swiss accounts should be somehow traceable. I always say this from a tax perspective or from the perspective of a tax audit.	Interview partner 11
Attention to companies that are too inactive	Well, as soon as I show my company on the market somehow, everyone asks how it's actually doing, how does it stand there? How is it judged? It's a bit strange when I have a service company that is completely inactive. You can't find it anywhere, not even on the web.	Interview partner 11
Corporate restructuring – Concrete approach		
Select companies in need of restructuring	I would look for companies that are in need of restructuring, and in this day and age, there are probably plenty to choose from.	Interview partner 17
Disguise beneficial ownership by using small, foreign investors (business angels group)	Then I, uh, pretend to have many, many small, smaller investments, uh, bring together a large amount and invest it as a single investor, behind whom there are supposedly many different ones. That way I can present it in a more or less credible way.	Interview partner 11

Generalization	*Representative Quote*	*Participant*
Borrow	So I would always take out a loan as a company, of course at the risk of being asked for more balance sheets. But I would somehow take it out on credit, but only to the extent that I could pay it back again gradually. But simply so that the company wouldn't notice it so much.	Interview partner 5
Check the plausibility of the origin of the equity capital	To declare smaller transactions or to actually pretend to have more in order to then credibly present a large fortune. And then I can invest it where I want. The origin is then, um, credibly presented and is not, significantly less questioned.	Interview partner 11
Use hidden reserves to justify profits	[Invest in] real estate or in a somewhat ailing enterprise and then officially bring it up to scratch and realize the hidden reserves and the potential, the performance potential. And with both, the question arises, how credible is it that I am putting money into this?	Interview partner 11
Assume a price fantasy	So one assumes a corresponding price fantasy then. The buyers then all sell and resell the company shares accordingly.	Interview partner 12
Corporate restructuring – Resources		
Firms in need of investment, distressed firms with jobs at risk	Um, where I can say, um, listen, it's maybe suffering, maybe even distressed, um, and there are a lot of jobs at stake.	Interview partner 17
Corrupt assessors	That is, of course, a question of how receptive someone is to writing a fake expert opinion.	Interview partner 9
Company conglomerate	Yes, you can deduct it again for tax purposes, so if you have a conglomerate of companies where you say, okay, I'm investing in a new company or in an ailing company and I'm now making a loss, can I then offset it against a part of the business that is run according to business principles, but that you can write off for tax purposes?	Interview partner 17

Generalization	*Representative Quote*	*Participant*
Corporate restructuring – Risks		
Banks and tax authorities demand a balance sheet	That's why we have to take a look; with companies, we feel sorry when we have a balance sheet of the company.	Interview partner 5
Business risks	[It's a] financial risk, so if you invest in a distressed company that is trying to be restructured, then there is a great risk that it will not be successful. So to speak, that you have to write off the investment.	Interview partner 17
Commercial register and notary	And then the question will probably arise with the new entry in the company register or with any other, let's say, actions, which in turn require a lawyer or a notary.	Interview partner 13
Involvement of groups subject to reporting requirements	Again, if there, if the transacting person falls under the reportable occupation, then they have to look.	Interview partner 13
Banks in Dubai – Concrete approach		
Establish a company in a free trade zone	Well, it's pretty easy to set up companies. There's 32 or 33 free zones in the UAE, most of them in Dubai and other smaller emirates. And you can set up a company there very quickly and easily for a bit of cash, erm, and then just – and then get a bank account and hide behind it.	Interview partner 1
Use stooges (domestic workers, professional secretaries)	You know, the Filipino maid or somebody will give you the passport to, you know, so it's pretty easy.	Interview partner 1
Set up an account with a correspondent bank	There is the famous keyword 'correspondent bank'.	Interview partner 4
Complex uses	With such large companies, it's a bit more complex. There is a concrete reference to invoices, to projects. It simply looks different.	Interview partner 8

Generalization	*Representative Quote*	*Participant*
Direct transfers	That is, if I make a payment instead of, I'll say some example now from Portugal to Switzerland, I make the diversions via Mexico, Singapore and I don't know where to, uh, then of course I have to clarify that and I have to say, why did they make these diversions, why no direct bank connection to Switzerland?	Interview partner 15
Document processes and justify legal background	A clarification also includes documenting the processes and then you also have to weigh up the legal background.	Interview partner 15
Avoid countries that give authorities access to financial transaction data	As a money launderer, it is important to avoid countries where the authorities have relatively direct access to financial transaction data.	Interview partner 16
Banks in Dubai – Resources		
Discreet, less cooperative banks	The credit institutions in the European area do not have the possibility to obtain certain information.	Interview partner 13
Incompetent or inattentive compliance departments	If I have someone sitting there in the area of compliance who really only adheres to the given rules and perhaps has relatively little foresight, as far as the phenomenon as a whole is concerned, then a money launderer probably wouldn't recognize it if it said money laundering in the subject line.	Interview partner 13
Unsuspicious environment	You need an unsuspicious environment. You need a highly professional financial centre that offers you everything you want.	Interview partner 16
Restricted freedom of the press	I think the free press factor plays a big role, because often cases are not discovered by investigators but by the media, or at least spread [by them].	Interview partner 16

Generalization	*Representative Quote*	*Participant*
Banks in Dubai – Risks		
Transactional analysis of financial intermediaries	The question is rather what standards of due diligence do our banks apply? That is, how do European banks deal with the fact that they have a counterpart in Dubai or somewhere else?	Interview partner 13
Dependence on compliance officers	So I think that especially in the money laundering compliance area, a lot really depends on the action and people.	Interview partner 13
Unfamiliar legal system	It is subject to a completely different legal system, which is probably a risk. I mean the risk for the money launderer.	Interview partner 7
Queries from the correspondent banks	Then a Swiss bank is involved, which is now the case with us, that was the case. The money came from Dubai to a bank account in Switzerland, and Switzerland ... the bank inquired with the accused and with its client where the money came from.	Interview partner 7
Transport of cash	Yes, and if they have larger quantities in the suitcase, the dogs sniff that out. That can be the same in Dubai.	Interview partner 5
Sale of information	Hm, and there is certainly also a leak sometimes, and information is sold.	Interview partner 17
Safe-deposit boxes – Concrete procedure		
Visit private safe-deposit box providers without identification requirements	But it's true that you don't know who is behind it, etc., if it's not declared or if nothing is identified, just like with the other financial intermediaries.	Interview partner 2

Generalization	*Representative Quote*	*Participant*
Transfer of assets by handing over safe-deposit boxes (keys, codes) including contents	That's not the general problem, whether they rent it, but the problem is that there is no one who has the right to pass it on, right? So they rent it, regardless of whether they are people from Switzerland. They can also articulate themselves accordingly and then always, I don't know, code or somewhere else and so on. And I'm the one who can enter the locker at any time.	Interview partner 12
Safe-deposit boxes – Resources		
Safe-deposit box provider who is not subject to the AMLA or comparable regulations	Safe deposit boxes is certainly also a topic that is relatively topical at the moment. Um, as I said, uh ... within the framework of a certain financial intermediary activity, the storage of assets is subject to the safe deposit boxes. So the one who offers this service is subject to the AMLA; the others who simply offer safe deposit boxes are not subject to the AMLA.	Interview partner 2
Safe-deposit boxes – Risks		
Insufficient concealment	But the concealment, the concealment does not take place, or the (unintelligible) does not take place, by putting it in our safe or in the post office in a box or somewhere.	Interview partner 14
Loss of value due to inflation	On the contrary, or the assets tend to decrease in value.	Interview partner 17
Safe-deposit box can be searched	If nobody knows, uh, clearly thwarted, if you have a clue, there are certain police possibilities, you can go open any locker.	Interview partner 2
Cash against cash – Concrete approach		
Involves (corrupt) central banks	I mean, what we also see in part is that, uh, ultimately, yes, state authorities also make use of money laundering means in part and, and ultimately channel funds past the official, uh, central banking or banking system.	Interview partner 9

Generalization	*Representative Quote*	*Participant*
Netting between criminals	But you have a Latvian in London who wants to transfer euros home, but then you have someone in Latvia who wants to transfer euros to the UK, and there is no transaction at all, let alone a physical transaction between Latvia and England, but not even an electronic one, but only the, only the difference is transferred, so to speak.	Interview partner 17
Bogus invoices as a tool	You trigger a transfer with a bogus invoice. Then 2 million are sent from A to B to clear the balance. So these are forms of cooperation that we have also already seen.	Interview partner 16
Find other money launderers via an app	So the system is so intelligent, so it brings people together and says okay, you want to have euros there and you want to have euros in another country, and sometimes that it is just transferred quasi from country to country; it is just calculated and the transaction only takes place within the, uh, state and the destination country and no longer across borders.	Interview partner 17
Cash against cash – Resources		
Financial intermediaries with criminal intent	If the financial intermediary himself brings criminal intent to light, then it is difficult to grasp. Because it is not because the control mechanisms would not be effective.	Interview partner 2
Professional foreign exchange traders	As a lawyer, I once had a client who lived on foreign currency exchange.	Interview partner 7
Other money launderers	Okay, I have dollars and you have euros; I need euros, you need dollars; we settle it at the same time.	Interview partner 17
App to find exchange partners	Um, and they say okay, um, we would like to transfer money even more cheaply, they have made an app for that; you can register and the system searches for it, so to speak.	Interview partner 17

Generalization	*Representative Quote*	*Participant*
Cash against cash – Risks		
Counterfeit banknotes	Now, of course, there are the big counterfeit notes, trade-in for real, yes, or contaminated with addiction, narcotics; certainly contaminated.	Interview partner 18
Exchange offices – Concrete procedure		
Establish a bureau de change	It would probably be much smarter to have a bureau de change myself, because then I could fake money exchanges that didn't even take place and would thus smuggle my cash into my completely comprehensible, plausible front business.	Interview partner 8
Using existing small businesses in the red-light district	But the, um, yes, who are perhaps based in the red-light district, that's just the way it is. Go to the Langstrasse district in Zurich; it's full of small bureaux de change and travel agencies that are being set up at the same time.	Interview partner 17
Fake customers	If a Saudi businessman will, uh, now, uh, change this amount and says he wants to shop at Bahnhofstrasse, that is quite plausible.	Interview partner 15
Transactions between CHF 400 and CHF 800	But there is a threshold for special clarifications, which is 5,000 francs. And most transactions are carried out below this threshold, i.e., most transactions are between CHF 400 and CHF 800.	Interview partner 15
Show profits	And then the question is, if I really want to launder, do I really have to show and report these turnovers, the profits on them?	Interview partner 11
Use prepaid cards for transporting foreign currencies	In this day and age, all these prepaid cards, well, they're just cards that you can top up, and if I go for a drive with a card like that, probably no one will check how much money I have with me.	Interview partner 13

Generalization	*Representative Quote*	*Participant*
Use bills of exchange as source of funds	If I were a customer, I could change money as if I had dollars before and euros afterwards. But I still have cash. The only thing I have is a bill of exchange receipt and maybe I can tell a bank, yes, that is my source of funds, but that is not a material source of funds, that is only a receipt for an exchange of money. But we have already seen that.	Interview partner 8
Exchange offices – Resources		
Forged passports	The problem here is that when I change over 5,000 and have to identify myself, you can't expect the person at the counter, whether it's at the train station or at the bank, to recognize whether a passport is genuine or not. That would be going a bit too far – he's not a customs officer.	Interview partner 15
City with tourists	In a bigger city or like Zurich now, for example, also in Geneva or in Bern or in Ticino, where there are tourists from Russia, for example, or from China or wherever.	Interview partner 17
Physical business with credible official activity	But here, too, there needs to be a certain, uh, official basic activity that is credible … fictitious turnovers, which are then not shown, or which are perhaps shown, but do not actually come from the exchange activity.	Interview partner 11
Exchange offices – Risks		
Exchange offices are a recognized risk factor	There is already the danger that this is of course a recognized risk factor, the bureau de change, and that is of course seen very critically. So it wasn't like that in the past, but today we as a bank/if we as a bank had a customer like that, we would make sure that the turnover is real.	Interview partner 5

Generalization	*Representative Quote*	*Participant*
Larger amounts attract attention	Someone changes, um, as you say, CHF 25,000, and looks, that's a very high amount, also for the holidays an extremely high amount, and you don't do something like that at the exchange counter, but with advantage at the bank. So in this case, you would have to clarify where the money comes from and then you would have to ask for the purpose for which you need so much money. If the person does not cooperate, for example, then one would have to check whether one makes a report.	Interview partner 15
Exceeding limit values	Amount XX standard is prescribed that the client is identified and then this is recorded in the system and then I would expect the financial intermediary to then check for these transactions that require identification.	Interview partner 17
Control mechanisms of the exchange offices lead to clarifications of origins	Large exchange offices of SBB Post Finance, um, have relatively large structures and measures to ensure compliance with money laundering obligations.	Interview partner 17
Smurfing made more difficult by monitoring	But of course there is also a monitoring of these transactions, and the monitoring is to ensure that no smurfing takes place, i.e., that the same person does not make several transactions below the threshold value and thus actually exceeds the threshold value.	Interview partner 15
Transport of foreign currencies	And it is, um, there we also have again, I say, to get a foreign currency into the country again, you have to travel through somewhere [else].	Interview partner 13

3.2.4 Quantitative Investigation

This section presents the results of the quantitative study. The results are presented descriptively since doing so is sufficient to confirm the following two hypotheses that were tested.

> *Hypothesis 1: Money launderers increasingly switch to less-regulated industries in order to escape the controls of the financial sector.*
> *Hypothesis 2: The forms of money laundering developed in this study occur in practice but rarely attract the attention of compliance officers.*

In order to present the results of the quantitative survey as clearly as possible, the author has opted for the use of horizontal histograms. Each question of the survey is presented below in a figure labelled with the original question text as well as the percentage results and the corresponding bar chart (Figures 3.1 to 3.17). Where useful, the presentations are supplemented by explanations by the author. Cross-tabulation analyses were deliberately omitted, as the questions are limited to general empirical values and are not aimed at specific cases. This means that a possible cross-tabulation analysis could only have shown very vague correlations, and it would not have been possible, for example, to link certain methods with certain predicate offences. However, this is not necessary to answer the research questions and thus does not represent a major obstacle.

Figure 3.1 How Long Have You Been Working in Compliance?

Answer	Graphic	Per cent
Less than 1 year		3.3
1–3 years		11.3
4–10 years		33.1
More than 10 years		45.7
Not specified		6.6

Figure 3.2 How Long Have You Been Working in This Company?

Answer	Graphic	Per cent
Less than 1 year		10.6
1–5 years		37.1
6–10 years		19.9
More than 10 years		32.5
Not specified		0.0

Figure 3.3 Have You Been Confronted with Cases of Suspected Money Laundering in the Last Three Years?

Answer	Graphic	Per cent
Yes		65.6
No		34.4

Figure 3.3a Approximately How Often Did This Happen?

Answer	Graphic	Per cent
1–20 times		75.0
21–40 times		10.0
41–60 times		2.0
61–80 times		6.0
More than 80 times (please specify)		7.0

A total of seven participants stated that they had been confronted with more than eighty cases of suspected money laundering in the last three years. The specific figures ranged from 100 to approximately 450 cases. This was partly due to the fact that these participants were responsible for reporting to the MLRO.

Figure 3.3b What Types of Predicate Offences Were Involved? Please List All Applicable Categories

Answer	Graphic	Per cent
Corruption		58.2
Fraud		75.5
Burglary		0.0
Robbery		3.1
Theft		10.2
Human trafficking		6.1
Arms trade		16.3
Drug trafficking		28.6
Tax fraud		38.8
Others (please specify)		22.4

Answers listed under 'Others (please specify)' included embezzlement, moonlighting, insider trading, forgery of documents, value added tax (VAT) fraud, price manipulation, misuse of data processing equipment and terrorist financing, among others. While these results are certainly interesting, they are not essential for answering this book's research questions, as predicate offences are not examined in detail.

Figure 3.3c Approximately How Many Cases Were Confirmed in the Course of Further Investigations?

Answer	Graphic	Per cent
0–20%		45.8
21–40%		16.7
41–60%		14.6
61–80%		12.5
81–100%		10.4

Figure 3.3d How Do You Become Aware of Suspected Cases of Money Laundering? (Multiple Answers Possible)

Answer	Graphic	Per cent
Electronic risk systems		69.4
Internal messages		71.4
External references		65.3
Others (please specify)		19.4

Answers listed under 'Others (please specify)' included newspaper reports, manual audit methods, supervisory activities, Internet searches and external databases, among others. All other methods mentioned, such as reports from authorities or other banks, can be filed under one of the other categories. In any case, the strikingly even distribution between electronic risk systems, internal reports and external indications is remarkable.

Figure 3.4 We Sometimes Hear That Money Launderers Are Switching to Less-Regulated Industries (Retail, Real Estate, Consulting Services, Etc.) Because of the High Compliance Standards of Financial Service Providers: Do You Share This Opinion?

Answer	Graphic	Per cent
Yes		74.5
No		25.5

Figure 3.5 Which Sectors Do You Consider to Be at Risk of Money Laundering? (Multiple Answers Possible)

Answer	Graphic	Per cent
Industries with cash payment		86.0
Industries with remittances from abroad		37.3
Industries or jurisdictions with little or no regulation		84.0

Figure 3.6 How Often Have You Come Across Cases of Money Laundering in Connection with the Trade in Antiques in the Past Three Years?

Answer	Graphic	Per cent
0 times		84.7
1–5 times		13.9
6–10 times		1.4
11–20 times		0.0
More than 20 times		0.0

Figure 3.7 How Often Have You Come Across Cases of Money Laundering in Connection with the Trade in Art in the Past Three Years?

Answer	Graphic	Per cent
0 times		73.2
1–5 times		25.4
6–10 times		0.7
11–20 times		0.7
More than 20 times		0.0

Figure 3.8 How Often Have You Come Across Cases of Money Laundering in Connection with Trading in Gold in the Past Three Years?

Answer	Graphic	Per cent
0 times		71.6
1–5 times		25.5
6–10 times		2.1
11–20 times		0.7
More than 20 times		0.0

Figure 3.9 How Often Have You Come Across Cases of Money Laundering in Connection with the Trade in Jewellery in the Past Three Years?

Answer	Graphic	Per cent
0 times		87.1
1–5 times		12.1
6–10 times		0.0
11–20 times		0.0
More than 20 times		0.7

Figure 3.10 How Often Have You Come Across Cases of Money Laundering in Connection with the Trade in Rough Diamonds in the Past Three Years?

Answer	Graphic	Per cent
0 times		79.1
1–5 times		19.4
6–10 times		1.4
11–20 times		0.0
More than 20 times		0.0

Figure 3.11 How Often Have You Come Across Cases of Money Laundering in Connection with Real Estate Purchases and Renovations in the Past Three Years?

Answer	Graphic	Per cent
0 times		65.7
1–5 times		30.0
6–10 times		2.9
11–20 times		1.4
More than 20 times		0.0

Figure 3.12 How Often Have You Come Across Cases of Money Laundering in Connection with Advisory Services in the Past Three Years?

Answer	Graphic	Per cent
0 times		52.9
1–5 times		34.3
6–10 times		7.1
11–20 times		3.6
More than 20 times		2.1

Figure 3.13 How Often Have You Come Across Cases of Money Laundering in Connection with Company Reorganizations in the Past Three Years?

Answer	Graphic	Per cent
0 times		83.3
1–5 times		15.2
6–10 times		0.7
11–20 times		0.0
More than 20 times		0.7

Figure 3.14 In the Past Three Years, How Often Have You Come Across Cases of Money Laundering in Connection with Banks in Offshore Centres (e.g., United Arab Emirates)?

Answer	Graphic	Per cent
0 times		59.7
1–5 times		26.9
6–10 times		8.2
11–20 times		2.2
More than 20 times		3.0

Figure 3.15 How Often Have You Come Across Cases of Money Laundering in Connection with Bureaux De Change in the Past Three Years?

Answer	Graphic	Per cent
0 times		77.8
1–5 times		17.0
6–10 times		3.7
11–20 times		0.0
More than 20 times		1.5

Figure 3.16 How Often Have You Come Across Cases of Money Laundering in Connection with Safe-Deposit Boxes in the Past Three Years?

Answer	Graphic	Per cent
0 times		80.5
1–5 times		15.8
6–10 times		1.5
11–20 times		1.5
More than 20 times		0.8

Figure 3.17 How Often Have You Come Across Cases of Money Laundering in Connection with Unofficial Foreign Exchange Dealers (Exchange of Cash Among Money Launderers) in the Past Three Years?

Answer	Graphic	Per cent
0 times		87.3
1–5 times		9.0
6–10 times		2.2
11–20 times		0.7
More than 20 times		0.7

The final question was open-ended and asked the participants if they would like to provide more details on a specific form of money laundering. Details were given on cash deposits, commodities, imports/exports, luxury goods business, price manipulation, distribution of services, antiques trade, shipping companies, charities and fertilizer distribution. It is obvious that all these industries lend themselves particularly well to money laundering. Specifically, the lack of regulation and existing business relationships seem to play an important role. Also, money laundering approaches involving goods that are hardly being controlled seem to be well suited to money laundering.

The actors involved seem to fall into one of two categories. Some are unwitting accomplices who do not know that they are participating in money laundering; others are often members of highly professional criminal groups from Southern Italy or Eastern Europe who pose as entrepreneurs, consultants, brokers, project developers or sports officials, for example. However, flying traders, traders that sell goods without having a stationary shop, also seem to be in operation in isolated cases. The described procedures also confirmed the findings of the qualitative study. The use of stooges, the charging of services not rendered and the use of companies as a cover were mentioned.

Finally, it can be stated that 74.5 % of the compliance officers surveyed are of the opinion that money launderers switch to less-regulated industries due to the high compliance standards of financial service providers. This confirms Hypothesis 1. Furthermore, it should be noted that the methods developed in the context of this book do occur in practice, but the compliance officers surveyed had only rarely come into contact with them. Hypothesis 2 can therefore also be confirmed. For a more detailed discussion of the results, please refer to Chapter 4.

Finally, it should be explained why further statistical analyses, such as the t-test, were not used. Due to the nature of the data and the hypotheses to be examined, it was sufficient to present the results descriptively. Of particular importance was the mode (i.e., the most frequent variable). This can clearly be seen from the bar charts.

Furthermore, while one could calculate the correlations between the individual methods, it was not apparent to what extent these would contribute to answering the research question or confirming the hypotheses.

CHAPTER 4
Discussion of the Empirical Results

In the following, the results of the empirical investigation are discussed. On the one hand, the focus is on the further development and optimization of methods of money laundering prevention through input from the author and references to the literature. On the other hand, the weaknesses and possible risks of the circumvention methods presented by the experts should also be pointed out. For this purpose, the perspective of the money launderer is taken. However, the author would like to emphasize at this point that the following guidance on money laundering is a scientific exercise and not intended as advice for money launderers. Ultimately, the explanations are intended to help those working for investigative authorities and in compliance departments to better understand the perspective of the money launderer. The author firmly believes that having a more informed understanding of the thought processes and actions of money launderers can ultimately help to identify attempts at money laundering in otherwise innocuous situations.

Some of the practices are very similar. For example, there is inevitably a great deal of overlap between the art trade and the antiques trade. Nevertheless, the author has presented both methods in full. On the one hand, this is due to the fact that the empirical results highlight quite different aspects of the two methods. On the other hand, there are also subject-specific differences to consider. In order not to exhaust the reader with all the overlaps, the author takes the liberty of referring to analogous applications of other methods at selected points. For example, within the framework of the antiques trade method, the construction of a fictitious shop is explained in more detail, whereas in the framework of the art trade method, only the analogous applicability of the fictitious shop is referred to and a flea market variant is included instead. However, the flea market variant would also be suitable for the antiques trade. This representation covers the greatest possible range of variants while avoiding repetitive scenarios.

Furthermore, the author would like to emphasize that the methods presented are by no means intended to be exhaustive. Rather, the intention was to investigate whether there are low-risk ways to launder money. The following commentary on the methods proves beyond doubt that it is possible to launder money with relatively little effort and sometimes very modest expertise. The methods can be adapted, extended, simplified or combined with each other. In order to answer the research question, it is not necessary to present all the available methods of laundering money.

In order to be able to assess the methods developed in the qualitative main study with regard to their risks for the money launderer, the results of the quantitative study are also discussed in this chapter. However, the results of the preliminary study will not be discussed again because the main study is already based on the results of the preliminary study, and a renewed presentation of the preliminary study would basically result in repetition.

This chapter focuses on the author's comments and reflections. The citations of evidence supporting the results of the qualitative study were presented in Chapter 3, section 3.2.2 in an unsmoothed form in Table 3.4 to ensure the greatest possible transparency. Nevertheless, the author does not want to miss including specific statements from the interview partners to support his comments in this chapter as well. Since these statements can already be found in an unsmoothed form in Chapter 3, as well as in Appendix, it is opportune to increase the readability of this chapter by slightly smoothing the statements; however, not all statements have been supported with a direct quotation from the participants.

4.1 GENERAL STATEMENTS

It is noteworthy that 74.5% of compliance officers surveyed said they believed that money launderers would increasingly move to less-regulated industries, such as retail, real estate and consulting services, due to the high compliance standards of financial service providers. This shows that the present work does have a solid raison d'être. It cannot be assumed that the current regulations are sufficient to successfully combat money laundering in the long term.

In particular, 86.0% of the compliance officers surveyed stated that they consider industries with cash payments to be problematic. In this book, these include the trade in antiques, art, jewellery, gold and rough diamonds. However, real estate, safe-deposit boxes and cash-against-cash procedures can also be grouped under this category, at least in part.

Furthermore, 84.0% of the compliance officers surveyed consider sectors with little or no regulation to be particularly at risk of facilitating money laundering. In contrast, only 37.3% of the compliance officers surveyed consider industries with remittances from abroad to be at risk of facilitating money laundering. This indicates that financial service providers recognize the signs of money laundering through remittances from abroad but that money launderers can switch to other industries to circumvent the banks' control mechanisms.

In principle, a distinction must be made between money laundering's three stages: placement, layering and integration. These stages have often been discussed in the literature, but for the purposes of this book, they should be defined once again in a uniform way. The money launderer obviously pursues two goals. The primary objective is to hide the incriminated assets; the secondary objective is to successfully obscure the incriminated assets' origins.

Placement, in the context of this book, refers to the successful hiding, bartering or smuggling into the economic system of incriminated assets needed to be laundered. An example of hiding would be depositing the assets in a safe-deposit box held by a private provider. Bartering takes place through foreign exchange trading at bureaux de change, for example. A first-level infiltration of incriminated funds into the economic system could refer to cash deposits at a bank or paying craftspeople cash in hand (i.e., making a cash payment without an invoice or receipt).

For the purposes of this book, layering refers to the concealment of the origins of funds through various steps. This can be achieved by making transfers between banks, for example, and it aims to make it more difficult to trace the origins of the funds. This is particularly effective if the transfers cross multiple jurisdictions.

Integration is, to a certain extent, the highest level of money laundering. Here, the incriminated assets are integrated into legal businesses. This typically happens only after layering in order to prevent supposedly legitimate businesses from seeming at all illegitimate. However, there can be exceptions here as well.

Distinguishing between the three individual stages of laundering money is often not possible as they can be combined in numerous ways. For example, incriminated cash can be 'placed' by paying a craftsperson in cash, and this simultaneously serves to integrate the money into the economic cycle. Therefore, these terms - placement, layering and integration - are critically assessed here and only used in the explanations of the individual methods in order to give the reader an approximate sense of what happens during each stage. However, the author explicitly emphasizes that a strict separation of the individual stages is not possible. Nevertheless, he considers it useful to designate the individual stages in order to prevent misunderstanding.

The primary objective of the money launderer appears to be to hide the incriminated assets. This is plausible insofar as he can thereby avoid any form of prosecution with regard to money laundering offences. In accordance with the principle of 'where there's no prosecutor, there's no judge', he can be sure that if he successfully hides his incriminated assets, or at least indications of their concealment, it will be unlikely that he will be charged with a violation of Article 305bis SCC.

In many cases, achieving the primary objective of hiding incriminated assets suffices. However, in certain circumstances, the money launderer does not want to reinvest his incriminated assets but wants to use them to meet his daily needs. This is likely to apply to those who have received a smaller sum as part of a one-off crime, in particular. In these cases, it is often sufficient to hide the incriminated funds in a safe-deposit box and occasionally withdraw smaller amounts from the safe-deposit box, as if withdrawing the money from a current account.

Of course, there are also numerous money launderers who regularly obtain large sums of money from illegal activities and do not want to use them to finance their livelihood. In these cases, the use of frontmen and legal entities seems to be particularly popular to ensure that the incriminated funds are not found in the course of an investigation against the money launderer.

If the assets are ultimately discovered, then the secondary objective comes into play with the aim being to break the connections between the evidence so that the funds can no longer be attributed to the money launderer himself. However, this objective only plays a subsidiary role since the money launderer normally wants to ensure that his assets are not found.

4.1.1 Concrete Approach

Some concrete approaches to money laundering seem to apply to many of the methods described in this section and are herewith briefly explained. There seems to be a broad consensus that engaging in identifiable actions falling within the scope of the AMLA should be avoided. Furthermore, the experts seem to agree that larger amounts can be split up and, under certain circumstances, merged again at a later stage as a means of evading detection. Investments in tangible assets are probably particularly well suited for money laundering. All methods aim to conceal the beneficial owner. This can be achieved through the use of frontmen. Ideally, existing structures are used to avoid attracting attention. In any case, money launderers must be careful to establish plausibility. Furthermore, money laundering chains are formed across several jurisdictions. In addition, legal and illegal assets are mixed.

In principle, it seems to make sense for money launderers to avoid the scope of application of the AMLA: 'I think there are certain areas in Switzerland that are not subject to the Money Laundering Act' (Interview partner 2). The ulterior motive for this is that much higher control standards apply in the areas of application of the AMLA than in other industries. While a bank must critically scrutinize a cash transaction of more than CHF 70,000 and will report it to the MLRO if there are grounds for suspicion of money laundering, a retailer in the art, jewellery, gold, antiques or rough diamond trade is free to accept the exact same amount without question. The retailer is not obliged to establish the identity of the customer. Thus, the money launderer would have to establish the plausibility of the origins of the cash at the bank but could convert it into a tangible asset via a retailer without facing any queries.

Avoiding the scope of the AMLA or comparable national laws is usually advantageous for the money launderer. However, exceptions confirm the rule here as well. This applies in particular to the bureau de change method and the use of financial intermediaries in offshore destinations. It is obvious that money launderers split larger amounts into smaller sums to avoid attracting suspicion: 'First and foremost, still the cash, because I can split that. I can divide it into small amounts and distribute it to different people. I can merge that again and so on' (Interview partner 13). After all, even the least sophisticated retailer would be concerned if a money launderer suddenly appeared in their shop with CHF 10 million. However, the exact breakdown of a larger amount of cash depends on the method chosen. While in the art and antiques trades a cash payment of more than CHF 50,000 would not be unusual, it would definitely be problematic with the bureau de change method.

At the same time, it seems to be common practice to at least partially merge assets once they have been split in a pooling process, even if this involves taking certain risks:

'But I think this pooling of ostensibly small turnovers, it's a bit of a risk' (Interview partner 11). On the one hand, this approach is plausible because it reduces the administrative effort involved. After all, it is rather complicated for the money launderer to have to manage ten thousand bank accounts. Investments can usually only be made with larger amounts that have already been consolidated. At the same time, however, merging also concentrates the risk, and with each transaction there is the threat of discovery of the incriminated funds. Therefore, money launderers prefer to find a balance between efficient management and sufficient risk diversification.

Investments in tangible assets seem to be popular with money launderers: 'I would always take refuge in tangible assets' (Interview partner 5). There are several reasons for this. On the one hand, tangible assets are often easy to acquire and transport. The market for rough diamonds is liquid, and the transport of the stones is quite feasible due to their small size. It is certainly easier to transport two hundred million dollars' worth of rough diamonds than the cash equivalent. On the other hand, cleverly chosen material assets offer the great advantage that their origins are very difficult to trace. Unless they are well-known individual pieces, it is probably almost impossible for the investigating authorities to determine the origins of a collection of antique jewellery acquired from a discreet private owner. Furthermore, tangible assets are often more stable in value than cash. While it will probably be difficult to introduce today's euro notes into circulation in forty years, gold can be stored for centuries with little effort.

The concealment of the beneficial owner seems to enjoy great importance as well: 'I would just exhaust as many of the possibilities as possible to actually make sure that the reference to me is disguised, so to speak, and that of course the reference before is also disguised' (Interview partner 13). This makes sense, as it promotes both the primary goal of hiding and the secondary goal of concealment. If the money launderer is not listed in the land register or a commercial register, the assets cannot be assigned to him. Concealment therefore initially makes it more difficult to locate the assets. Should the assets nevertheless be found, it must first be proven that they can also be attributed to the money launderer. If the money launderer has transferred the assets in cash, attribution is unlikely to be possible without the testimony of the straw man.

It also makes sense to exploit existing structures: 'It uses structures that already exist' (Interview partner 16). This has the added benefit of not attracting attention. If a newly founded company suddenly reports an enormous turnover, this can quickly lead to questions, whereas if an established company increases its turnover by 20%, this usually causes less of a stir. Furthermore, using already existing structures prevents the money launderer from having to create structures himself. This saves time and money.

Money launderers usually have to establish plausibility: 'If I were a money launderer, I would try to establish plausibility' (Interview partner 14). A money launderer anticipates that questions may arise about his activities. He prepares meticulously for this moment so that, in case of doubt, he can immediately alleviate all concerns. This means, for example, that he prepares fictitious contracts professionally and in good time. At the same time, he keeps in mind that his transactions must stand up to third-party comparison and should reflect local and industry customs. No sausage shop with one employee on the payroll will report CHF 10 million in profit per year, and no independent third party will sell a mint Ferrari F12 for CHF 30,000. Such conspicuous transactions would lead to queries in most cases. The money launderer therefore makes sure that his transactions do not go beyond the scope of reason, and, in the event of queries being raised, he makes sure that he has all the documents he needs to further support the plausibility of his story.

Another option is concealment across multiple jurisdictions: 'Whether then different jurisdictions that have jurisdiction log in Offshore Destination 1, that there are executive offices in Offshore Destination 2 and the account is in Offshore Destination 3. Very often, these offshore companies are in further offshore destinations' (Interview partner 12). Doing so offers the advantage that national law enforcement agencies usually have great difficulty analysing international transactions. The legal assistance guide, which helps Swiss authorities and courts with evidence collection and official notifications to foreign legal authorities, is regularly provided by the Swiss Federal Office of Justice and reveals which destinations make investigative work more difficult. Even if one jurisdiction's or another's request for legal or administrative assistance should actually be successful, this does not jeopardize the cover-up. After all, a clever money launderer builds constructs across various countries. This delays any investigations for years before ultimately coming to nothing.

In the final step, legal and illegal funds are mixed together: 'As soon as it is mixed with legal assets, and you can no longer prove that the EUR 3 is incriminated money and the EUR 3 is legally acquired money. That's when you get out' (Interview partner 13). This step helps to at least make the confiscation of the assets more difficult in certain jurisdictions, and in certain cases, it even helps to prevent it. Ultimately, the commingling of assets must be carried out in such a way that it is no longer clearly comprehensible whether the assets are legal or illegal. It must also not be apparent through which detours the funds have found their way to each other.

4.1.2 Resources

This section identifies some resources that are critical to most of the money laundering methods that are described in this book. These include alternative payment methods and banks with weak or corrupt compliance departments. In addition, the money launderer needs detailed contracts and, in most cases, access to experts with in-depth knowledge.

Alternative payment methods help to circumvent traditional placement risks and overcome banks' transaction analyses: 'With all the payment methods, technologies, like reloadable prepaid cards. So everything where the physical presence is reduced' (Interview partner 12). The spectrum of alternative payment methods is broad and ranges from prepaid cards to netting amounts between criminals and virtual currencies. The money launderer usually strives to have payment instruments that are suitable for his activities. A precise selection can only be made after the method has been chosen.

Banks with weak or corrupt compliance departments are needed because the money should be channelled through the financial system at some point during the process of laundering the money, regardless of the method chosen: 'Which bank is suitable here? A small one that is under great customer pressure. Here, you might be more likely to accept transactions without questioning them' (Interview partner 8). Although tangible assets such as jewellery, antiques or gold can be acquired with cash, it is beneficial if the money launderer can consider resale via a bank transfer. In order for the bank not to become suspicious, either an incompetent or corrupt compliance department is advantageous. The money launderer provides the compliance officer with flimsy stories about inheritances, which in case of doubt can justify the fact that no SAR was filed. Small banks under pressure from their customers or with compliance officers in financial distress seem to be welcome partners for money launderers.

Possessing detailed contracts help to nip any initial doubts about the money launderer's business right in the bud: 'Detailed contracts, maybe even with product lists to go with them, that don't even exist' (Interview partner 8). For this, it is essential that these contracts are not based on a standard template, which can be prepared by laypersons quickly and cheaply. If the business is to look solid, then the contract must also make an impression that inspires confidence. This means that contracts should be highly individualized and not shared with other people. In addition, attachments and supplementary documents, such as (fictitious) product lists, can complete the picture.

In addition, the money launderer often needs the help of external experts to acquire expertise: 'Then I would have to get people who have been doing this for many years and can tell me how to plausibly present it to the bank official in a trial and who will take it off my hands' (Interview partner 14). This is particularly important when trading in tangible assets. Rough diamonds, jewellery, antiques, art and other high-value objects often have to be tested for authenticity. This is not normally easily done by laypersons. It is therefore important for the money launderer to have a loyal, reliable and discreet expert at his side. Ideally, this person lives abroad so that he is unavailable to be interviewed by the authorities in the course of an investigation.

4.1.3 Risks

In addition to business risks, attracting the attention of banks and the authorities is considered a major danger for the money launderer. However, the money launderer also faces risks resulting from cooperating with other criminals. For example, embezzlement can quickly occur with straw men, and business partners could defraud the money launderer.

Like any other economic activity, money laundering also entails certain business costs and risks: 'Sure, so for money laundering you always have to pay something' (Interview partner 4). For example, foreign currencies' price fluctuations often cannot be calculated *ex ante*. Tangible assets can also drop in value. Furthermore, bribes often need to be paid. However, the money launderer is generally prepared to accept a limited loss in order to turn incriminated assets into supposedly legal funds. Thus, business risks are only marginally dealt with in the context of this book.

Attracting the attention of the banks poses a great danger to the money launderer: 'You have to expect that the bank will question where the money comes from and why this is being done. And a good money launderer is prepared for this situation' (Interview partner 16). Often, indirect ownership structures or certain transactions are questioned. Banks often use computer systems that highlight suspicious transactions and trigger queries from the compliance department. This is especially the case if the transaction does not match the client. Ideally, the money launderer knows the parameters of these computer systems and controls his transactions so that he does not trigger any checks. Nevertheless, this is a risk that should not be underestimated, and the money launderer should be thoroughly prepared to answer such queries.

Attracting the attention of the authorities represents a major risk for the money launderer. While banks primarily aim to reduce their compliance risks, the authorities are interested in the material truth. Therefore, the money launderer should deliberately avoid attracting the attention of the authorities. This can be achieved, among other things, by paying all taxes and fees on time and through an exemplary administration of all transactions.

Furthermore, it should be considered that criminals could also cheat each other: 'He would be well advised to take a closer look at what it is and where it comes from. There is also a lot of fraud in the classical sense' (Interview partner 10). Thus, it is quite possible that the material assets offered to the money launderer are counterfeits of supposedly high-quality goods. The money launderer wants to protect himself from this risk because he would not be able to call on the help of the authorities in the event of a loss without incriminating himself. Therefore, the money launderer needs to have access to the appropriate expertise or experts at his side to help him avoid being defrauded.

The use of stooges greatly facilitates the concealment of the beneficial owner. However, it also leads to stooges being able to dispose of the assets. Theoretically, they could embezzle them: 'Trustors have to be paid well. So if someone appears as an account holder and gets enough money for it, he has to think ten times before he goes against the trustor, as long as he gets enough money for it every year' (Interview partner 16). It is therefore important to select loyal stooges who can be put under pressure if necessary. A family man with a wife and three small children tends to be more suitable than a bachelor with no relatives, as the risk of flight is too high with the latter since he has no family ties and a low opportunity cost. Moreover, stooges should be well paid so that they have a great incentive not to embezzle assets.

4.1.4 Overall Assessment

The general procedures outlined apply to most methods of money laundering. However, as mentioned, exceptions confirm the rule here as well. Not all statements apply to each of the methods. Therefore, a differentiation as well as a presentation of the individual methods follows in section 4.2.

4.2 GOLD

4.2.1 General Suitability

Gold seems to be suitable for both the placement and layering of incriminated funds. The change in the value carrier is always in the foreground. With melting the gold down an option, the illicit origins can be disguised with little effort.

By buying gold, the money launderer can place incriminated cash and in return receive a medium of value that can usually be resold without incurring a loss if he has a little patience. Since cash payments in the gold trade are often overlooked, and the origins can only be traced to a limited extent, this method is exceptionally well suited for the placement stage.

In the course of melting gold down, further concealment is carried out, which is most likely to be assigned to the layering stage. The gold is melted down and recast, and by deliberately mixing different stocks, any analysis of the origins of the gold becomes impossible. This means that sufficient concealment can be successfully implemented very discreetly and with minimal effort.

4.2.2 Concrete Approach

First, the money launderer must create a realistic paper trail for the gold. It is a good idea to fake an inheritance that takes into account the deceased's financial circumstances and tax returns. Afterwards, the money launderer can buy gold and recast it. Alternatively, storing the gold in bonded warehouses can be considered. This offers the advantage that the property rights can be transferred directly inside the bonded warehouse. Both variants offer the possibility of profit-taking in the event of a positive price trend.

Procuring documentation for the gold before purchasing it makes the most sense; otherwise, there would inevitably be a period of time during which the money launderer possesses gold but is unable to explain its origins in the event of an investigation. Should the investigating authorities find the goods during this period, this would be a serious problem for the money launderer. However, if the investigating authorities were to find the documentation without the associated goods, the money launderer could comfortably argue that unfortunately he had lost the gold.

A possible paper trail for the origins of the gold could be created by feigning an inheritance. In this case, assets are listed in the estate register that were not actually inherited. However, with this variant, the plausibility of the origins must be ensured: 'The wealthier someone is, the more there is in it. I can come along with ten pictures or 20 kilos of gold as a family inheritance. That is more credible than if I, as a simple wage earner, suddenly come along with 20 kilos of gold' (Interview partner 11).

It is unlikely that a poor pensioner would have left behind tens of millions' worth in gold, but a wealthy lady may well have discreetly kept a million or two in the form of gold for tax reasons. This explanation cannot be easily dismissed, especially in view of the wealth tax. The money launderer can then argue that, as an honest heir, he would naturally also like to pay tax on his aunt's black money. When faking an inheritance, the national tax laws and the degree of relationship must be considered in each case.

The next step is for the money launderer to acquire the gold: 'Of course, I can also buy up gold somewhere with my black money and then melt that down' (Interview partner 11). In this case, it is advisable to use incriminated funds to buy up privately owned gold stocks or to do business with jewellers. Precious metal dealers are subject to the AMLA according to Article 2, paragraph 3, lit. c, and thus they have to fulfil special duties of care. Private individuals, on the other hand, often have unofficial gold holdings which they wish to treat very discreetly for tax reasons. A bank transfer would therefore not be ideal for these private individuals, as one could ultimately question which assets they have sold. Therefore, they may agree to the cash payment preferred by the money launderer. However, it is not always easy for a money launderer to find wealthy individuals with significant gold holdings that they wish to sell. Consequently, alternative approaches make more sense, such as buying gold from a jeweller. Jewellers can usually obtain gold in various ways, and no one would question why a jeweller would need to buy gold. However, in many countries, there is also a black market for precious metals or there are no identification requirements in the precious metals trade. A black market exists in Italy, for example.

The next obvious step is to have the gold melted down. In this way, any serial numbers disappear and tracing the origins becomes much more difficult. Melting down gold is not a problem, especially in corrupt EU countries, because in exchange for a small compensation, officials look the other way. Finally, it is also difficult to trace whether a trader has melted down 10 kilograms of gold more or less per day.

Storage and transfer of ownership of gold can also take place in bonded warehouses: 'You can leave that in there and transfer ownership there' (Interview partner 17). The transfer of ownership in bonded warehouses significantly reduces the transport risks. In addition, the money launderer never has to come into personal contact with his gold. Moreover, storage in bonded warehouses can be carried out in the name of a company. It goes without saying that people acting in the name of a company can act as the company's beneficial owners. Thus, these assets are very difficult to attribute to the money launderer.

Finally, it is a good idea to take the profit if the price trend is positive: 'After all, you can see that as an investment, and when the price goes up, it's common to sell that again. Profit taking' (Interview partner 10). Of course, it is possible that the money launderer will have to be patient and wait for prices to trend upwards. However, and especially in the case of larger amounts, it is important to bear in mind that the money launderer does not necessarily need the money to finance his daily life and can therefore exercise the requisite patience.

4.2.3 Resources

The most important resource when using gold as a method of laundering money is documenting the origins: 'I will have to document where I bought it' (Interview partner

12). The money launderer must be able to explain plausibly where he got the gold. Ideally, he can do this by pretending to have inherited it. If he can plausibly claim that he inherited the gold from his grandparents thirty years ago and has so far refrained from declaring it in order to avoid the wealth tax, it may no longer be possible for the authorities to prove that the gold originated from a crime.

4.2.4 Risks

Using gold as a method is a relatively low risk. However, there are some factors that the money launderer must consider nonetheless. First of all, there are many fraudsters in the gold trade who sell fake gold. There is also a risk of theft. Furthermore, the purchase of gold may be registered. Gold traders are subject to Article 2, paragraph 3, lit. c AMLA and thus have to fulfil the due diligence obligations associated with the AMLA. Furthermore, gold is a volatile asset. Due to the standardized prices on the gold market, the transaction amount is easily traceable. Furthermore, the weight and volume of gold make it difficult to transport.

First of all, it should be pointed out that people sell fake gold: 'We personally have big scams with gold, that is, gold bullion' (Interview partner 18). These fakes can sometimes easily be recognized due to their weight. An experienced gold dealer knows the correct volume of gold in proportion to the weight and can quickly determine whether it is fake. Chemical tests can also provide information regarding authenticity.

Furthermore, the risk of theft associated with trading in gold must be considered: 'There's a risk of it getting lost along the way' (Interview partner 17). Unlike antiques or art, gold is relatively easy to transport and extremely liquid. Whereas a thief would have trouble selling an antique vase, he could trade in his gold at a jewellery dealer's shop. Therefore, an intelligent money launderer relying on gold takes the appropriate security measures. In particular, he makes sure that as few people as possible know about his dealings in gold and he ensures its safekeeping by storing it in a safe-deposit box held by a private provider.

What is extremely dangerous for the money launderer is that the acquisition of gold may be registered: 'Gold has to be acquired somewhere. There, too, it has to be registered again' (Interview partner 5). Since it could become known that he is carrying large amounts of cash, the money launderer should buy gold from traders who do not require registration.

In Switzerland, it is difficult to avoid registering the acquisition of gold. The problem is that gold traders are subject to Article 2, paragraph 3, lit. c AMLA, and thus many of them fulfil the due diligence obligations associated with the AMLA: 'These businesses are subject to the Money Laundering Act according to Article 2 para. 3 AMLA. Accordingly, we receive reports from these gold dealers, et cetera, again and again' (Interview partner 2). Therefore, an intelligent money launderer acquires gold from private sellers or from abroad. In Italy, as is well known, there is a lively black market among jewellers trading in larger quantities of gold. This is due to the fact that jewellers in Italy prefer to sell goods without an invoice, and thus the gold may not appear in the accounts. The gold trader could easily take advantage of this circumstance.

The gold market is also extremely volatile: 'The disadvantage is high volatility. If you're a money launderer and you invested everything in gold three years ago, you've also lost quite a bit in the meantime' (Interview partner 16). This means that a money launderer relying on the gold trade either needs patience or has to be willing to take a loss. Alternatively, he can also try to resell the gold immediately. In this case, any loss should be limited to a few percentage points.

Due to the standardized prices of gold, it is easy for banks and investigating authorities to trace how much money the money launderer has spent on a certain amount of gold: 'So, if they take 50,000 to the bank in one day and say I sold so-and-so many gold pieces, you know exactly, aha, it must have been so-and-so many goods or so-and-so many kilograms to generate that' (Interview partner 5). However, this is only problematic if the perpetrator takes the money to the bank or the authorities actually find the gold. By keeping the gold in a private safe-deposit box, finding it can be prevented in most cases.

Its volume and weight can also pose a challenge when transporting gold: 'But of course, gold already has a specific weight. So, a kilo of gold is a kilo of gold and not so easy to transport' (Interview partner 17). However, the gold does not necessarily have to be transported. Possession can also be transferred to the vault of a private safe-deposit box provider. In case of doubt, the money launderer can split the gold and transport it in several pieces. As a result, this risk does not really pose a sizeable threat.

4.2.5 Overall Assessment

In conclusion, it can be said that the gold trade is a suitable method for both professional and 'casual' money launderers. Trading in gold is a low-cost method that requires only limited expertise. The risks are manageable and can be almost completely offset. The applicability of the AMLA is not an obstacle to using this method since gold can be bought by private individuals or purchased abroad and subsequently find its way into the legal economic cycle, as supposed integrating inherited property.

The practical use of gold as a method of money laundering is demonstrated in a case from 2013. A criminal organization bought 4,100 kilograms of gold and 11,000 kilograms of silver with incriminated funds in Italy within a period of twelve months and then had them melted down in Switzerland. The money launderers came to the attention of investigators when they transported gold hidden in medium-sized cars across the Italy–Switzerland border.[165] Cash-for-gold shops also seem to be very popular with organized crime for money laundering purposes.[166] However, it must also be noted at this point that the customs authorities are already targeting gold as an instrument of money laundering.[167] This is especially true for money launderers of

165. Stefano, 2013.
166. Tagesspiegel, 2012, pp. 1 ff.
167. Sonntagszeitung, 2014, pp. 1 ff.

South American origins.[168] Smaller money launderers, on the other hand, can devote themselves to the anonymous purchase of gold bars and only have to make sure that they fall below any regulatory limits.[169]

Despite the practical relevance of using gold for money laundering, 71.6% of the compliance officers surveyed stated that they had not come across any cases of money laundering in connection with the gold trade in the past three years; however, 28.4% of the compliance officers surveyed had come into contact with this method in the past three years. Nevertheless, it can be stated that trading in gold rarely attracts the attention of compliance officers. Either trading in gold is a rarely chosen form of money laundering or the money launderers using this method do not usually get caught.

4.3 JEWELLERY

4.3.1 General Suitability

Jewellery is particularly suitable for the placement and layering phases of money laundering. The fact that there are normally no fixed market prices for jewellery is a decisive advantage for the money launderer. Its anonymity, excellent value retention and the liquidity of the market make it an ideal instrument for any money launderer to use.

Jewellery is obviously suitable for placement since all the money launderer has to do is go to the nearest jewellery shop and buy jewellery there with incriminated funds. At the time of purchase, he changes the medium of value and makes tracing the origins of the incriminated funds considerably more difficult. By operating his own jewellery shop, however, he could also mix incriminated funds with legal assets and trigger a layering process. Ultimately, the resulting profits could even be invested in further official and legal activities until the incriminated assets are fully integrated into the legal economic cycle.

Another advantage of the jewellery method is that there are often no fixed market prices. Apart from some renowned brands that publish fixed price lists for standardized works, most dealers deal in unique pieces. It goes without saying that there cannot be a fixed price for unique pieces. Value is ultimately in the eye of the beholder and is determined by the customer's willingness to pay. At the very least, massive price fluctuations can be justified using this line of argument.

Furthermore, the actual origins of jewellery are normally difficult to trace. This leads to anonymity, which is very useful for the money launderer. No one can determine with any degree of certainty - not even an expert - from which Turkish bazaar a gold chain originates. The same applies to antique jewellery that has not caused a stir at an auction in the last thirty years because of its rarity.

168. Goldhill, 2014.
169. Süddeutsche Zeitung, 2011.

Jewellery offers high-value retention compared to other assets that raise questions for money launderers, such as cars or electrical appliances. Of course, fluctuations in the value of commodities must be taken into account, but ultimately, jewellery can be stored for decades and presumably resold at the appropriate moment without losing value.

When reselling a piece, the money launderer benefits from the high liquidity of the market. This applies in particular to mass-produced goods that are also affordable for a broad middle class. As long as the jewellery is not a fancy collector's item, the money launderer should be able to resell it within a short period of time without incurring a great loss of value.

4.3.2 Concrete Approach

With regard to the concrete procedure, money launderers posing as private individuals should be differentiated from those operating as official jewellery dealers. An official jewellery dealer must first establish an actual official activity in the jewellery trade. He can achieve this, for example, by distributing leaflets advertising that he purchases jewellery. He then fakes customers buying jewellery from him and thus channels incriminated funds into an official activity. A money launderer posing as a private individual, on the other hand, might buy jewellery while in a holiday destination. He then declares it as inherited property and records it in the estate register of a recently deceased relative. Alternatively, he might declare it as a gift.

A money launderer posing as an official jewellery dealer first engages in real activity within the jewellery trade: 'If such jewellery purchases are feigned to launder money, then that just needs some actual activity' (Interview partner 11). For this purpose, the money launderer establishes a legal entity. Normally, he chooses a limited liability company or a joint-stock company. He then sets up a website on which he advertises his jewellery business. This website should normally have various subpages and contain specific information on the opening hours of the shop. In addition, he needs an actual shop, which should be furnished in a more or less representative manner, depending on the design of the business activity. If the money launderer also serves customers in this shop, he should have an attractive salesroom that meets the average requirements of his customers. Here it is important to pay attention to creating plausibility. If the money launderer is planning an eight-figure turnover in his jewellery shop, he needs a shop in a prestigious location. If, on the other hand, he plans to engage in a rather small-time, inconspicuous activity, a small shop on a side street would suffice.

Typically, the money launderer does not want to invest too much time and energy in attracting clients. Often, a relationship of trust must first be established. This is often followed by lengthy sales talks. Nevertheless, it is important for the money launderer to carry out transactions with real clients in order to maintain the appearance of engaging in real, legitimate activity. Therefore, he distributes leaflets and positions himself and his employees in shopping centres and restaurants on weekends: 'That's where people come and sell. You can pump up this business with black money. Who knows how much I really bought and sold that weekend?' (Interview partner 11).

Of course, security is taken into account and permission is obtained from the respective landlords. In the leaflets, the money launderer advertises that he buys jewellery. The money launderer does in fact buy jewellery on these occasions and thus gains witnesses of his legitimate activities. He pays for this jewellery with clean funds. In doing so, he makes sure that he does not attract attention either through excessive generosity or through fraudulent dealings. As a result of this purchasing activity, he now has a wide pool of jewellery to resell.

In the next step, the money launderer sells this jewellery to fictitious customers. Of course, these 'customers' pay in cash. In this way, the incriminated funds enter the official jewellery business. The trick is that the money launderer resells the jewellery at significantly higher prices than the purchase price and the jewellery's actual value.

Naturally, the jewellery remains in the possession of the money launderer. After all, he has sold it to fictitious customers who will therefore never claim it. This means that in the next step, he fakes a fictitious transaction in order to be able to officially take the jewellery back into the inventory of the jewellery shop. Of course, this transaction takes place at a much lower price than the previously achieved sales price. This cycle can be repeated almost as often as desired. Should anyone enquire about the jeweller's actual business activities, the money launderer can show evidence of the numerous transactions in shopping centres and restaurants that actually took place.

Employing this mechanism is only worthwhile for money launderers who regularly have large sums of incriminated funds at their disposal and need to launder them. Someone who has to launder only a small or medium sum from a one-off transaction will not necessarily set up a jewellery business for this purpose. In the latter case, engaging in the following procedure would probably make more sense.

As a private individual, a money launderer is entitled to buy jewellery and pay for it in cash. He can do this either in his home country or in holiday destinations: 'There are cases where a lot of jewellery is bought with cash in holiday destinations in order to avoid creating a paper trail. Officially, the jewellery is then said to be from a friend' (Interview partner 18). Bazaars in Arab countries are often particularly suitable locations for purchasing jewellery because the money launderer will not be known there and his anonymity is thus guaranteed. However, for this purpose, he must bring the incriminated money with him into the foreign country and then transport the jewellery back into his home country. Customs controls could be an obstacle here. However, it would not be a problem for him to import or export money and jewellery within the EU.

Regardless of where the money launderer buys the jewellery, he always proceeds in an astonishingly banal manner. He enters various jewellery shops and selects pieces there that have a high value retention and a high degree of anonymity. This means that the pieces of jewellery should not have serial numbers. Furthermore, they should not be overpriced due to an exclusive sales location. Rather, the money launderer pays attention to the substantial value of the jewellery, which he subsequently purchases and pays for in cash. In doing so, he must make sure that he consistently falls below any limits for cash transactions that might attract attention.

Once he has done that, the money launderer now has jewellery instead of incriminated funds. Normally, he then declares the jewellery as inherited property: 'As they say in our country – it turned up in probate' (Interview partner 14). If a relative who appointed the money launderer as the sole heir in his will has recently died, the money launderer lists the jewellery as part of the estate in the estate register. If the last relative who appointed the money launderer as the sole heir died a long time ago, he can claim that he forgot to list the jewellery as part of the estate. Of course, certain plausibility must be ensured here as well. A deceased unskilled worker living on social welfare is unlikely to leave an inheritance worth millions. However, a wealthy aunt who inherited several million herself may well have left behind jewellery worth CHF 3 million.

Alternatively, one could also pretend that the jewellery was a gift: 'In the case of endowments, we don't have a single regulation with the source of funds' (Interview partner 18). However, it must of course be borne in mind that the authorities could enquire of a person who is still alive where he or she originally got the jewellery which he or she so generously gave away. Therefore, claiming that the jewellery is a gift only makes sense in exceptional cases.

4.3.3 Resources

To launder money using jewellery, the money launderer needs two critical resources. On the one hand, he needs specialist knowledge about the processing of and any materials from which the jewellery was made. On the other hand, he needs access to goods with poor comparability.

The money launderer acquires as much expertise in the processing of jewellery and raw materials as possible: 'It's quite good if they have mineralogical knowledge, that is, if you can tell reasonably easily what the source materials are' (Interview partner 6). Alternatively, he can of course also pay for access to this expertise. However, this makes him vulnerable to the supposed experts who could theoretically also work together with his negotiating partners to defraud him. Nevertheless, the risk is ultimately limited since the money launderer de facto sells and buys the jewellery himself. If he were to acquire inferior jewellery in the first step, the same jewellery would keep moving around in circles.

Furthermore, the money launderer needs access to goods with a lack of comparability: 'There, a piece of jewellery can cost EUR 1,000. They can sell the same one for maybe EUR 10,000' (Interview partner 5). Requiring a lack of comparability is not an obstacle because it is easy to obtain. It is therefore not a scarce resource. A trip to a jewellery shop would ultimately be enough to procure goods.

Of course, the money launderer also needs business premises as part of his activity as an official jewellery dealer. When equipping these premises, he pays attention to meeting high-quality security standards. In addition, he takes all measures customary in the market, such as taking out appropriate insurance policies and contracts with security companies.

4.3.4 Risks

Using jewellery to launder money is an extremely low-risk method, with the biggest risk being related to appraisals, although pawnshops are probably already being targeted by the authorities. These risks need to be considered but are not serious enough to discard the model.

Appraisal risks are undoubtedly a non-negligible risk factor for pawnshops and jewellery dealers: 'With antique jewellery, you might have a hard time estimating [its value]' (Interview partner 13). However, this risk can certainly be reduced through the use of qualified personnel. It is true that forgeries cannot be completely ruled out due to the time pressure and the often limited technical proficiencies of those working in pawnshops and at train stations. However, due to the abundance of transactions, the money launderer has a solid risk spread and can thus face the risks calmly.

More problematic, however, is the fact that the authorities already know that pawnshops are suitable locations for money laundering: 'Pawnshops are on the radar' (Interview partner 4). This means that pawnshops may be subject to stricter controls. However, this does not discount the utility of this model. After all, it is hardly possible for the authorities to trace every single transaction made by a jewellery dealer.

4.3.5 Overall Assessment

In conclusion, the method described in this section is well suited for laundering large sums of money. Although certain expertise is required and certain costs may have to be accepted, the method is extremely low risk. Small sums can easily be laundered by a money launderer posing as a retail customer.[170] It is true that governments have partly tried to curb money laundering in the jewellery trade. However, background checks in the retail trade, as they are to be implemented in Germany, for example, are only of limited use. After all, no money launderer will conduct transactions himself if he has to identify himself.[171]

Interestingly, 87.1 % of the compliance officers surveyed stated that they had not come across any cases of money laundering in connection with jewellery in the last three years. This figure is not surprising. Finally, it must be borne in mind that jewellers do not normally employ compliance officers. A money launderer who pays cash and does not involve a bank in the transaction can therefore easily place his incriminated funds with a jeweller without expecting to be queried. It is therefore obvious why the jewellery trade rarely attracts the attention of compliance officers. Either trading in jewellery is too complicated for money launderers or they are simply able to do it without getting caught.

170. Buomberger, 2012.
171. Ungerman, 2011; Ramthun, 2012.

4.4 ROUGH DIAMONDS

4.4.1 General Suitability

Rough diamonds are suitable for all stages of money laundering. In their simplest form, they are suitable for placement. However, in combination with complex structures, they can also be used for the layering and integration stages. Rough diamonds are easy to transport and offer good value retention. Furthermore, their origins are difficult to trace.

Rough diamonds are suitable for placement because the money launderer can arrange for cash payment with the seller of the diamonds. Once the money launderer has exchanged incriminated funds for rough diamonds, he has succeeded in placing the funds. When exchanging the diamonds for other valuables, the origins can be disguised, which also makes layering successful. Integration takes place when the diamonds are officially sold to a reputable dealer and the proceeds of the sale are subsequently reinvested.

Since rough diamonds are usually very small in size and weight when compared to gold, art, antiques or jewellery, the money launderer has fewer transport problems to contend with. The storage of rough diamonds, apart from certain security risks, also poses no significant challenge. The value retention is also not affected by improper storage.

The origins of rough diamonds can only be traced by means of complex mineral analyses. Nonetheless, these analyses cannot reveal when or from where the diamond was acquired. Unlike gold bars or jewellery, rough diamonds do not have serial numbers. They are therefore a very intransparent commodity.

4.4.2 Concrete Approach

First, the money launderer acquires rough diamonds. Then he imports them in a briefcase or in his trouser pocket. It is also possible to store them in bonded warehouses. In the next step, the money launderer buys certificates of origin to comply with the Kimberley Process. Through subsequent processing, he justifies a high price premium. In doing so, he benefits from non-transparent pricing. For the layering and integration stages, it is also necessary for him to set up a company for the purposes of trading in gemstones in order to ensure the necessary plausibility has been created.

In the purchase of rough diamonds, placement has to be differentiated from the other stages of money laundering. For placement purposes, it is a good idea to purchase rough diamonds directly from mine owners in their countries of origin. These sellers are not usually averse to cash transactions. In this approach, the rough diamonds are paid for entirely with incriminated assets. This approach offers an advantage in that the diamonds can usually be acquired at a deep discount due to the lack of Kimberley certificates. However, exporting the diamonds from their countries of origin poses a challenge. Couriers could possibly be used for this purpose. Importing diamonds into destination countries such as Switzerland is not much of a challenge because the diamonds can be sewn into clothing, for example, and are therefore difficult for customs officials to find. Particularly brave money launderers transport the rough diamonds in their trouser pockets or briefcases: 'It used to be common practice to import diamonds in a small suitcase or trouser pocket' (Interview partner 7).

If the money launderer intends to use the rough diamonds at the layering or integration stages, he needs to acquire them using official assets but at a heavily discounted price. This mixes legal and illegal funds. In the process, the money launderer officially buys rough diamonds. The amount specified in the purchase contract is transferred to the seller from an official account with legal assets. At the same time, the seller receives a partial payment in cash that is not documented. Rough diamonds are thus officially in the possession of the money launderer. Any differences in value are due to the money launderer's negotiating skills. It is important that the value differences remain realistic. Fluctuations of 30% are justifiable, but differences exceeding this could attract unwanted attention.

For the official acquisition of the diamonds, and especially for the eventual official sale of the diamonds, it is recommended that a legal entity be established in Switzerland for the purposes of trading in precious stones. Swiss joint-stock companies are recognized worldwide and are usually considered very reputable.

Officially acquired rough diamonds do not normally have to be imported illegally. In this case, legal import and storage in a bonded warehouse is the best option. There, the rough diamonds are kept relatively protected and cumbersome customs formalities are avoided. Furthermore, there is no risk of being caught by customs controls when importing them illegally. A clever money launderer declares part of the goods officially and mixes unofficial goods into the delivery: 'I can smuggle stuff in there, i.e., goods that are not inventoried and may not be discovered. One part is then official and something floats along behind it' (Interview partner 11). Due to the small size of rough diamonds, it might not be easy to spot them in a larger shipment of various goods.

In order to be able to legally resell rough diamonds, the money launderer needs Kimberley certificates. These certify that the rough diamonds are not so-called blood diamonds. However, these certificates can also be purchased on the black market and are therefore not a serious obstacle to overcome: 'Certificates of origin. I've also been to Africa a few times on business, and I know you can get anything there for money' (Interview partner 17). Thus, obtaining certificates of origin is not a major problem, at least not in certain African countries. Furthermore, it should be mentioned at this point that there are also numerous buyers in Europe for rough diamonds without Kimberley certificates.

The subsequent processing of the rough diamonds (i.e., the cutting) further enhances the value of the diamonds and obscures their pricing: 'I can play with the price. I can say it's a much bigger cut and then worth more' (Interview partner 16). Furthermore, traceability, especially for law enforcement agencies, is becoming increasingly difficult since most laymen do not know how many and which cuts can be extracted from a single rough diamond. Numerous expert opinions would have to be obtained to even begin to calculate this.

The next step is the sale of the diamonds. The money launderer's company now has the possibility of selling the diamonds to common diamond dealers at home and abroad. In doing so, it quotes the market prices. In this way, the company makes a significant profit on which it pays Swiss taxes.

4.4.3 Resources

First and foremost, using rough diamonds to launder money requires diamond experts who can reliably assess their value. Furthermore, Kimberley certificates are required. This means that a money launderer needs access to the black market to get Kimberley certificates. For the further processing of the diamonds, one needs access to qualified experts who specialize in the cutting of rough diamonds.

First, the money launderer needs to either have solid expertise or access to an advisor: 'Do I have a glass bead or a rough diamond? I always have to rely on some expert' (Interview partner 18). Diamond experts are relatively easy to find. The biggest challenge here might be the fact that the diamond expert knows the real value of the rough diamonds and thus knows about any differences in value and misreported purchase prices. Therefore, it is important to choose a trusted person for this.

In addition, a proof of purchase must be created: 'With gemstones, I will eventually have to document where I bought them' (Interview partner 12). Kimberley certificates are easy to obtain on the black market, but it is important that the certificates look genuine so that they do not attract attention during further processing. After all, the money launderer does not want to be targeted by law enforcement agencies because of badly forged Kimberley certificates.

Finding diamond cutters to further process the rough diamonds is also easy to organize. Especially abroad, these services can be obtained relatively cheaply and discreetly. Transporting the diamonds to the cutters and back to Switzerland is done with the help of specialized security companies.

4.4.4 Risks

The money launderer's lack of expertise and subsequent dependence on professionals is certainly one of the greatest risks associated with the rough diamond trade as a method of money laundering. Furthermore, the presence of counterfeits in the rough diamonds markets must be expected. A certain degree of comparability can also be assumed for diamonds due to standardized valuation criteria. Ultimately, it is a high-risk industry that could possibly cause a stir at banks and attract increased attention from compliance departments. Purchasing Kimberley certificates on the black market is also associated with a certain degree of risk.

Ideally, the money launderer himself has knowledge in the field of rough diamonds, but in-depth expertise on rough diamonds is rare: 'This is an area where a lot of people don't really know their stuff' (Interview partner 12). Ultimately, possessing this knowledge is the only way to really reduce the dependence on professionals. It stands to reason that the money launderer either acquires sound knowledge himself or at least has a person he trusts who is trained in this area. However, this is of course also associated with certain risks.

It is important to bear in mind that the money launderer wants as few confidants as possible: 'Relying on an expert to tell the difference between a glass bead and a diamond, I already involve some persons with the knowledge and this seems too risky to me' (Interview partner 18). If his heirs have sound knowledge in this area, this is ultimately helpful. After all, they have a vested interest in advising the money launderer honestly so that they ultimately inherit diamonds and not glass beads.

Furthermore, there is the risk that the money launderer himself becomes a victim of criminal activities: 'There are perfect certificates for fraud. That is, where you have given a higher value than you have sold your bling for' (Interview partner 12). There are numerous fake rough diamonds on the market, which are often not visible to the naked eye. It is therefore important that he trusts his business partners and thoroughly investigates their backgrounds and reputations. A careful check of the rough diamonds and their certificates should nevertheless be carried out for every transaction.

Applying standardized evaluation criteria to rough diamonds is challenging to a certain extent: 'With diamonds, you have a fixed value again. If I had a high cash turnover, people would say, aha, he must have sold so-and-so many diamonds per day' (Interview partner 5). Ultimately, these criteria can be largely circumvented by cutting the diamonds, as the value changes massively through further processing and it is no longer possible to trace exactly what the value of the original rough diamond was. Nevertheless, too-high value differences should be avoided.

Finally, it should also be borne in mind that rough diamond trading is not part of the everyday business of many banks: 'That is not our field of business. I would also not accept any company that is active in the rough diamond trade. I have already received several enquiries about this. We reject that because we don't know anything about it. We cannot judge that. We don't know how it works' (Interview partner 14). While many banks categorically reject companies involved in the rough diamond trade, others at least scrutinize them in more detail. Since these business relationships are not commonplace, such transactions are often scrutinized more closely. This can pose a certain risk for the money launderer.

4.4.5 Overall Assessment

The rough diamond trade is undoubtedly a niche method for money laundering, but it is very suitable for money launderers with expertise in the field because it can be very lucrative. This is particularly due to the fact that uncertified blood diamonds can sometimes be acquired at a deep discount. If the money launderer then succeeds in providing them with Kimberley certificates and reselling them on a par with the prices charged for legal rough diamonds, he has not only laundered his money but also made a considerable profit. However, it should also be mentioned at this point that a solid infrastructure is needed for this, and the involvement of any external experts increases the risk as they become potential witnesses to the money launderer's crimes.

Furthermore, it must be kept in mind that the diamond trade has been known as a paradise for money launderers since the 1990s.[172] Antwerp and London in particular have played a major role in this trade in the past. Governments have therefore tried several times to lower the thresholds for identification requirements.[173] However, a large number of fictitious transactions below the threshold can be faked by justifying official activity in the diamond trade.

Rough diamonds are, to a certain extent, considered vulnerable to criminal activity. It is therefore not surprising that 20.8% of the compliance officers surveyed stated that they had come into contact with cases of money laundering in connection with rough diamonds in the past three years; however, these compliance officers do not normally work with diamond traders but with financial service providers. This means that they only record those transactions that are processed via a bank. It can therefore be assumed that the number of unreported cases is high since rough diamonds can conveniently be traded for cash.

4.5 ANTIQUES

4.5.1 General Suitability

Antiques seem to be suitable for placement as well as for layering and integration. The antiques market in Switzerland is not regulated. It has high turnover, and pricing is often influenced by collectors' prices. The actual value of antiques is difficult to determine objectively. Therefore, the antiques market is in principle very well suited for money laundering.

Antiques are suitable for placement because cash payment is common in the antiques trade. The money launderer could therefore purchase antiques from private individuals as well as from retailers or auction houses and pay in cash, thus placing the money. However, further concealment can also be achieved by reselling these antiques, which means that the antiques trade can in principle also be considered a vehicle for layering. Ultimately, the money launderer can also set up an antiques business and manipulate transactions in such a way that he can record a high cash turnover. This is done so that the profit from the antiques trade is shown on the company's balance sheet at the end of the business year. After this balance sheet profit has been taxed, the integration of the incriminated funds into the economic cycle is complete. The money launderer can then use the funds at this point for any other legal or illegal activity.

Since the antiques trade in Switzerland is not regulated, anyone can trade in antiques. If the threshold values of the AMLA, namely CHF 100,000 for cash payments, are not exceeded, there is no obligation for sellers to report the transaction, and the customer does not have to be identified. The law enforcement authorities therefore

172. Der Spiegel, 1997.
173. Thompson, 2003; The World, 2013a.

have no way of knowing when antiquities are bought or sold in Switzerland and by whom.

Another advantage of the antiques trade for the money launderer is the high turnover that is common in the industry. While it is extremely difficult to justify a turnover of CHF 100,000 per week in a fictitious restaurant or bar, doing so is not a challenge in the antiques trade. To achieve this, the antiques dealer only needs to maintain a small infrastructure and requires no employees. It is quite plausible that an individual with good contacts in the antiques trade could achieve a six-figure turnover each week. This means that this method is also suitable for money launderers needing to process larger sums.

Furthermore, pricing in the antiques trade is often influenced by collectors' prices. Ultimately, the value of antiques, as in the art trade, lies in the eye of the beholder. Whether an antique cabinet is worth CHF 100,000 or CHF 300,000 cannot ultimately be determined objectively. Experts can undoubtedly write appraisals and give guide values, but if a collector wants the cabinet badly enough, he is free to pay a price above the market value. This means that the money launderer can actively control the price of his antiques.

4.5.2 Concrete Approach

The money launderer must first acquire expertise in the antiques and antiquities trade. Then he sensibly selects rather unknown objects. For this, he prefers to operate in non-transparent markets. If necessary, the money launderer obtains false papers and expert opinions from renowned experts. Then he mixes legal with illegal goods. As for the transport, the goods are made unrecognizable and hidden in a larger load of modern art. The goods chosen are preferably as robust as possible, such as clay vessels or jewellery made of semi-precious stones. These goods are declared the 'property of a private gentleman' when they are resold. Auctions are a good way of reselling. However, there are alternative ways whereby supply and demand can be actively managed. The money launderer could, among other things, set up a shop with overpriced goods. This business generates plausible turnover and regularly declares cash as cash turnover. In doing so, all threshold values are consistently observed.

First, the money launderer must acquire expertise in the antiques and antiquities trade. This step seems very challenging at first, as it undoubtedly requires some time and intellectual effort. It is obvious that the required expertise is a barrier, and this method is not suitable for every money launderer. However, at the same time, it should be kept in mind that not every criminal is ignorant and uneducated. There are highly intelligent criminals in almost all areas – not only in white-collar crime. Furthermore, the required expertise must be put into perspective at once. Ultimately, the money launderer may specialize in a niche area of the antiques trade. This means that he needs significantly less expertise than the average antiques dealer because he only has to know about a very small area.

Should the money launderer nevertheless find it too tedious to acquire basic specialist knowledge, he is free to call in experts and trust their expertise. However, this not only makes the money launderer dependent on the expertise of third parties but also creates witnesses who are informed about his transactions. Therefore, it makes sense to switch to trading in worthless antiques instead. In this case, the antiques dealer does not need any expertise since the goods he buys are worthless anyway. Subsequently, he feigns a fictitious trade in these goods in order to generate cash turnover. It should be mentioned, however, that this method entails the risk of a lack of plausibility. Thus, it is recommended that the money launderer actually has basic knowledge in the field of antiques and conducts plausible transactions with high-value antiques.

Ideally, the selection of the objects to be acquired is made in such a way as to ensure the greatest possible anonymity and non-transparency. This presupposes that the money launderer acquires rather unknown antiques or antiquities in a non-transparent market: 'They should actually be things that come fresh from the earth. In other words, things that are not yet known to science. Nowadays, if they find a life-size Roman bronze statue somewhere in the Mediterranean and put it on the market, it's worth millions' (Interview partner 6).

Antiques or antiquities that have recently been shown at an auction and sold or auctioned off at a publicly communicated price are in principle unsuitable for the money launderer. After all, the origins and the approximate market price could be determined. The money launderer therefore prefers to acquire antiques from private owners and agrees with the seller not to disclose the price.

If the antiques or antiquities originate from an incriminated source, as is often the case lately due to the financing of terrorism, the money launderer may have to obtain false papers and appraisals. There are several ways to do this. One possibility is to seek contact with the most unscrupulous scholars possible: 'This renowned archaeologist had no reservations whatsoever and examined everything that was shown to him. He then also published the things. By publishing, the layman has an entry point to be able to judge whether the things are rare' (Interview partner 6). This approach is particularly recommended for very rare antiquities. The scholar gets the opportunity to be the first to examine them and write about them, and in return, he does not ask any questions about their origins. He offers a free expert opinion to the money launderer and benefits by being the first to have written about a rare individual piece. For less unique pieces, the money launderer commissions expert opinions from tolerant but also recognized experts.

Of course, one could argue that the money launderer should refrain from incriminating antiquities since this would ultimately allow him to avoid the problem of obtaining false papers or fake appraisals. However, one should also bear in mind that terrorist financiers, just like the money launderer, depend on a high degree of anonymity and a discreet handling of the transaction. The markets are non-transparent and often grant high-profit margins due to the origins of the goods: 'You can sell Madonnas there, you can sell a painting there and whether you then make a discount or a knockdown, no one can evaluate that' (Interview partner 5). This applies in particular to antiquities that have come into the possession of terrorist financiers in the course of looting in war zones, such as Syria or Iraq. However, it should also be mentioned at this point that not all antiquities require an appraisal - appraisals are most often required for only very high-priced pieces.

After acquisition, mixing the illegal goods with antiques of legal origin is done in order to achieve further concealment: 'You can mix legal assets with illegal goods, so it becomes even harder to determine what is illegal' (Interview partner 16). In the course of a search of the dealer's storage rooms, it may become difficult for the investigating authorities to determine which antiquities were purchased with incriminated assets. On the one hand, this can be achieved by the money launderer paying for part of the purchase price officially with legal funds and the remainder with incriminated funds, with the invoice only showing the official part of the purchase price. On the other hand, commingling can be achieved by issuing less concise invoices and accumulating less unique antiques. If the invoice reads 'cabinet 1920s, 120 cm x 180 cm', it is not obvious at first glance which cabinet in the inventory the invoice refers to. If there are ten cabinets with these dimensions from this period in the same warehouse, such receipts make it much more difficult to determine the origins of the cabinets.

If the money launderer is forced to transport the goods, he makes them unrecognizable and hides them in a load of modern art or antiques:

> *For example, he smuggled things out of Egypt and made them really ugly beforehand. For example, he covered them with masses, real sculptures with malleable mass, and then painted them very garishly, colourfully, so that they looked like bazaar kitsch, and every customs officer who looked at something like that immediately said, no, that's bazaar kitsch, that's horrible, and that's how he brought them to Great Britain* (Interview partner 6).

For example, the money launderer might cover antique vases with plasticine in order to declare them as worthless junk from a market trader during an inspection. Alternatively, he will carry fake invoices and receipts for the goods. For a customs officer, it is thus no longer obvious at first glance whether the vase is valuable or not. Since customs officials usually have to cover a wide range of specialist areas, they do not normally have in-depth specialist knowledge of antiques. Ultimately, it might not be obvious at first glance, even to an antiques dealer, whether the vase is valuable or not. It is important to bear in mind that the plasticine must not simply be removed. If the vase is indeed a valuable piece of modern art, the removal of the plasticine may cause considerable damage to it.

In addition, the money launderer prefers to deal in very robust antiques, such as clay vessels and jewellery made of semi-precious stones: 'Other things, for example, clay vessels or even jewellery made from semi-precious stone, from this gemstone, are a bit more robust' (Interview partner 6). On the one hand, this prevents the pieces from being damaged during transport. On the other hand, these objects often do not require costly restoration work to ensure that they retain their value. An antique manuscript, for example, must be stored professionally, whereas a clay vase can ultimately be stored in a hiding place in a dry cellar that maintains a constant temperature.

A question then arises as to how the goods can be declared for resale. Ideally, the money launderer succeeds in convincing a reputable auction house to include the goods in its catalogue, labelled the 'property of a private gentleman', and to auction them off: 'X has basically put the whole thing on the market under the heading "property of a private gentleman"' (Interview partner 6). The auction house transfers the proceeds to the money launderer. Alternatively, the money launderer offers the antiques to other dealers. In both cases, however, there is a risk that the money launderer will be asked where he got the goods. Furthermore, there could be a search of his storage rooms by the investigating authorities before the sale. In order to be prepared for these queries, the money launderer repeatedly acquires antiquities by official means. Furthermore, he might declare the goods as an untaxed inheritance. Any queries from dealers and auction houses are likely to come to a quick end at this point. After all, one does not necessarily want to upset a wealthy customer, and there is no legal basis for asking further compliance questions.

In the context of auctions, it is important that the money launderer remains anonymous. This wish is respected by the vast majority of auction houses. Furthermore, the money launderer can use the auction to launder further incriminated funds. A straw man from abroad could travel to participate in an auction in Switzerland. There he buys the goods at a completely inflated price. He pays the purchase price in cash. Although the straw man may have to identify himself, his data is of very little value to the investigating authorities. A Kazakh businessman living in Dubai who buys a vase or a cabinet and pays in cash does not appear to be committing a crime, even if the price is inflated, and the seller (i.e., the money launderer) has simply made a good deal. In the process, the money launderer only loses what he has to pay in commission to the auction house.

Supply and demand can also be controlled outside of auctions. This means that the money launderer in principle also has the possibility of acquiring antiquities with legal funds and subsequently sell them to a straw man at an inflated price: 'Of course, supply and demand come into it [laughs], which of course you can control' (Interview partner 12). As a result, the money launderer has a receipt for the purchase and a receipt for the sale. If the transaction is below the national threshold, he does not have to identify the buyer. He is therefore free to buy a vase for CHF 10,000 and then sell it for CHF 70,000. He cannot be required to know the name of the buyer.

Should the money launderer engage in fictitious transactions more frequently, he should set up a shop selling overpriced goods: 'And in this shop, they hang a few worthless pictures or put up a few figurines or a few chamber pots ... and then when you look in, you just see, aha, he's actually selling something' (Interview partner 5). For example, the money launderer could take over an existing retail business with low turnover at a relatively low price. In this way, he gains plausibility and still does not have to make too high an investment. Moreover, he does not have to invest time in setting up the infrastructure. He then expands the assortment of goods available for purchase in the shop. If he does not want to make any actual transactions, he only has to adjust the prices and the opening hours so that visiting the shop ceases to be an option for the average customer. However, he also loses plausibility by doing so. In any case, both in an antiques shop that is actually operating and in a shop without real customers, the money launderer can conveniently smuggle large amounts of cash into the system through fictitious transactions.

The plausibility of the turnover must be observed regardless of the methods of purchase and sale. Particularly in the context of a commercial activity, care must be taken to ensure that the sales are as customary and inconspicuous as possible for the industry: 'Yes, and if you plausibilize the sales there' (Interview partner 7). Admittedly, there is nothing to be said against doing somewhat better than the competition in terms of earnings. This may ultimately be due to the antiques dealer's exceptional negotiating skills and range of contacts. However, it would be short-sighted for the money launderer posing as an antiques dealer to earn ten times more than his competitors. Doing so would attract suspicion, and the tax authorities might start asking questions. A clever money launderer therefore takes care not to attract unwanted attention.

For money launderers, declaring cash as cash turnover is extremely tempting: 'So if we had an antiques dealer as a customer, we wouldn't find out how much he actually gets for his Madonna figurines or paintings ... has just got a good deal' (Interview partner 5). However, certain principles must be observed here as well. For example, the bank might question excessively high cash transactions and ask the antiques dealer to document the exact origins thereof. However, this problem can be conveniently circumvented by the antiques dealer having accounts with at least ten different banks. A cash amount of CHF 10,000 per week is in no way unusual for an antiques dealer. A cash amount of CHF 100,000 per week attracts considerably more attention. Cash amounts are thus cleverly split across accounts and banks. At the same time, cash turnover should fluctuate somewhat. Declaring overly consistent amounts as cash turnover every week would be implausible. In the summer holiday period in August, for example, sales could drop somewhat. In the pre-Christmas period, however, turnover might increase. These seasonal fluctuations are partly recorded by banks as part of the transaction analysis.

Furthermore, there hardly seems to be an upper limit with this method: 'There is no upper limit of an amount above which it would become critical' (Interview partner 7). Nevertheless, the money launderer must observe all thresholds. These vary from country to country. Therefore, the money launderer must inform himself precisely about the specific values and make sure that he not only falls short of them but also keeps a significant distance from the values relevant for control reports. A prudent money launderer falls below the thresholds by at least 30% in each case. This is due to the fact that banks often look particularly closely at transactions that are just below the threshold.

4.5.3 Resources

Probably the biggest challenge with this method is the expertise required in a particular field of antiques or antiquities. Furthermore, the money launderer may need access to restorers as well as non-transparent markets and volatile prices. Ultimately, however, the resources required are manageable.

To be successful, the money launderer must acquire a certain expertise in a specific area: 'But for that you would first have to learn to read different languages and cuneiform writing' (Interview partner 6). For this, the money launderer essentially needs time and possibly contact with existing experts. In most cases, a careful reading of the relevant specialist literature should lead to the desired results.

More difficult, however, is the selection of a suitable restorer. In some cases, pieces have to be restored. In other cases, certain measures must be taken to preserve their value: 'Metal objects are often very fragile, they are often already very corroded due to storage in the ground and would then actually have to be restored in order to be secured so that the corrosion process does not continue' (Interview partner 6). While restorers are easy to find, it should be kept in mind that these people can ultimately testify to what pieces the money launderer has or has had in the past. Therefore, money launderers call in restorers from abroad. In order not to have to transport the antiques, it makes sense to have the restorer travel to the country where the goods are stored. For example, a Russian restorer could travel to Switzerland for a few weeks as a supposed tourist, restore the goods and then return to his home country. In Russia, the Swiss authorities are limited in the questions they can ask him.

Non-transparent markets and volatile prices are ultimately not hard to find: 'Between private parties, prices are extremely volatile' (Interview partner 2). Almost every antiques market is also opaque and volatile. The non-transparency is due to a lack of regulation on the one hand and discrete antiques buyers on the other. The volatility results from collectors' prices and shifting market demand.

4.5.4 Risks

Due to the suspicion of terrorist financing, the antiquities trade has recently received increased attention from the authorities. An additional risk is that it can be assumed that the money launderer could come into contact with forgeries. Furthermore, tracing the origins of certain pieces is possible because of serial numbers. Finally, the risks resulting from customs controls and the volatility of the antiquities market should not be underestimated. However, based on an overall assessment of this method, the risks are ultimately manageable.

Terrorist financing is an increasingly central issue for the antiquities industry: 'One of the five or six ways ISIS is financed is effectively through antiquities. They destroy some stuff, but only stuff they can't really sell' (Interview partner 2). Admittedly, the effectiveness of the current measures to combat terrorist financing can be questioned, as it is even more difficult to gather evidence in the area of terrorist financing than in the area of money laundering. However, no Western government wants to be accused of not having done everything possible to combat global terrorism. This means that markets suitable for terrorist financing attract the special attention of law enforcement agencies. This also includes the trade in goods that change hands in the course of looting in terrorist-controlled areas, such as central banks' gold reserves as well as antiques and art from museums.

It is also important to bear in mind that forgeries make a regular appearance on the antiques market: 'The risk of me getting a fake antique is huge after all' (Interview partner 18). Some fakes are easy to recognize, even for lay collectors. Others have been carefully crafted and look deceptively real, even to experts. Thus, it is clear that this risk can only be reduced and not eliminated. By spreading the risk well (i.e., by buying as many small items as possible), the risk can be mitigated. At the same time, counterfeiters are less likely to dedicate a lot of time to make an item in the lower price segment look deceptively genuine.

When purchasing incriminated goods, it must be assumed that the origins could possibly be traced on the basis of serial numbers: 'They have photos of things that have serial numbers that have then been picked up again' (Interview partner 6). This means that the money launderer must consistently ensure that the objects he acquires do not have serial numbers. It is obvious that an attentive money launderer can eliminate this risk with very little effort.

Customs controls do pose a considerable risk, especially in the cross-border transport of antiquities, but the extent of the controls depends on the expertise of the customs officers onsite, which is difficult to predict: 'That depends, I would think, on how good these controls are, and it also depends on how well trained the customs officer is' (Interview partner 6). It is obvious that the money launderer wants to avoid customs formalities in order not to attract the attention of authorities unnecessarily. However, should he come across a control, failing to declare his goods could quickly be his undoing. Therefore, the intelligent money launderer avoids the cross-border transport of these goods.

The volatility of the antiques market should also not be underestimated, as it can lead to losses as well as gains: 'Then there is just the threat of a financial loss' (Interview partner 17). On the one hand, high price volatility is a great advantage for the money launderer, as it allows him to set prices in a non-transparent and arbitrary manner. On the other hand, it could also be to his detriment. If he has acquired valuable goods and is dependent on reselling them in a timely manner, he may have to reckon with losses in value.

4.5.5 Overall Assessment

In conclusion, this method of money laundering is suitable for laundering both small and large amounts. While an occasional money launderer can launder small amounts through retail and by reselling items at auction, a professional money launderer can build up an official business in the antiques trade. All that is required is a certain level of expertise. The risks are manageable and the costs extremely low.

Some governments have already begun to recognize the risks posed by the antiques trade and have tried to react to it through legislative measures.[174] Various studies have also drawn attention to the potential for money laundering in this sector.[175] Providers of forensic services are already soliciting clients in the antiquities trade.[176] However, even in this case, a clever money launderer can feign engaging in a brisk trade in goods below the threshold by setting up his own business.

174. Jahn, 2012.
175. Transparency International, 2014.
176. Deloitte, 2014.

Trading in antiques seems to attract the attention of compliance officers rather rarely, as only 15.3% of the compliance experts surveyed stated that they had encountered money laundering in connection with antiques trading in the last three years. This stands to reason, as cash payments can easily be made in this industry as well. Retailers in the antiques trade do not have compliance departments and are not obliged to scrutinize cash payments under CHF 100,000.

4.6 ART

4.6.1 General Suitability

Art, like other tangible assets, is suitable for all three stages of money laundering (i.e., placement, layering and integration). The art scene successfully resists stronger regulation and subordination under the AMLA. Its combination of a lack of regulation and non-transparent determinations of value makes it an ideal instrument for money laundering.

The art trade, like the antiques trade, is dominated by cash transactions. It is therefore obvious that through the acquisition of art objects, such as a painting, incriminated cash can be exchanged for a material asset. Through the subsequent resale, further concealment is ensured. As soon as the profits from the sale have been taxed, they can even be considered integrated. After all, these are official profits that are legitimized by a tax assessment.

The art scene very successfully resists almost any form of regulation. Lowering the thresholds for cash transactions is considered extremely unlikely, at least in the near future, and requiring the registration of buyers and sellers has similarly been rejected. Many legitimate art collectors are also extremely wary of publicity and prefer to trade in secrecy, even with legal assets, and agree to keep quiet about their transactions. This has made it almost impossible to tell whether a dealer is a discreet private individual with a strong need for discretion or a money launderer.

Another advantage for money laundering in the art scene is that the art trade is not subject to the AMLA. While the money launderer might have trouble buying gold bars for CHF 20,000, he could easily purchase a painting for CHF 80,000. In view of the fact that art objects are always considered an interesting alternative investment and that there are now even investment funds that specialize in trading in art, making this distinction between gold and art in the AMLA seems almost arbitrary.

However, works of art have another advantage over gold. Their value cannot be precisely determined. This means that in the end, what the art dealer found in an attic or bought in a flea market might actually have considerable value. While it is unlikely that someone would mistake 20 kilograms of gold for worthless scrap and sell it at the flea market for CHF 50, it is quite possible that a flea market dealer might fail to recognize the true value of a painting due to a lack of expertise in fine art.

4.6.2 Concrete Approach

Through actual or fictitious cash payments, incriminated funds are converted into material assets via the art trade. Auctions, as well as flea markets, are suitable venues for trading. For those operating within the professional art trade, they need to maintain good relationships with banks and, under certain circumstances, to indicate that legal entities are the owners of the objects. Domiciliary companies seem to be particularly suitable for this. For resale, it is usually sufficient to locate art dealers via common Internet search engines, such as Google. Under certain circumstances, however, it would also make sense to seek out reclusive art collectors in order to obtain a better price. It should also be mentioned that bonded warehouses offer ideal conditions for low-cost, secure and relatively discreet storage.

The author deliberately refers to actual or fictitious cash payments because this already indicates an initial differentiation of the methods. The money launderer can actually acquire high-value art objects and spend larger amounts of cash on them since cash payment is quite common in the art trade: 'Cash payments have historically been accepted at auctions' (Interview partner 7). This cash is placed by the money launderer once the counterparty has received it and transferred ownership of the artwork to him in return. Alternatively, the money launderer may only pretend to have sold a painting at a certain price and to have received cash in return. In this case, the money would be placed as soon as his bank accepts the cash deposit from the proceeds of the sale of artwork. The procedure for setting up a dummy company for this purpose is analogous to the mechanisms already outlined for trading in antiques.

Flea markets are particularly suitable for carrying out fictitious transactions. The occasional money launderer can argue that he has made a 'lucky find' at a flea market: 'We've seen cases where someone actually bought a book at a flea market and then sold it on for 10 million because it was supposedly a rare work of art or a rare collector's copy' (Interview partner 9). The money launderer may claim that he purchased a painting for CHF 50 and hung it in his office. During a visit by a foreign art lover, the true value of the painting was then realized. This foreign art lover, based in Russia or Kazakhstan, had spontaneously offered him CHF 50,000 for the painting. Using a professional civil law contract, the deal was consummated. The art lover either paid cash or transferred the amount owed from Russia or Kazakhstan to Switzerland. The flea market trader could not be traced due to the money launderer's bad memory. Clearly, this method cannot be used three times a week. However, not every money launderer has millions that he needs to launder on a regular basis.

The flea market example, which could be applied analogously to other methods, such as antiques, shows that money laundering is also possible with a very small infrastructure and a single contact abroad. The special thing about it is, among other things, that this method does not require any expertise. After all, the money launderer does not have to have a profound knowledge of art when he buys a painting for CHF 50. Furthermore, in the case of a fictitious cash payment, the straw man cannot embezzle the money because it does not have to be entrusted to him. It is sufficient if the money launderer claims that he received CHF 50,000 from the art lover. Further verification of the facts is almost impossible, as the money launderer will only deposit the cash amount at the bank once his straw man is safely back in Kazakhstan. Questioning the art lover in Kazakhstan is likely to be difficult for the authorities to achieve.

Furthermore, the money launderer may contact other art dealers in order to acquire or sell art objects. Both private (i.e., hobbyist) art dealers and commercial dealers come into play for this purpose. In both cases, cash payment is agreed upon and care must be taken to ensure that the pieces to be acquired have not recently changed hands publicly. Reclusive private collectors and discreet galleries seem to be particularly suitable for this method.

Of course, auctions are also a popular instrument in the art trade, just as they are in the antiques trade. The money launderer can sell art objects at auctions. He is also free to purchase works of art at auctions. However, it is important to bear in mind that the market prices for certain objects sold at auction become public. This can lead to restrictions in the plausibility of resale. Furthermore, it becomes known exactly when the money launderer acquired the art object and at what price. Should the investigating authorities learn of this and question the validity, he would have to be able to explain the means with which he settled the purchase price. Therefore, auctions are more suitable for the sale of art rather than its purchase. A referral from a reputable auction house is likely to meet with little to no resistance from compliance departments, and the money launderer claims to have privately acquired the objects to be auctioned.

To evade suspicion from compliance departments, the intelligent money launderer maintains good contacts with his banks. He builds up a relationship of trust over several years and presents himself as a serious businessman and art lover. He repeatedly tells his advisor about his family's long tradition of collecting art. He then mentions that he occasionally parts with less beloved pieces: 'If we had a client whom we had known for a long time and who said he had a work of art that he would sell, and we weren't talking about million-dollar sales, but about medium amounts, then that would probably be possible' (Interview partner 14). Should the compliance department ask the client advisor for details about the client relationship, a glance at the dossier would be sufficient to establish that the money launderer is a supposed art lover. Of course, certain plausibility must be ensured here as well. A corrupt public official with a university degree will tell this story more credibly than an inner-city drug dealer without a high school diploma.

Should the money launderer have larger sums of incriminated funds to process, he will take a somewhat more professional approach. In this case, the art objects would be acquired through domiciliary companies to ensure further concealment takes place: 'Especially when it is in the fine art sector, that is, really paintings by great masters et cetera, that is not done in cash. These art objects usually belong to legal entities. A separate domiciliary company is made and it is then the owner of this painting' (Interview partner 17). Ideally, the beneficial owner of the domiciliary company is not the money launderer himself but a supposedly independent third party (i.e., a straw man). The joint signing authority of two straw men can reduce the risk of the art objects being sold without the money launderer's consent.

Moreover, duty-free warehouses seem to be particularly well suited for storage purposes: 'Then there are these opportunities via bonded warehouses to store things for years' (Interview partner 2). In bonded warehouses, relatively inexpensive, discreet and secure storage is guaranteed. Furthermore, the money launderer avoids cumbersome customs formalities which could lead to queries. Possession can even be transferred directly inside the bonded warehouse. Of course, storage in private safe-deposit boxes is also an option, whereby reference is made to the safe-deposit box method described in this book.

4.6.3 Resources

The money launderer may need access to experts and a secure storage facility to utilize this method. He also needs large amounts of cash and contacts in the form of dubious art dealers. He should also have solid civil contracts of sale. Small assets seem to be particularly suitable for this method as well.

Should the money launderer decide to acquire valuable art objects, it is obvious that he needs to ensure that they are not forgeries. It is helpful, but usually not sufficient, if he acquires sound expert knowledge himself to avoid being fooled. In any case, he should also seek the advice of experts: 'Again, I need special experts' (Interview partner 18). These experts must be chosen in such a way that they are very difficult for the investigating authorities to access in case of doubt. It is therefore also advisable to consult an expert from abroad who will return to his or her home country after the work is done.

Small assets seem to be better suited for money laundering than large assets. There are several reasons for this. First, small assets spread the risk of large losses in value due to counterfeiting. Furthermore, many small works of art are often more liquid than one large one, and the sale of a rare work by a world-renowned artist is more likely to attract attention than the sale of fifty small works of art by moderately well-known artists.

The money launderer also needs larger amounts of cash: 'It's easy to get in if you pay with cash' (Interview partner 17). This is not a problem, however, as money launderers usually have access to cash. If they only have access to electronic means of payment, then they can use another method.

Contacts with dubious art dealers are very useful in any case: 'I'd have to have contacts in dodgy art dealer circles first' (Interview partner 6). This applies in particular to the resale of works of art and the establishment of contacts. The money launderer normally refrains from buying works of art from dubious art dealers because he does not want to risk attracting attention of the authorities due to the stolen goods.

Furthermore, the money launderer needs a secure warehouse to store the art objects. Duty-free warehouses seem to be particularly suitable for this purpose: 'These huge warehouses are relatively new. You can store things there duty-free in a no-man's land. Works of art and I think even cars can be stored in these things' (Interview partner 10). Security has a dual meaning with regard to the storage facilities. On the one hand, the art objects must be secured against theft. On the other hand, they should ideally also be stored in such a way that authorities cannot access them. Ultimately, the money launderer will only have to prove the origins of the artworks once the authorities have learned that these items are or could be present. Therefore, bonded warehouses and private safe-deposit boxes are suitable for secure storage. In both cases, the contracts for safekeeping can be made through companies that are, if possible, not attributable to the money launderer.

Finally, the role of civil law sales contracts should not be underestimated: 'Often, simply civil law contracts are sufficient' (Interview partner 9). Should the art objects or their proceeds upon resale come into the focus of the law enforcement authorities, the money launderer will have to provide a plausible explanation for the business transactions in order to remove any suspicion of money laundering. While an inheritance, finding a good deal at a flea market or discovering treasure in the attic (in combination with the convenient presence of a knowledgeable Russian art lover) may certainly be suitable explanations in individual cases, they cannot explain a professional art trade. Therefore, the money launderer needs solid civil law contracts of sale which inspire such confidence that they cannot be classified as fakes.

4.6.4 Risks

First and foremost, the risk of being hoodwinked must also be mentioned with this method. Furthermore, it must be considered that there are dishonest experts. Together with poor self-assessment, this can lead to making the wrong decisions. It should also be mentioned that reputable art dealers may report alleged money launderers to the authorities. Finally, the volatility of the art market should not be underestimated.

First of all, it should be noted that the money launderer could buy counterfeits: 'It's just insanely difficult to establish or have confirmed that the artwork is not real' (Interview partner 17). This risk can be mitigated by adapting the method outlined above, namely by trading in already worthless art objects that are sold at inflated prices. Otherwise, acquiring specialized knowledge and consulting suitable experts also helps reduce the risk.

However, the possibility of the experts being dishonest must also be considered: 'After all, there are people who know much better and pretend that something has value' (Interview partner 17). On the one hand, these experts could deliberately declare fakes as genuine art objects or at least adjust the price of genuine objects upwards in order to collect a kickback payment from the seller. This risk can be mitigated by the money launderer himself acquiring certain expertise in order to be able to somewhat confirm the work of the experts. It is also a good idea to involve several independent experts. However, this also creates further potential witnesses for the investigating authorities to question. Therefore, it is obvious that the primary risk reduction measure should be to use experts whom the money launderer can reprimand for their mistakes in case of doubt.

The poor self-assessment of many art lovers must also be considered: 'The fascinating thing about fine art is that a lot of people don't want to admit that they don't know anything about the subject matter and are madly dazzled' (Interview partner 17). It is helpful if the money launderer acquires knowledge and is able to independently assess the value of an art object to a certain extent. However, assuming that he does not deal with this subject full-time, the money launderer should bear in mind that even professional art experts repeatedly fail to recognize forgeries. Exercising some humility probably protects against unpleasant surprises here.

Furthermore, the possibility of serious art dealers reporting the money launderer to the investigating authorities must be considered: 'Art dealers who are serious pay a lot of attention to who else is on the market' (Interview partner 11). The art scene has so far successfully resisted increasing regulatory pressure. However, the players in this scene are probably well aware of how vulnerable their industry is. Money launderers are likely to bring unrest to the art market through their unusual practices. Inevitably, there is a risk that legitimate art dealers will feel threatened by the presence of money launderers and report them to the authorities. This risk can be reduced by the money launderer behaving as discreetly and inconspicuously as possible. Furthermore, he should try not to annoy other art dealers.

Furthermore, the volatility of the art market should not be underestimated: 'Unlike gold, silver or jewellery, for example, where the precious metal has a market value, the value of art is always in the eye of the beholder. Who wants to tell me whether this Picasso painting is really worth a million or 5 million?' (Interview partner 9). Fluctuations in value in the art market can bring both opportunities and dangers for money launderers. On the one hand, they help the money launderer to justify and feign differences in value. On the other hand, they can also bring financial disadvantages to the launderer if they work against him. This can be prevented by maintaining a very long-term investment horizon and exercising patience.

4.6.5 Overall Assessment

Trading in art is a method that can be used on many levels of money laundering. It is suitable for both small-time, occasional money launderers and professional, large-scale money launderers, requiring more or less expertise. However, maintaining plausibility poses a challenge. An inner-city drug dealer without a high school diploma will have a harder time using this method inconspicuously than a supposedly serious public servant who has regularly attended art gallery openings for years.

Nonetheless, there is little demand for tougher rules to be implemented in the art trade.[177] Thanks to Art Basel, Switzerland is often referred to as the global centre of the art trade. Since banks are more strictly controlled in Switzerland, money launderers can use the art market to disguise the origins of their incriminated assets.[178] An attempt at self-regulation in the Swiss art scene failed, and the possibility of safely storing artworks in warehouses in Switzerland also seems to play a certain role in making this an attractive method of money laundering.[179]

The art trade also seems to rather rarely attract the attention of compliance officials. Overall, 26.8 % of the compliance experts surveyed stated that they had come into contact with money laundering in connection with art in the last three years. This

177. Mair, 2013a.
178. Handelszeitung, 2013.
179. 3sat, 2014; The World, 2013b.

can also be explained by the fact that art dealers generally do not have their own compliance departments. Thus, it can be summarized that the art trade is ideal for money laundering.

4.7 REAL ESTATE

4.7.1 General Suitability

Real estate seems to lend itself both to the placement and integration of incriminated assets into the economic cycle and to the subsequent concealment of the origins of these assets. This is due to both a lack of awareness of money laundering risks in the real estate sector and the international nature of many real estate transactions. The enormous disproportion between the potential risk in the real estate sector and actual number of SARs suggests that the real estate sector is in principle well suited for money laundering.

The real estate sector is suitable for the placement of incriminated assets because cash payments within the framework of so-called sub-securitizations are often considered desirable for tax reasons in real estate purchases and sales. In this case, a lower purchase price than the actual sale price is stated in the public notarization in order to reduce or completely avoid paying any real estate transfer and capital gains taxes. Money launderers can therefore suggest to property sellers that an unofficial cash payment of the purchase price would be in both parties' interests. Often, unsuspecting sellers accept cash to save on paying taxes and in return deliver an asset which now belongs to the money launderer. The latter can sell this asset at any time.

An alternative approach to the placement of incriminated assets is the purchase of properties in need of renovation. Subsequently, craftspeople are commissioned to renovate these properties. Part of the renovation work is officially paid for by invoice and with non-incriminated money. The remaining part is paid in cash. In this way, incriminated assets are channelled into the economic cycle.

However, buying real estate is also an excellent way to integrate already placed funds into the economic cycle. In this case, real estate is securitized at the actual purchase price. The purchase price is then settled by a transfer from abroad. The only thing to watch out for is that the transfer looks plausible. Normally, the seller does not suspect anything. The property can then be rented out to generate legal and unsuspicious income.

It should also be mentioned that the resale of a property, which may have considerably increased in value due to possible renovation work, is an ideal form of concealment. In the event of an investigation by the authorities, the money launderer could declare his funds as the proceeds of a property sale. The same applies in the case of a reinvestment of these funds.

The lack of awareness of money laundering issues in the real estate sector is certainly particularly advantageous for money launderers. Real estate is often sold by private individuals who do not have basic legal knowledge. In principle, these private individuals have no obligation to report because they are not financial intermediaries.

Money launderers could specifically look for naïve private individuals selling property in order to benefit from such real estate transactions.

Even if professionals, such as real estate agents, are involved in the transaction, there is still no guarantee that any money laundering activities will be detected. Real estate agents usually have only rudimentary legal knowledge and are rarely trained in criminal law. Furthermore, as non-financial intermediaries, they are not subject to any special supervision in most countries.

In most countries, real estate transactions have to be publicly notarized, which means that notaries and other notarial staff could report suspicious transactions. However, doing so would conflict with their professional secrecy standards and commercial interests.

Craftspeople are a central element in money laundering in the real estate sector. For tax reasons, they often have no interest in refusing any cash payments. Furthermore, even if they suspect that money laundering is taking place, they have a strong commercial interest to ignore the possible risks. Finally, it should also be emphasized that craftspeople do not normally have sufficient knowledge of criminal law to recognize the signs of money laundering.

It should also be mentioned that engaging in real estate transactions abroad could be particularly suitable for money launderers. After all, certain plausibility can be established by buying a supposed holiday property. Furthermore, the holiday property can be bought in a country where not too many questions are asked. Ultimately, this makes the investigative work of the law enforcement agencies more difficult since receiving administrative and mutual assistance can sometimes take a long time.

4.7.2 Concrete Approach

Properties in large cities with very liquid real estate markets as well as problematic properties in need of renovation in more remote areas seem to be suitable for money laundering. To acquire the properties, either straw men or legal entities are used. In the case of companies, the acquisition and leasing of real estate are stated as the purpose of the company. Furthermore, offshore companies can be integrated into a corporate network. Subsequently, a false purchase price is publicly notarized. If necessary, this is done by the company's own notaries. Care must be taken to ensure that the official purchase price is paid with unsuspicious funds. Therefore, direct transfers from offshore destinations should be avoided. Under certain circumstances, loans can be faked. Subsequently, the property is subjected to a luxury renovation in order to invest further incriminated assets. In the process, amounts of less than CHF 100,000 are settled in cash. Finally, the property can either be rented out for real or rental contracts can be faked. Alternatively, the property can also be sold. In this case, even incurring minor losses could be acceptable. Depending on local requirements, the value of the property can be controlled via easement agreements.

Properties in larger cities with liquid real estate markets are very well suited for money laundering for several reasons. First, the anonymity of the big city ensures greater protection from nosy neighbours and indiscreet villagers. Furthermore, it is plausible that a foreign investor group would invest in condominiums in a big city such as Zurich, Geneva, Frankfurt, Munich, Milan, Madrid, Moscow or London. On the other hand, it would seem unusual if an international real estate company were looking for properties to purchase in small villages in Appenzellerland or Thurgau. At the same time, the real estate market in large cities is often very liquid, which facilitates any resale: 'In big cities, there are liquid real estate markets where you know exactly how much the property will be worth in half a year' (Interview partner 16).

It should also be mentioned that very liquid real estate markets are normally very transparent. The recent economic crisis in particular has shown that real estate in large cities can be subject to massive fluctuations in value. If in a residential building in the centre of Frankfurt, twelve identical flats change hands in a year, there is little room for manoeuvre in the case of sub-securitizations. Any price fluctuations would presumably be noticed at the first tax audit.

However, remote properties, which are preferably in need of major renovation, are also quite interesting for money launderers:

> *These are usually not the properties in the best locations. I go to neighbourhoods with a high proportion of foreigners and buy properties that are in need of renovation. I buy the land plus the building, renovate it and then sell it again individually on a condominium basis. In the process, I still make a nice profit* (Interview partner 17).

One thinks at this point, for example, of a remote, run-down villa in Italy. First of all, the advantage is that there are hardly any comparative values. If the 5-kilometre radius surrounding the villa only consists of farmland and vineyards, tax and law enforcement authorities will struggle to make a comparison. This offers an advantage in that properties can be securitized at fictitious prices. Furthermore, the attraction of properties in need of renovation is that incriminated funds can easily be invested in the property by making repairs.

The use of frontmen helps money launderers to disguise who actually purchased the property: 'So anyway, with a name that doesn't stand out or with a business background that can be explained. The whole environment makes the decisive impression' (Interview partner 7). Even if the beneficial owner himself comes under suspicion, it will be almost impossible to attribute the assets to him if there is an independent third party in the land register. When selecting a stooge, care should be taken to ensure that there is no obvious connection to the beneficial owner. For example, the beneficial owner's wife or direct descendants tend to be less suitable than persons outside the family. At the same time, they must be loyal.

As indicated, there is a risk that straw men will dispose of the assets entrusted to them independently and against the interests of the beneficial owner. Therefore, creating a legal entity is an alternative way of disguising the true identity of the beneficial owner. For the acquisition of a property in Italy, an Italian limited liability company could be used which belongs to a German limited liability company. The German company belongs to a Swiss limited company which belongs to another Swiss limited company that in turn belongs to a Dutch holding company. The Dutch holding company belongs to a British company which belongs to a company in the Channel

Islands. The Channel Islands company is owned by a company based in a free trade zone in Dubai. The Dubai company is owned by a company in Kazakhstan. The Mutual Assistance Guide provides information on which other levels might be appropriate in order to make any request for administrative or mutual assistance as time-consuming as possible. Ultimately, the beneficial owner cannot be found out if there is sufficient concealment. When acquiring real estate, one will at most enquire as to who is behind the acquiring company. A German limited liability company that is controlled by an Austrian limited liability company would not seem very suspicious. However, in the course of a more detailed examination, such an elaborate corporate network as the one described here would probably be noticed.

Of course, using a combination of straw men and companies is also possible. The most inconspicuous and least risky variant is probably a combination of one straw man and two companies: 'Let's say the company in Zug buys a property, it is then paid for by its Cayman Islands subsidiary' (Interview partner 7). The straw man does not appear at first because the companies are upstream. Should the company model be critically questioned, there is an unsuspicious natural person at the end of the inconspicuously short chain.

Public certification of a false purchase price also ensures that incriminated cash can be placed: 'As we know, the amounts are not all always declared as they should be, and cash is probably flowing' (Interview partner 2). To do this, it is first necessary to find a seller who is willing to accept part of the purchase price in cash. This should not be a problem in view of the associated tax advantages. However, it must be assumed that the seller will attract attention with the cash. If he is clueless, he might even take it to the bank and thus trigger a SAR. A purchase price is chosen that does not fall too far below market value. If the seller is targeted by the investigating authorities, the buyer can argue that he negotiated skilfully and as a result got a good deal. The purchase price can be about 25% below market value. This also prevents the tax authorities from becoming suspicious and asking questions because the land transfer tax is considered too low.

Of course, the certifying officer is also chosen in such a way that he or she does not ask any questions. On the one hand, this can be achieved by using one's 'own' deputies: 'If it's criminals who behave directly like this, there's a scene that also has its "own notaries". Of course, they don't do a damn thing to report anything then. There are involved notaries and lawyers for every purpose, also in the OK' (Interview partner 10).

However, the accumulation of various incriminated transactions with the same deputy can lead to a concentration of risk. If the prosecuting authorities focus on this notary, it is quite conceivable that any further transactions carried out by the same notary will be investigated in the course of the investigation. It is therefore advisable, insofar as possible, to use different certifying agents and to structure the transactions in such a way that they appear relatively unsuspicious and are not questioned further by a person who may well profit from the transaction.

The official part of the purchase price (i.e., the amount stated as the purchase price in the course of the public notarization) is to be paid with unsuspicious funds:

> *Now the question is, where does the money come from? It is transferred for the purchase of real estate. The bank is satisfied with that because it is also plausible with the story that the client told me in Austria. It's just the question of where the money comes from beforehand, if it keeps coming from the Cayman Islands, so I would question that again* (Interview partner 8).

Ideally, these funds are the proceeds of legal transactions in seemingly reputable countries: 'If I have the origin and the money is not incriminated, then I lack the pre-interpretation. Then the use per se is also relatively difficult to recognize as money laundering' (Interview partner 14). For example, earning real estate income from properties in the country of the property to be acquired creates an ideal paper trail. Dividends from listed companies also look very credible when questioned. In any case, direct transfers from offshore centres should be avoided in order not to attract attention.

The remaining part of the purchase price (i.e., the 25 % that was concealed in the course of the public notarization) must be paid in cash in any case. Care must be taken to ensure that the cash is handed over in an extremely discreet manner. Should the seller of the property with the cash be the target of an investigation, neither he nor the authorities should be able to prove from whom he received the cash. Thus, one should refrain from touching the cash barehanded in order not to leave fingerprints. The case containing the cash should be handed over by an anonymous assistant who never gives his name. This ensures that the official buyer of the property can easily deny that the money came from him.

In the next step, the newly acquired properties are extensively redeveloped. This will result in further incriminated assets being invested in the properties: 'If, on the other hand, I have an existing property and simply renovate it in a luxurious way with a lot of money, then it looks a bit different. Even if the companies all invoice properly and account for it and book it for themselves. But they are not obliged to report anything' (Interview partner 11). In doing so, the money launderer makes sure that in each case, some of the tradespeople's invoices are paid off using legal funds and some are paid for using incriminated assets. In this way, legal and illegal funds are mixed together. This makes it difficult for law enforcement authorities to prove which parts of the property were paid for with incriminated funds. Furthermore, this approach ensures that all services rendered can be supported by an official invoice. This is essential in several respects. First of all, attentive neighbours or authorities observe craftspeople working on the site. If the money launderer were then unable to prove that they were paid officially for the services rendered by showing an invoice, he could find himself in trouble. It is also possible that building tradespeople might not use their cash income from this project discreetly and take it to the bank instead or even tell friends and acquaintances about their lucrative business. Although suspicion would initially focus on the tax offences, in the event of criminal proceedings for money laundering taking place, these same building tradespeople would be important witnesses. If, however, around 50 % of the services rendered were officially paid for by bank transfer with an invoice, the money launderer could always argue that he had all the work done perfectly legally.

Cash payments in excess of CHF 100,000 should generally be avoided so that the recipient of the cash does not have to make major efforts to place the money. In doing so, they would ultimately run the risk of being discovered: 'In the revised Anti-Money Laundering Act, payments for use were limited to 100,000, above which they must be processed through a financial intermediary' (Interview partner 15). A building craftsperson can make a living with smaller cash payments and finance everyday luxuries such as holidays, clothes and watches. With a cash payment of more than CHF 100,000, an ordinary building craftsperson normally comes up against certain limits in terms of utilizing it to pay for his expenses. There is a risk that he will try to place the money with a bank. Assuming that building tradespeople are not necessarily familiar with the compliance mechanisms of banks, it is likely that this will trigger a SAR. There is also a risk that he will be targeted by the tax authorities for evasion.

In order to prevent the money launderer from coming under pressure when several builders are being scrutinized by the tax authorities at the same time, it is advisable to withdraw large amounts of cash from a legal account before the start of construction. If the cash payments can no longer be denied, the money launderer can claim that he made them with these legal funds. Although he would then have to answer for tax offences, it would be much more difficult to prove money laundering at this point. After all, the money launderer can prove the origins of the cash beyond a doubt. This also prevents building tradespeople from blackmailing the money launderer. Finally, in the event of an investigation, the building tradespeople would have to answer for tax offences themselves.

A freshly renovated property should ideally be rented out first to avoid an excessively large increase in value within a short period of time from attracting attention, which it would surely do if the property were immediately sold. It is therefore advisable to either look for real tenants or create fictitious tenancy agreements. Renting the property out to genuine tenants means that legal income is generated, which is beneficial. The tenants should be chosen in such a way that their identity can be easily traced in the event of a possible investigation by the law enforcement authorities. This offers the advantage of ensuring that the money launderer can argue that he is earning honest rental income from the letting of his property as an upstanding businessman. Once the tax assessment becomes legally binding, this income has a flawless paper trail.

Of course, the money launderer could also fake rental contracts: 'Then you can falsify rental contracts. Produce rental income that then turns illegal assets into legal assets, so to speak. Because rental inflows come in that in reality were not there at all' (Interview partner 10). The advantage of this solution is that the money launderer can declare incriminated funds as rents. However, this business model also entails considerable opportunity costs. Ultimately, he would have to leave the properties unrented, as double rentals would undoubtedly attract attention. Furthermore, he would have to establish false identities for the tenants. This solution is therefore only attractive if the properties cannot be let regularly.

The culmination of the real estate method is the resale of the property. Here, it is first necessary to wait for any speculation periods to have passed in order to avoid an excessive tax burden. Then the property is sold to an independent third party at the regular market price. The buyer should preferably be a trustworthy person with an impeccable reputation. At this moment, the incriminated funds are laundered. Any differences between the original purchase price and the selling price can be attributed to commercial skill, renovation work and volatile real estate markets.

It is true that the money launderer could also sell his property at a loss in an emergency. However, this solution tends to be avoided. Based on the commercially sensible approach outlined above, it is not clear why the money launderer should deliberately accept losses. In doing so, he would ultimately attract unwanted attention from the authorities who might wonder why an estate agent would deliberately take a loss.

Easement agreements can be used as a complementary tool by money launderers to control the value of real estate as needed: 'That's where certain encumbrances or usufructuary rights control the market value' (Interview partner 12). The value of a property can be massively reduced by the registration of a usufruct. Rights of way can also have a value-reducing effect. This can be helpful if money launderers have to justify making payments to each other or engaging in transactions in unusual market conditions.

4.7.3 Resources

For this method of money laundering, the money launderer needs first and foremost a liquid real estate market, which allows one to buy and resell properties. It is also essential to have gullible and inattentive lawyers, notaries and estate agents. You also need cash-happy sellers.

The money launderer first needs a liquid real estate market: 'If I have a reasonably liquid property market, where I know I can buy and sell and not have to take a big drop in value, then of course I can use that to bring big money into circulation' (Interview partner 16). A liquid real estate market is usually easy to find. Especially in the major cities mentioned above, this should not be a problem. Since money launderers are not usually tied to a specific location, it should be easy to locate and use liquid markets.

Finding gullible and inattentive lawyers, notaries and estate agents presents a bigger challenge: 'If I now make such a purchase, then both the notary and the broker must register and record this purchase price and the brokerage contract accordingly. Now an idiot comes along in good German who pays an excessive price and there you would have a lead' (Interview partner 5). However, this must be contextualized. In cash-intensive societies and in countries with high taxes, sub-securitizations and related cash payments are often common. This means that the corresponding lawyers, notaries and brokers do not have to be bona fide. They must simply refrain from exercising their full due diligence with regard to their clients' tax obligations.

In addition, the money launderer must find suitable property sellers: 'First, you still have to find someone to sell you a property for cash' (Interview partner 7). Ultimately, the money launderer also needs sellers of real estate who are willing to accept part of the purchase price in cash and at the same time declare a lower purchase price at the time of public notarization. Again, properties for sale in countries with a high tax burden seem to be suitable targets. In Spain and Italy, such sub-securitizations are probably still possible with relative ease.

Furthermore, it could be argued that the money launderer also needs to employ building tradespeople who are willing to accept cash and issue lower invoices in return. However, in view of the tax savings resulting from this approach, this should not be a serious obstacle to overcome, especially in countries with a relatively high tax burden. Therefore, it is only mentioned here in passing.

4.7.4 Risks

Using real estate is such a complex and lucrative method of money laundering that it entails certain risks. First of all, it should be mentioned that the attention of the media, law enforcement agencies, tax authorities and banks represents a considerable risk. Furthermore, lawyers or notaries could also become suspicious of the money launderer's activities. In case of initial suspicion, the extensive documentation associated with real estate transactions in the context of land registries becomes a risk. Business risks and general queries about the source of funds should not be underestimated, either.

The attention of the media poses a significant risk: 'The media, especially in real estate, love it when you say "Ah, the daughter of a Central Asian ruler has bought a villa for 75 million in the Lake Geneva area"' (Interview partner 17). Should journalists become aware of unusual transactions, this can lead to incriminating research and publications. This ultimately attracts further attention. However, this risk can also be significantly reduced by consistently avoiding high-profile transactions. The purchase of ten single-family homes in inconspicuous suburbs is usually less conspicuous than a record-breaking transaction on Lake Geneva.

At the same time, of course, it is also important to avoid attracting the attention of law enforcement agencies: 'If you stand out, there are always people from the law enforcement scene, police officers and maybe even prosecutors, who take a look at something' (Interview partner 17). The attention of law enforcement can be avoided by the money launderer carrying out transactions as inconspicuously as possible and avoiding contact with suspicious persons. It would be of limited foresight to buy a brothel from a well-known pimp at conditions that are not in line with the market. On the other hand, it would be clever to buy a holiday home from a pensioner with an unimpeachable reputation.

Furthermore, it is important to avoid attracting the attention of banks' compliance departments: 'The bank would have to ask where the money came from. If the broker says he got it from a house sale, then you would have to ask "Aha, who gave you that in cash?"' (Interview partner 4). In this context, it is advantageous to know the compliance guidelines of the respective bank. Ideally, the money launderer maintains good relations with the responsible compliance officer. In any case, however, he does not engage in any conspicuous transactions. This means that the legal funds come from traceable and legal sources. The seller is advised not to take the cash to a bank. In this way, the incriminated assets do not enter the bank's sphere in the first place.

Lawyers and notaries are inevitably involved in real estate transactions in most jurisdictions. They enjoy insight into numerous documents and, due to their local knowledge, usually have the possibility to assess whether a transaction stands up to a third-party comparison or not. Therefore, they potentially pose a great risk: 'Then we usually have lawyers and notaries who are responsible for signing the contracts. I believe that there is already a safety net there. If a situation were totally suspicious, I believe that someone from the parties involved would report it' (Interview partner 13). However, this risk can be reduced by choosing inattentive and tolerant lawyers and notaries. It should also be noted that lawyers and notaries do not normally face massive sanctions if they fail to recognize indications of money laundering offences. It can therefore be assumed that offering financial incentives to lawyers and notaries could be beneficial. Furthermore, lawyers and notaries could be chosen in countries where sub-securitizations are common.

Brokers also pose a considerable risk because they usually know the actual purchase price of the property. However, real estate transactions can be conducted without the involvement of real estate agents. Therefore, it is advisable to consistently search for properties being sold by the owner without a broker.

In addition, there is a risk that the tax authorities could become aware of the transaction due to the purchase price being too low and a correspondingly low real estate transfer tax: 'The tax authorities are not very cooperative' (Interview partner 4). Ultimately, this risk can only be mitigated to a limited extent. However, the money launderer can simply accept higher tax assessments. Thus, the interest of the tax authorities in further clarifications should be low.

The extensive documentation usually associated with real estate transactions poses a certain risk in the event of an investigation by law enforcement authorities: 'It may not be as easy as one imagines. The real estate market is relatively highly regulated with the land registry and notarized contract and so on' (Interview partner 17). This risk can be reduced by producing plausible documentation. All files should be kept clean and without gaps in order to avoid possible complaints. Solid manipulations are therefore possible. Ultimately, the purchase price may be misstated but this must first be proven.

Of course, all real estate transactions also involve taking certain business risks: 'There's a business risk that's there, but I think people are happy to take that' (Interview partner 17). Many money launderers seem to accept the risk as the cost of doing business. Moreover, especially in times of financial crisis, real estate is considered a relatively safe form of investment. The risks should be limited by a prudent investment strategy and, above all, spread. Excessive cluster risks in certain geographical locations should be avoided. Ultimately, developing an international portfolio is also quite advantageous in the event of a possible investigation by domestic prosecuting authorities. Compared to other methods of money laundering, the economic risks associated with this method are quite limited.

Finally, queries about the sources of funds should of course also be mentioned as a risk: 'Especially with real estate, I have to ask myself where the money is coming from' (Interview partner 14). This is particularly relevant with regard to the cash intended for the building tradespeople and the sellers of the property. However, by withdrawing a large amount of legal funds from their house bank, the skilful money launderer can also prepare himself for answering any possible queries here and thus ultimately limit the risk. Should there be any queries, he can finally produce a withdrawal receipt and thus largely eliminate any justified initial suspicion.

4.7.5 Overall Assessment

London's real estate market was recently described as a 'true money laundering wonder'.[180] In Switzerland, too, the real estate sector seems to offer many opportunities for money launderers to thrive.[181] Real estate seems to be just as attractive as the luxury goods sector. While it is true that there are efforts to introduce a national land register, this will likely take some time.[182] If this were to happen, money launderers would have to buy real estate in other countries in order to smuggle incriminated assets into the legal economy.

The majority of the compliance officers surveyed (65.7%) stated that they had not come across any cases of money laundering in connection with real estate in the past three years. Conversely, this means that more than one-third, namely 34.3% of the compliance officers surveyed, had indeed come across cases of money laundering in connection with real estate in the last three years. This is a conspicuously high figure and suggests that this can be explained by the fact that, in contrast to the retail sector, banks - and thus compliance officers - are almost always involved in real estate transactions.

In conclusion, this method of money laundering is inexpensive and relatively low risk. The money launderer even enjoys a competitive advantage in comparison to conventional real estate dealers due to the tax advantages in the area of VAT, real estate transfer tax and speculation or capital gains associated with the procedure described above. He can thus generate further income through commercially sensible transactions and does not have to accept losses as is otherwise common in money laundering. At the same time, however, it should be mentioned that this method is only suitable for money launderers who also have substantial legal funds at their disposal.

4.8 CONSULTING COMPANIES

4.8.1 General Suitability

Consultancies seem to be particularly suitable for the layering and integration stages of money laundering. They are legal and recognized entities that are largely uncontrolled due to their consistent avoidance of operating in regulated areas. Non-transparent pricing as well as a performance that is difficult to quantify and thus only measurable to a limited extent reinforces their suitability for money laundering.

180. Trettmann, 2014.
181. Fahmi, 2010.
182. Handelszeitung, 2015.

As cash payment is rather uncommon in the consultancy industry, consulting companies are obviously of limited suitability for the placement stage. Higher cash amounts are usually questioned by the compliance departments of the banks as part of the deposit process. However, provided the cash has already been deposited, consulting companies can be used for layering and integration. Money launderers in jurisdictions that do not scrutinize deposits of large amounts of cash can funnel the cash into the banking system and then transfer it to a consulting company abroad. Said consulting company can then use the services of other companies, which ideally are also owned by the money launderer, and ultimately invest the money into legal activities such as listed public companies.

Consulting companies offer a great advantage in that legal and recognized entities can be created with relatively little effort. Think here, for example, of a public limited company in Switzerland. Placing CHF 100,000 in a foundation account is sufficient to cover the start-up costs. A further CHF 5,000 can be used to establish a serious Internet presence. It should also be possible to rent a small office for a relatively low amount. This is how a legal entity based in Switzerland presents itself as legitimate in international business dealings.

By avoiding work in regulated areas, consulting companies evade the authorities' vigilant scrutiny. Financial advisory firms or insurance brokers tend to be less likely to engage in money laundering than marketing advisory firms. A marketing consultancy does not have to join a self-regulatory organization and is not the focus of financial market supervision.

Furthermore, advisory services are often very difficult to quantify and are thus hardly measurable. The example of marketing advice mentioned above helps to illustrate this. While the value of a legal opinion or investment advice should still be in proportion to the value of the dispute or the assets to be invested, there is still a much greater margin of discretion in the development of a marketing strategy. The value of a new brand is difficult to establish concretely. Should the development of the brand not succeed, this is not necessarily the fault of the advisory firm.

4.8.2 Concrete Approach

First, the money launderer must set up a corporation in a country that inspires confidence, preferably Switzerland. In doing so, he should conceal the beneficial owner. He then sets up subsidiaries abroad. The money launderer specifies the provision of advisory services in Switzerland and abroad as the purpose of the company. In the next step, he sets up a professional website and a representative business address. It is essential that the money launderer actually provides some of the advisory services the business claims to offer. For this, it is necessary to involve existing companies. Only then does he shift the focus of the services abroad. In doing so, he chooses destinations that make it almost impossible to verify the actual provision of the services. He then charges for services that are difficult to quantify, such as developing brands, compiling market analyses and brokering deals. Payment for these services is made by bank transfer from Russia, Latvia and Kazakhstan. By faking business expenses, the money launderer plausibilizes his business. Creating complex structures with several levels of concealment makes investigations of these activities more difficult. For this purpose, various neighbouring countries and offshore centres are involved. Ideally, the network of companies should have accounts in different jurisdictions. Finally, meticulous care is taken to ensure that the ratios of the sums involved stand up to industry comparison. Tax assessments are consistently accepted and any taxes owed are promptly remitted.

Setting up a public limited company in a country that inspires confidence is not a major problem: 'An example: Someone from Latvia has a million in cash. He deposits this in Latvia, transfers it to a trustee in Switzerland and instructs him to set up a Swiss limited company' (Interview partner 7). Thanks to the express procedures of the commercial registers in Switzerland, the company's set-up is usually completed within two weeks. The advantages of a public limited company over other legal entities relate primarily to its higher credibility in international business dealings. Especially when establishing further business relations in Germany and Austria, a joint-stock company is clearly more recognized than a limited liability company. Money launderers depend on this credibility. Switzerland is still considered a safe haven in international business transactions and is clearly more trustworthy than other jurisdictions. A company registered in South Africa or the Cayman Islands already looks suspicious at first glance in European business dealings. A Swiss public limited company, on the other hand, appears reputable.

When setting up the public limited company in Switzerland, care must be taken to disguise the beneficial owner. This can be done, for example, via subsidiaries and parent companies abroad: 'You certainly have to have [laughing] sisters abroad' (Interview partner 7). In times of increasing pressure from the OECD and the infamous Base Erosion and Profit Shifting programme, the possibilities of concealing the beneficial owner for fiscal reasons have reached a historic low. In terms of long-term concealment, bearer shares are no longer a serious solution. Instead, the choice is between the use of nominees and legal entities. In the case of the latter, it makes sense to question the beneficial owner. However, it may be possible to disguise the beneficial owner abroad on several levels. The use of nominees is by far the most discreet method of concealment, but it is also fraught with risk. After all, nominees can freely dispose of the company. Thus, there is the risk that they will no longer act in the best interests of the money launderer.

Deciding the company's main purpose is of central importance. In principle, it is already stated at this stage that the company aims to provide services at home and abroad: 'A company in Switzerland can officially offer services in Switzerland and abroad' (Interview partner 11). This makes it easy to justify an international client base later on. Advisory services and so-called family office services seem to be particularly suitable because they cannot be quantified. In the case of family office services, however, care must be taken to ensure that no financial services are provided since otherwise the company might have to join a self-regulatory organization.

In order to withstand superficial checks by authorities and banks, it is of enormous importance to have a professional website: 'If I saw a test case like that, I would probably Google the consultancy company first and see if they even existed'

(Interview partner 8). Purely domiciliary companies tend to be more suspicious and less trustworthy than companies with their own offices and employees. A website without subpages, which is obviously not optimized for search engines and thus only conditionally suitable for attracting new clients, already looks dubious at first glance. Therefore, the clever money launderer makes sure that his website corresponds to the standard of medium-sized consulting firms.

Furthermore, the prudent money launderer chooses a prestigious business address: 'I would also look there where I can buy additional services, like representative business addresses where I just have a forwarding order, address lists and so on' (Interview partner 12). It does not have to be chosen in such a way that the costs are excessive or even attracts the watchful gaze of the neighbours due to being empty. However, it should also not be located at an address in the canton of Zug that is well known for domiciliary companies. A small office near the University of St Gallen is affordable and seems plausible at first glance. Due to the proximity to the university, it can be argued that one has access to international know-how.

This is followed by what is probably the biggest hurdle of this method of money laundering. The newly established advisory company must actually provide advisory services to easily verifiable clients in Switzerland: 'Care must be taken to ensure that some part is actually provided' (Interview partner 11). By proving that advisory services have actually been provided, any initial suspicion of money laundering could be weakened or even eliminated in the event of an investigation. It is therefore of central importance that established and trustworthy companies are advised by the consulting company claiming to offer these services.

The client companies are selected in one of two ways. On the one hand, it is obvious to offer advisory services to the money launderer's other companies. If the money launderer already has catering or similar companies, he will of course 'advise' them. On the other hand, existing consulting companies could be bought up and business consultants with a solid client base recruited: 'I would stock up with companies, which were already founded years ago. Of course, that can also document a certain history, that this company has been around for a while' (Interview partner 12). In doing so, a solid customer base can be faked.

The next step is to create fictitious customers abroad: 'Services abroad, for which a fee is then obtained in Switzerland, would be feasible because you just can't check the performance' (Interview partner 11). These clients are located in jurisdictions where it is possible to smuggle large amounts of cash into the banking system. Jurisdictions in Eastern Europe are particularly suitable for this. On the one hand, the supervisory authorities there are sometimes less strict than in Switzerland; on the other hand, the high level of corruption in these countries suggests that even strict controls can be circumvented.

Then, fictitious Eastern European clients take advantage of the company's various advisory services offered. Market analyses seem to be particularly popular: 'Invoicing other services or market analyses and so on, in order to then raise funds from a neighbouring country and then pass them on again at a percentage rate' (Interview partner 18). However, not only market analyses but also concepts are suitable offerings for fictitious consulting services. For example, a money launderer has a new brand designed to introduce a sweet-tasting soft drink on the global market in order to compete with existing brands in this area. There are hardly any limits to the sums of the consultancy fees that could be charged. Other clients take advantage of slightly less sophisticated services and ask for recommendations for schools or universities in Europe for their children to attend, for example.

The next step is to feign operating expenses since a consulting company without personnel expenses would not seem very plausible. Expenses for the company headquarters and company cars must also be considered. These expenses should correspond to an industry average so that they can withstand a possible comparison by the investigating authorities. The exact amount of the expenses therefore depends on the size of the consulting firm.

The personnel costs mentioned above are usually a very significant cost factor for consulting companies. It is therefore important that these funds do not end up in the private pockets of auxiliary persons but ultimately remain within the economic sphere of the money launderer. This can be achieved by hiring subcontractors abroad. For example, agencies in Russia could receive lavish fees for referring Russian clients. Consulting companies in Dubai could provide part of the services that are then charged for on the basis of standard transfer pricing methods. In this context, the cost-plus and resale minus methods seem particularly suitable.

The inclusion of foreign companies creates complex networks that can only be checked with considerable effort: 'The more complex the thing becomes, the more financial centres are involved, the more complex basically the structures become … the more appropriate the whole thing is' (Interview partner 2). It is quite conceivable that such a consultancy firm would have holdings in other consultancy firms and intermediary agencies in more than twenty countries. This means that administrative and legal assistance from the authorities in more than twenty countries is required to examine the corporate network in the event of an investigation. This massively delays and complicates any investigations that might take place.

Care should also be taken to ensure that all subsidiaries have bank accounts in different jurisdictions: 'The company is an offshore company and the account is somewhere else' (Interview partner 12). This ensures that the company is even more convoluted and, ideally, additional jurisdictions would have to be included in any investigations. In addition, the company should be flexible at all times. If one bank suspects it of money laundering, then the company has other accounts at home and abroad with other banks. This means that it remains capable of reacting quickly.

The aforementioned consulting companies consistently accept tax assessments and promptly settle any tax debts: 'So even if I reduce tax burden, of course I will accept the payments I have to make' (Interview partner 12). This means that it is not necessarily advantageous for money launderers if the tax authorities take a second look at their accounts. After all, these companies are not supposed to be scrutinized closely. This is best achieved through meticulously kept books, employing a trustworthy tax expert with contacts in the competent tax authority and having a certain level of tolerance towards any possible mistakes made by the authorities.

4.8.3 Resources

To implement the money laundering method described, the money launderer primarily needs placement possibilities for possible cash deposits. This requires banks with correspondent banks abroad. Furthermore, a solid network of offshore companies with bank accounts in Dubai and other destinations must be created. The money launderer also needs a company in Switzerland with advisors, directors and a good reputation.

Placement through cash deposits is definitely a challenge with this variant: 'The cash has to come into circulation somewhere' (Interview partner 5). Ideally, the money launderer has good contacts in banks in Russia and Kazakhstan and deposits his incriminated funds there. He then transfers them twice within Russia. In the next step, the money launderer must transfer the incriminated funds abroad. In the third transfer, the money launderer makes sure that the funds end up in an account that allows him to transfer them abroad: 'You need to find institutions that have correspondent banks' (Interview partner 9).

Due to current sanctions, the route goes via Kazakhstan. Since European banks have established themselves in these countries, a bank with correspondent banks in Switzerland should be easy to find. At the same time, the money launderer needs companies in free trade zones in the UAE with bank accounts in Dubai: 'Letterbox companies in Dubai with bank accounts in Dubai are difficult to see through' (Interview partner 7). Establishing these companies is not a challenge. As soon as one can present evidence of such a company and a letter of recommendation from another bank, establishing a bank account in Dubai is no longer a difficult hurdle to overcome.

Setting up a company in Switzerland is also easy. However, one needs advisors, directors and a good reputation there as well. It is therefore worth considering whether the purchase of an existing company with an established infrastructure and a solid client base would be worthwhile. Should the money launderer set up a new company, he must in any case take care to select competent advisors in order to be able to exercise effective dominion over the funds:

> *But the Russian didn't know that you don't need the whole million and simply told the trustee to find him a joint-stock company. He took the whole million as share capital and then it was formally bound in the company. The Russian was of the opinion that he had the money at his disposal and could easily take it out of the company again. He was not aware that share capital cannot be reduced so easily. Of course, the Russian almost couldn't get his money that way* (Interview partner 7).

To avoid such surprises, the money launderer makes sure that his advisors are competent and that any language barriers are avoided or overcome.

Directors are also needed to ensure that services are actually supplied: 'There is the possibility of using directors so that I really have an offer' (Interview partner 16). It goes without saying that an advisory company without a director does not appear very credible. If real people are presented as advisors on the Internet and clients can actually talk to them when they call the company, the company will easily stand up to superficial scrutiny. Directors with a good reputation are particularly suitable: 'A good name and familiarity with the local conditions always help. Let's say a trustee you know' (Interview partner 7). If the local prosecuting authority has doubts about the company, a director with a good reputation as an honourable businessman and an impeccable record will certainly help to reassure the investigators. Ideally, the director is well connected locally.

4.8.4 Risks

International administrative and legal cooperation is certainly among the main risks associated with this method of money laundering. This could ultimately make the lack of anonymity of the beneficial owner a serious problem for the money launderer. Transaction analyses by banks should also not be underestimated. Cash fees are uncommon in the advisory industry and receiving payment in cash would certainly be significantly risky. A detailed audit by the police, the public prosecutor's office or the tax authorities could quickly reveal fees that are too high or companies that are too dormant.

International administrative and legal cooperation is sometimes a natural enemy of money launderers: 'In the EU and Double Tax Agreements, we share bank data, bank information with EU countries and third countries' (Interview partner 18). However, this enemy is also easy to fight. Ultimately, the Legal Aid Guide, which explains in detail which countries make the work of the investigating authorities more difficult, reveals which jurisdictions are not very forthcoming in terms of cooperating with foreign jurisdictions. The clever money launderer lines up some of these destinations to conduct wire transfers with the intention to layer the funds. This means that although information provided by the first destination in the chain might be available after twelve months, it is ultimately only a reference to the second destination in the chain. This buys the money launderer time. It is obvious that such a chain of companies is in itself suspicious. However, this risk is accepted in order to make it impossible to prove anything.

Banks' transaction analyses pose a further problem. Swiss banks could make enquiries based on conspicuous transactions and ultimately file reports with the MLRO in order to protect themselves from compliance risks. It is therefore important to appear transparent and cooperative with the banks and to bring them lucrative business. Small private banks are arguably better suited for this than large corporations, as the individual customer carries more weight with smaller banking houses. It is therefore important to suggest to the bank, through commercial interests and the proper fulfilment of all formal compliance regulations, that it refrains from reporting. Alternatively, it helps to choose banks with less competent compliance officers: 'Unless the bank has the brightest head at the top, they wouldn't realize that the turnover from this company is way too high' (Interview partner 5). However, it is not easy to determine *ex ante* which compliance officer will review the transaction. Thus, it may make more sense to search for banks with corrupt compliance officers.

Cash fees are unusual in the consulting industry and would immediately attract attention: 'Even though these can be documented with an invoice, I find cash payments for consultancies, it's not standard at all' (Interview partner 17). Thus, payment of fees in cash should be avoided. In the context of transactional analysis, cash fees would cause a stir.

Ultimately, a detailed examination of the companies by the police, the public prosecutor's office or the tax authorities must always be expected: 'There is also the question of how credible is that? If I am active in Switzerland and abroad, at least the Swiss clients should be somehow traceable. I always say this from the perspective of a tax audit' (Interview partner 11). In this case, it is wise to have some real clients in Switzerland. It is also essential to be well prepared. If the money launderer has to start falsifying contracts after the first search is carried out, it is usually already too late. The money launderer with foresight anticipates a search of his business premises and maintains a complete, plausible and serious-looking record of all important business transactions. In this way, he can succeed in eliminating any initial suspicion right away.

Companies that lie dormant could also become dangerous for the money launderer as they raise suspicion: 'As soon as I show my company on the market, everyone asks, "How does it stand? How is it rated?" It's a bit strange when I have a service company that is completely silent. You can't find it anywhere, not even on the web' (Interview partner 11). It is therefore important that the money launderer gives the appearance of being active in order to reduce the risk of being caught. Having a website that is easy to find using the usual search engines can be helpful here.

Another serious problem is the large number of experts involved in consulting companies. In the end, these are always potential witnesses. By creating plausible companies, several people are involved with access to the companies' business records. Therefore, it is advisable to appoint close confidants in these positions and maintain small companies.

4.8.5 Overall Assessment

The method presented above offers many advantages for the money launderer. In particular, it is suitable for laundering large amounts while incurring relatively low costs. Whereas companies like restaurants have to deal with the high cost of goods and maintaining large premises, an advisory company has to bear considerably lower operating costs. However, this model also entails certain risks. The number of potential witnesses that maintaining this model generates should be considered first and foremost.

Money laundering through consulting firms is not only a lucrative business in Switzerland. Such front companies also seem to enjoy great popularity in London.[183] Law firms are also repeatedly associated with money laundering.[184] However, a simple Google search quickly reveals that the press has apparently not yet paid much attention to this form of money laundering. Nonetheless, this does not automatically mean that the method presented here is irrelevant in practice. Rather, it suggests that due to its

183. The Independent, 2014.
184. Financial Times, 2014.

complexity and the involvement of several jurisdictions, it is more difficult to prove than the somewhat clumsier methods of trading in gold or antiquities.

However, it should be borne in mind that this method attracts the attention of compliance officers comparatively more often. In the context of this study, 47.1 % of the compliance officers surveyed stated that they had come into contact with cases of money laundering in connection with advisory services in the last three years. This is due, among other things, to the fact that advisory services are usually not paid for in cash but by bank transfer. This inevitably involves banks and thus also compliance officers. However, to what extent any evidence of money laundering could be hidden if the above-mentioned steps were taken by the money launderer is unknown.

4.9 CORPORATE RESTRUCTURING

4.9.1 General Suitability

Corporate restructuring seems to lend itself to all three stages of money laundering (i.e., placement, layering and integration). In the process, a detailed paper trail (i.e., precise documentation of all transactions) is deliberately procured in order to provide the incriminated funds with a credible paper trail. The non-transparent pricing of corporate restructuring and the subsequent resale of the company play a decisive role here.

Corporate restructuring is suitable for all stages of money laundering. By faking fictitious transactions in the company to be restructured, turnover can be increased. At the same time, incriminated cash finds its way into legal accounts. This is a considerable advantage for the money launderer, especially in the case of companies operating in the retail sector. When paying the purchase price for the takeover of the company to be restructured, and through subsequent capital increases, freshly placed funds from abroad can flow into a legal business. These funds are then used to carry out further transactions within the same group and to conceal the origins of the incriminated funds. This takes place over several layers until the money ends up in a completely legal construct after sufficient concealment through transactions with supposedly independent companies. This completes the integration.

Corporate restructuring is particularly suitable for producing a so-called paper trail. The money launderer deliberately tries to create a false trail in order to be able to present rebuttals in the event of an investigation. The incriminated funds are thus provided with a paper trail. This means that they find their way out of the black economy into the fully documented balance sheets of recognized companies in countries with an excellent reputation.

A particularly interesting aspect of corporate restructuring is that the resale of the supposedly reorganized company represents a further opportunity for money laundering. If the money launderer sells his restructured company to himself, there are hardly any limits to what he can do due to the non-transparent pricing of companies and the multitude of available valuation methods, as well as market price fantasies. Of course, it is necessary to disguise the buyer and the seller in order to avoid attracting the attention of the tax authorities. This variant is tax optimized, as the money launderer in Switzerland benefits from the participation exemption, provided he has held the company to be restructured as a subsidiary of another company for more than one year.

4.9.2 General Procedure

In principle, the money launderer should select companies in need of restructuring. The money launderer can disguise the beneficial owner by using small, foreign investors, so-called business angels. For the purposes of passing plausibility checks, outside capital can also be raised even if it is not needed. In any case, the origins of the equity capital must be made plausible. In the subsequent resale, hidden reserves and a fictitious price fantasy can be used to justify exaggerated prices.

First, the money launderer must locate suitable companies: 'I would look for companies that are just in need of redevelopment. In this day and age, there's probably plenty to choose from' (Interview partner 17). Selecting suitable companies should not be a problem for those who have help from the right advisors. Often, trustees know which of their clients are currently experiencing economic difficulties or are thinking of selling their business for personal reasons. It is therefore helpful to bring local trustees on board.

Of course, it would be of very limited foresight to disclose to the trustees the actual reasons for the money launderer's desire to invest. It is true that one could argue that the money launderer could specifically seek out dubious trust offices in order to be able to count on a corresponding tolerance from the trust office in the subsequent transaction. However, this argumentation is flawed in that the money launderer could not benefit from the reputation of a reputable trust office, which he needs. If the trustee is also involved in other criminal activities, this could also cast a shadow over the money launderer and attract unwanted attention from the authorities. It therefore makes more sense to work with reputable trust offices that are not aware of the money launderer's actual intentions.

Rather, the money launderer pretends that he wants to diversify his investments in order to achieve a solid risk spread. He tells the trustee that he is interested in private equity transactions and investments in companies in need of restructuring. In this context, attention must be paid to the plausibility of the story. An Eastern European businessman may argue that doing business in Russia and Kazakhstan is too risky for him and that he therefore wants to invest in Switzerland due to its stability. A Swiss businessman might argue that he wants to expand his existing portfolio of companies in Switzerland.

Ideally, however, the money launderer does not act himself but sends advisors in his place. Between him and the advisors, he inserts various smaller investors who act as so-called business angels. This has the advantage of making it easier for him to justify the origins of the funds from abroad. If a large number of small investors transfer six-figure sums from Russia, this will probably trigger fewer controls than if a single investor transfers a seven- or eight-figure sum from Russia. This is due to the fact that controls in Russia are difficult to enforce due to the sluggish administrative and legal assistance it offers. Banks have only very limited possibilities to check on the exact origins of funds. An investor group that wants to buy a company in need of restructuring and then plans to increase its equity sounds relatively plausible and serious. Once the funds have been transferred, the money launderer can invest the total amount as a representative of various investors: 'Then I pretend to have many small investors, raise a large amount and invest it as a single investor who is supposedly backed by many different people. That way, I can present it in a more or less credible way' (Interview partner 11). On the surface, the money launderer acts as the head of an investor group and invests in legal businesses.

In certain circumstances, the company to be restructured could be chosen in such a way that the bank has a vested interest in not taking its compliance obligations too seriously, or at least in exercising some discretion in favour of the investors. This is particularly the case if the bank has financed the ailing company. In this case, the bank struggles with a massive conflict of interest. On the one hand, it has to fulfil its compliance duties and make enquiries regarding the investors' money. However, should it come across irregularities, it would have to reject the transaction and would ultimately be left with the financing of the ailing company. This could result in massive write-offs. In some large banks, attempts have been made to prevent these conflicts of interest by erecting so-called Chinese walls between departments. However, even then, people at work could still meet occasionally in the canteen and ask each other for favours. In smaller banks, such meetings in the canteen are almost unavoidable. The more familiar the contact within the bank, the more likely it is that people will also exchange information about possible business deals. If the financing is of great importance for the respective bank, management is probably also involved in the transaction.

The money launderer could take advantage of banks' conflicts of interest in various ways. On the one hand, he could try to get to ailing companies via a bank instead of via a trustee. This would almost guarantee a conflict of interest. On the other hand, he could enquire at the companies identified by the trustee as to which banks are providing the financing. The group of investors then opens accounts with these banks through which the transaction can be processed.

Debt capital can be raised for the restructuring. This has the advantage that the bank is granted another business from which it can profit. Of course, these loans must be guaranteed with sufficient collateral; otherwise, the bank could make losses again. This approach is certainly supported by the fact that it is common practice in the private equity sector to finance company restructurings largely with debt capital. An investor who works only with equity capital could quickly attract attention. However, the fact that the money launderer is restructuring the company in order to accommodate his own incriminated funds argues against taking on outside capital. If he solves any possible liquidity problems of the company to be restructured with outside capital, he may no longer be able to make the company solvent with his own funds. Moreover, in the context of financing, he would have to provide the bank with regular insight into the course of business even after the acquisition of the company. Therefore, borrowing from a bank is not advisable.

However, from the point of view of the money launderer, there is nothing to be said against providing the company to be restructured with loans from various companies owned by the money launderer. For this purpose, separate financing companies could be founded abroad. The advantage of this approach is that the money launderer does not attract attention through unusual business practices, such as foregoing outside capital, and at the same time can bring further incriminated funds into the company to be restructured. Financing companies based in Dubai, for example, would be particularly suitable for this. A combination of company restructuring with the 'banks in Dubai' method is quite conceivable at this point.

Probably the biggest hurdle to overcome when using company restructuring to launder money is ensuring the plausibility of the origins of the equity capital. Companies are not usually acquired in cash but by bank transfer. This means that the incriminated money must first be placed with a bank. Since it is not easy to deposit millions in cash in Switzerland, the money launderer cleverly switches to using banks abroad.

When selecting banks abroad, care is taken to ensure that transfers to the destination country, such as Switzerland, are readily possible. In the present example, banks in Eastern Europe and Dubai would be particularly suitable. In Eastern Europe, the money launderer ideally has the opportunity to place his funds with financial institutions without much questioning due to the widespread corruption: 'Then I can invest where I want. The origin is then presented in a credible way and is not questioned or is questioned significantly less' (Interview partner 11). After a few national transfers, the funds then end up in a bank with good correspondent banking relations in Switzerland. The Dubai method is the same as the 'banks in Dubai' method.

However, making a partial cash payment is also quite conceivable in the case of a company acquisition. Analogous to the real estate transaction, one could also think of a partial cash payment as beneficial for tax reasons. This is particularly interesting if the company owner holds the company as private assets and cannot claim the participation exemption.

In any case, the money launderer must be able to plausibly explain the origins of his equity capital. Normally, the banks and the seller, as well as possibly any professional secret holders involved, will enquire about the composition of the investor group and the origins of the funds. As a rule, these questions are not too detailed since one only wants to ease one's conscience but in no way intends to annoy the investors. It is therefore advisable for the money launderer to prepare himself conscientiously to answer these questions in order to nip any doubts in the bud and thus prevent further enquiries. It is a good idea to explain that the investors are businesspeople from Eastern Europe who want to diversify their portfolios. This also makes the subsequent transfer of funds from Eastern Europe more plausible.

The resale of the acquired company after the successful reorganization represents a good opportunity for the money launderer to integrate further incriminated funds into supposedly legal structures. For this purpose, it is advisable to acquire the company to be restructured by means of a Swiss public limited company. First, this would ensure that the tax laws applicable to legal entities apply; second, the prestige of a joint-stock company in international business transactions carries considerably more weight than that of a simple partnership or a limited liability company.

As soon as the restructuring of the company is complete, the money launderer sells the restructured company to a supposedly foreign conglomerate of companies. This conglomerate claims to have plausible reasons for making the investment. For example, an Eastern European conglomerate could be seeking to enter the Swiss market. Since the foreign conglomerate is a supposedly independent third party, the price of the reorganized company can be determined almost freely. However, it is still advisable to have a value appraisal prepared according to standard market criteria.

Expert opinions on the value of companies are extremely imprecise. Thus: 'One can assume a corresponding price fantasy' (Interview partner 12). Although there are numerous methods that are supposed to support determining the value exactly, even with a banal discounted cash flow method, the value can be determined almost freely just by adjusting the interest rate risk. With more complex methods, other parameters can be manipulated, which ultimately makes an accurate and precise determination of the value of the company increasingly unlikely. Nevertheless, care should be taken to ensure that the disposal price appears plausible.

The parent company that sells the restructured company receives a transfer from a foreign group in this way, which buys the successfully reorganized company from it at a fair market price. The resulting funds come from the official sale of a subsidiary and can thus be legally invested in further businesses in Switzerland. As a result, more incriminated funds can enter Switzerland from abroad. In addition to manipulated valuations, hidden reserves can also serve as a possible justification for a capital gain.

4.9.3 Resources

The money launderer needs access to distressed companies in need of investment, preferably with jobs at risk, in order to use corporate restructuring as a means of laundering money. Furthermore, corrupt appraisers are of great service to the money launderer. Access to a conglomerate of companies into which he can integrate the existing company may also be very helpful.

The money launderer must first find a company in need of restructuring that meets his needs. Ideally, this company should suffer from massive liquidity problems but pursue a business model that is sustainable in itself. After all, the money launderer does not want to risk incurring too great a loss. Ideally, jobs are already at stake. This usually means that all parties who might ask the money launderer unwanted questions about the origins of the funds do not want to stand in the way of a swift and smooth transaction.

Furthermore, the money launderer needs corrupt appraisers: 'That is, of course, a question of how receptive someone is to writing a fake report' (Interview partner 9). Supposedly federally certified auditors who work independently and have a lack of solvent clients are suitable candidates for this role. As a rule, renowned auditing firms should be avoided in such transactions so that no doubts arise as to the legality of the transactions. The tolerant auditors used by the money launderer can also be used for a limited or ordinary audit, if necessary.

Furthermore, it is advisable for the money launderer to set up a small conglomerate of companies before acquiring the company to be restructured, so he can integrate the company to be acquired into the conglomerate: 'If you're a conglomerate of companies ... you invest in a distressed company and you make a loss, you can offset that against a part of the business that's run on business principles, so you can deduct that for tax purposes' (Interview partner 17). A public limited company in Switzerland, which may belong to a company in Eastern Europe, is suitable for this purpose. Behind the company in Eastern Europe, there are usually various people operating in the background. In addition, other companies can be incorporated between the public limited company in Switzerland and the company in Eastern Europe.

4.9.4 Risks

When raising outside capital, it is important to remember that banks usually want to see the company's balance sheet and numerous other documents. The tax authorities may also examine the company's records. The same applies to a limited extent to the commercial register. Furthermore, in the case of mergers and acquisitions, professional groups that are obliged to report are usually involved. Finally, business risks should of course also be considered.

As already indicated in section 4.9.2, raising debt capital is associated with considerable risks. This is especially true if the debt capital is provided by banks. As a rule, banks require the balance sheet of the company to be financed. When reviewing the company's books, the banks may come across irregularities: 'With companies, we do it easily when we have a balance sheet' (Interview partner 5).

As a rule, therefore, it is not advisable to raise outside capital from banks. If necessary, a separate financing company, which is under the control of the money launderer, can provide the company to be restructured with liquidity or guarantees. The money launderer can deny the bank's insight into the business ledgers, but this strategy will not work with the tax authorities. Therefore, he makes sure that the accounts are kept properly and do not have any gaps. The inspection of the records of the company to be restructured should be made as easy as possible for the tax authorities through extremely cooperative and courteous collaboration. Furthermore, wherever possible, profits shall be declared so that capital gains taxes are payable. All tax assessments are to be accepted, and any taxes owed are to be paid promptly. This is to prevent the tax authorities from taking a closer look at the company.

It should also be borne in mind that the commercial register also carries out a superficial check of various documents, such as the articles of association. The money launderer makes sure that the documents to be submitted to the commercial register are prepared in an exemplary manner. Critical documents, such as the foreign ownership structures of any companies, must be disclosed proactively. Here, too, maximum cooperation is required in order to avoid attracting attention. It is advisable to work with a local law firm that maintains good contacts with the local commercial register. In this way, a very direct, informal approach can be taken in the event of queries being raised.

The acquisition of companies inevitably involves holders of professional secrets, such as lawyers and notaries, who may be subject to reporting obligations in certain countries: 'Then the question will probably arise with the new company register entry or with any other actions that again require a lawyer or a notary' (Interview partner 13). These professional secrecy holders often have a high level of professional competence, which could allow them to recognize a less than obvious violation of Article 305bis SCC. Therefore, the skilful money launderer is particularly careful when dealing with these professional groups. In particular, he tries to find lawyers who can also act as notaries. He rewards them with lucrative contracts to keep them happy.

Finally, it should be mentioned that the method described almost inevitably involves exposure to various witnesses. Although many of them, such as the seller and the notary, are relatively clueless, some will already suspect criminal machinations are in play. The stooges and the bribed appraisers, as well as the corrupt bankers abroad, are inevitably aware of the criminal transactions taking place. The money launderer can protect himself here by (in principle) sending one or two frontmen to take over the correspondence with these potential witnesses. Although this creates a dependency on individual frontmen, it at least succeeds in concealing the true beneficial owner. Even if an investigating authority were to succeed in getting a banker in Russia to testify, this would still not reveal the identity of the money launderer. At the same time, it is very unlikely that the Swiss investigating authorities would succeed in getting a banker in Russia to testify.

4.9.5 Overall Assessment

In conclusion, it can be said that corporate restructuring as a method of money laundering is particularly well suited for perpetrators with basic business and legal knowledge and strong networks in various countries. Of course, there are less complex methods that could be used instead, but different money launderers have different needs. This method enables the money launderer to integrate his incriminated assets into the economic cycle and, under certain circumstances, make a considerable and almost tax-free profit. The particular advantage of this method is its ability to place very large sums in one transaction and to place some during the preparatory work. Of course, this also results in a cluster risk, which the money launderer can accept.

However, it should be noted that the success of this method accepts only a very small margin of error due to its complete documentation requirement, which is of fundamental importance to ensure the money launderer is not caught. Should the money launderer make a mistake, the entire construct is in danger of being exposed. Therefore, this method is only suitable for money launderers with the highest level of professionalism.

Given the sophisticated design of this method, it is not surprising that the general public has not yet looked more closely at the issue of money laundering in the context of corporate restructuring. It is true that private equity firms are seen as ideal vehicles for money laundering.[185] However, few people know how to launder money in the context of corporate restructuring. Therefore, this innovative method of money laundering has not yet been sufficiently presented in the literature.

This method also seems to have only marginally caught the attention of compliance officers. Of the compliance officers surveyed in this study, 83.3 % stated that they had not come into contact with this form of money laundering in the last three years. This suggests that this method is not yet in the sights of compliance officers.

4.10 BANKS IN DUBAI

4.10.1 General Suitability

Banks in Dubai are suitable for placement as well as layering and integration. As a cash-intensive city and an offshore banking centre, Dubai offers all the advantages a money launderer could wish for. It is a recognized, not too exotic financial centre that is increasingly gaining international importance. While the UAE government has implemented strict anti-money laundering standards in an exemplary manner, these do not seem to be fully implemented by all banks, at least not yet. The free trade zones also facilitate the concealment of beneficial owners.

It is obvious that banks in Dubai are suitable for all stages of money laundering. The money launderer can place his funds there, withdraw it and deposit it in another bank or transfer it directly. After several stages of concealment between different banks, he can legally invest the money in listed companies' securities. Alternatively, he could use it for other investments.

Dubai is a cash-intensive city. Thus, a money launderer with large amounts of cash will not immediately attract attention. Since Dubai is known for its extravagance, and even unusually lavish events do not necessarily cause too much of a stir, the money launderer operating in Dubai benefits from a relatively tolerant environment. In Dubai, people have become accustomed to displays of extreme wealth. A guest who wants to pay cash for an expensive hotel room is as unlikely to attract attention as a tourist who wants to pay cash for jewellery. Thus, spending large amounts of cash in Dubai is fairly common.

Furthermore, offshore banking centres like Dubai are naturally relatively tolerant with regard to what would normally be considered unusual financial transactions. It is true that the government of the UAE has significantly tightened money laundering prevention measures in recent years; nevertheless, Dubai is still considered an extremely popular tax haven.[186] It is therefore not surprising that many banks readily accept a customs declaration form from the domestic tax authorities. This is of great importance for the money launderer at the placement stage. It is true that the money launderer cannot admit that the funds to be placed originated from a crime, such as trafficking in narcotics; however, he can pretend that these are tax-neutral assets which

185. Hunter, 2012.
186. Arnold, 2014.

he wants to keep safe in Dubai's financial centre for fear of expropriation by the government in his home country.

Another advantage that Dubai offers is that it is an internationally recognized financial centre and is not considered overly exotic. It is of little use to the money launderer to place his incriminated funds in Vietnam or in Central African states. A transfer from these countries to Switzerland would pose a real challenge and would in any case give rise to a large number of queries. A transfer from Dubai, on the other hand, is already part of the daily routine of many banks and can be plausibly explained in most cases. Since other offshore destinations, such as Singapore, have been trying for years to establish themselves as open and legally compliant financial centres, it is no longer true that small financial centres have a bad reputation. Singapore has long been striving to become an open financial centre following strict anti-money laundering rules.[187]

4.10.2 Concrete Procedure

To use banks in Dubai to launder money, it seems obvious to first set up a company in one of its free trade zones using stooges. In doing so, the money launderer could make use of domestic employees or professional secretaries. Subsequently, an account must be set up with a correspondent bank. In principle, money transfers should be made directly. The purpose should be as complex as possible. All transactions should be documented and legally justified. Transacting with countries known to grant the authorities access to financial transactions should be avoided.

Setting up a company in a free trade zone can be achieved within a few days and does not require any special expertise: 'Setting up a company in one of the 32 or 33 free zones in the UAE is quite easy. It's quick and easy for very little money' (Interview partner 1). The money launderer can turn to a local trustee office for support in setting up the company. It will not usually ask any probing questions, especially if the money launderer appears as unsuspicious as possible.

Stooges can be used in several ways. On the one hand, it is possible in Dubai to use the papers of domestic workers who are often willing to provide their passports in exchange for a small extra fee: 'The passport of the housekeeper from the Philippines or any other person is easy to obtain' (Interview partner 1). Due to their lack of legal expertise, these groups of people often fail to recognize money laundering risks. Alternatively, professional secrecy holders could be used. Here, however, it is to be expected that they will normally scrutinize the transactions more critically than simple domestic workers.

Subsequently, the money launderer needs to open an account at a bank with numerous correspondent banks: 'There's the famous keyword of correspondent banking' (Interview partner 4). Establishing an account with a correspondent bank is rarely difficult. After all, it is a customer relationship with a legal entity within the UAE.

187. Pieth & Aiolfi, 2004.

Since any individuals operating in the background are normally also resident in Dubai, there should not be any major queries raised in the process.

A smart money launderer handles money transfers in a direct manner and the purposes are intentionally complex: 'For large companies, specific reference is made to invoices and projects' (Interview partner 8). Thus, an intelligent money launderer makes sure that his remittances appear authentic. For example, he can refer to invoice numbers and periods of performance.

A wire transfer that passes through five offshore destinations within a few days raises red flags at many banks, thanks to modern transaction analysis, and makes one bound to ask why a direct transfer was avoided: 'Then of course, I have to clarify that, and I have to say why did they make this diversion, why not a direct bank connection to Switzerland?' (Interview partner 15). In combination with banal intended uses, a transfer with detours can lead to an investigation. Direct transactions with complex purposes, on the other hand, are inconspicuous because it is difficult to distinguish them from supposedly legal transactions.

In principle, it is also obvious to document the transactions: 'A clarification also includes documenting the processes and then you also have to weigh up the legal background' (Interview partner 15). If one day there is an inspection, the money launderer can show why the money was transferred. It is therefore common to draw up complicated contracts that cannot be recognized at first glance as forgeries or pretexts.

In the context of an investigation, it is advantageous if the money launderer has avoided transactions with countries that are willing to provide information to the authorities: 'As a money launderer, you have to avoid as much as possible those countries where the authorities can access financial transaction data relatively directly' (Interview partner 16).

At this point, reference should again be made to the Legal Aid Guide. It is freely available at www.rhf.admin.ch.

4.10.3 Resources

To apply this method, the money launderer needs access to discreet banks and, above all, banks that do not cooperate with the authorities. Furthermore, banks with incompetent or inattentive compliance departments offer a clear advantage. Ideally, the money launderer operates in an unsuspicious environment. He will also prefer banking in countries with limited freedom of the press.

Discreet banks that do not cooperate willingly with the authorities are a clear advantage for the money launderer using this method: 'That's where the credit institutions in the European area don't even have the possibility to obtain certain information' (Interview partner 13). However, it is important to differentiate between the stages of money laundering. In the placement stage (i.e., the first deposit of incriminated cash in the UAE), the bank should not ask any questions. In the further stages, more reputable banks can be chosen because a national transfer within the UAE should not raise any further questions.

Of course, the entire bank does not have to be incompetent or inattentive - only the compliance department: 'If I have someone sitting in the compliance area who really only follows the given rules, but perhaps has relatively little foresight as far as the phenomenon as a whole is concerned, then he wouldn't recognize a money launderer even if it said money laundering in the subject line' (Interview partner 13). Money launderers can research in advance how banks staff their compliance departments. If a bank is looking specifically for highly qualified compliance experts from all over the world who have to meet demanding minimum requirements for employment, it probably attaches great importance to compliance with all laws. If, on the other hand, a bank is specifically looking for compliance staff from guest worker countries who will accept low pay, it can be assumed that the compliance department is more concerned with fulfilling minimum regulatory requirements than with specifically combating money laundering.

Furthermore, the money launderer needs an unsuspicious environment in which to operate: 'They need an unsuspicious environment' (Interview partner 16). If entering the money launderer's name in common Internet search engines immediately reveals investigations by the public prosecutor's office for various crimes, he has already probably been caught using this method. However, having a plausible story can help nip any initial suspicions in the bud. An unemployed twenty-year-old cannot turn up at the bank in Dubai with large sums of cash without raising suspicion, but a man in his mid-thirties could pretend to be a building contractor and rave about receiving tax-neutral cash payments from his clients without attracting unwanted attention.

Banks in Dubai usually require a letter of recommendation from the new client's house bank. This letter of recommendation is easy to obtain. Nevertheless, this should not be done carelessly. After all, the party writing the letter ultimately knows about the money launderer's extended business relations. It would therefore be of limited foresight to ask one's house bank for such a letter. On the one hand, this would immediately raise suspicions at the respective house bank. The compliance department could thereby become aware of a previously unsuspicious client. On the other hand, however, there is also the risk that the employees of the house bank could become valuable witnesses for the investigating authorities in the context of possible proceedings. Furthermore, they could also try to blackmail the money launderer. Therefore, this letter should be obtained from a bank with which the money launderer does not have any significant business relations. Ideally, this bank should be located in a reputable country, such as Austria. The money launderer - resident in Switzerland - could deposit a small amount of non-incriminated funds there (at least CHF 40,000) and leave it there for years. After three years, he asks the Austrian bank to confirm in writing in English that an exemplary business relationship has existed between the two for three years.

Once the money launderer has successfully placed the incriminated funds in a bank in Dubai, he starts to distribute them within the UAE. For this purpose, he can either transfer them or withdraw them and then deposit them again. Transfers have the disadvantage of leaving a paper trail (i.e., a data trail). The paper trail is interrupted by a withdrawal and a subsequent deposit. If the original account is discovered, the money launderer can claim that he spent the money. This means that ideally, it is not possible to discover that the money launderer has redeposited the money at another bank. However, when transporting cash, caution should be exercised: 'If they have larger quantities in the suitcase, the dogs sniff that out. It can be the same in Dubai' (Interview partner 5). This risk should be low unless the money launderer is frequently transporting cash through airports.

The money launderer must be able to plausibly explain what he has spent the incriminated money on. Supporting a supposedly lavish lifestyle is usually a suitable justification. Regular visits to prostitutes in connection with excessively high tips are also extremely suitable explanations for this. The discretion valued in the red-light district makes it impossible for the authorities to track down the prostitutes.

Finally, it should be mentioned that if third countries are involved, care should be taken to ensure that the freedom of the press in those countries is severely restricted: 'I think the free press factor plays a big role, because often cases are not discovered by investigators, but by the media, or at least spread' (Interview partner 16). Curious journalists are in principle a latent danger for money launderers. This risk can be easily mitigated in countries with limited freedom of the press.

4.10.4 Risks

Financial intermediaries' transaction analyses are probably one of the main risks with this method. Furthermore, a certain dependence on compliance officers could arise. It should also be borne in mind that the money launderer in Dubai is probably operating in an unfamiliar legal system. In addition, possible queries from correspondent banks also represent a certain risk. The transport of cash to Dubai is also risky. Finally, the trade in information, especially so-called tax CDs (storage media containing stolen bank data of customers), should also be considered in light of the current situation.

Banks' transaction analyses could draw attention to the money launderer's suspicious actions and unusual business partners: 'The question is rather what standard of due diligence do our banks apply? That is, how do European banks deal with the fact that they have a counterpart in Dubai or somewhere else?' (Interview partner 13). These systems are often very standardized and therefore also predictable. It goes without saying that overly suspicious transactions should be avoided. This can be done, for example, by cleverly denominating the funds to be laundered.

Likewise, a certain dependence on certain compliance officers could arise: 'So I think that especially in the money laundering compliance area, a lot really depends on the action and people' (Interview partner 13). This is particularly the case if individual compliance officers are used as a loophole in the system and become correspondingly tolerant in return for payment. It is therefore important to avoid building up dependencies on individual persons. If a compliance officer approaches the money launderer and demands a bribe, it must be paid in an emergency, but all future transactions must be processed through other banks.

Furthermore, the money launderer in Dubai operates in a legal system that is completely foreign to him, which should be mentioned: 'Dubai is subject to a completely different legal system. That is probably a risk. I mean the risk for the money launderer' (Interview partner 7). Provided there are no differences with contractual partners, this obstacle is surmountable. However, a money launderer should spread the risk because facing a possible legal dispute in an unfamiliar legal system could become particularly unpleasant. Consequently, different contractual partners should always be involved.

Queries from banks also represent a certain risk with this method: 'The money came from Dubai to a bank account in Switzerland. The Swiss bank has enquired with the accused and its client where the money came from' (Interview partner 7). The best way to reduce this risk is for the money launderer to prepare meticulously for these questions before the first transaction takes place. This means, above all, that he should produce plausible-looking documents in order to be able to produce them promptly when needed.

Finally, it should be mentioned that in the past, employees of financial institutions have sold information to tax authorities: 'There's bound to be a leak, a piece of information being sold' (Interview partner 17). The money launderer can counter this risk by using frontmen. Should information about his accounts actually be sold, his name ideally does not appear.

4.10.5 Overall Assessment

Using banks in Dubai continues to be suitable for money laundering. However, the money launderer should by no means underestimate the logistical effort required for this method. Specialized knowledge and a serious appearance are required in any case. Those who already have established structures in Dubai can benefit greatly from this method. Those who do not yet have structures in place in Dubai should probably first make two or three trips to the UAE before their first transaction in order to establish the right contacts there. Nevertheless, the risks associated with this method should not be underestimated. In this context, it is worth remembering in particular the suggestions of the OECD, which are difficult to predict.

The simplicity of setting up a company in the free trade zones of the UAE makes it much easier to conceal the beneficial owner.[188] By establishing a company in one of the free trade zones, the money launderer has a legal entity in UAE. This means that he no longer has to set up any accounts in his own name, necessarily.

In the quantitative survey, 40.3 % of the compliance officers interviewed stated that they had come into contact with cases of money laundering in connection with banks in offshore centres in the last three years. However, only 37.3 % of compliance officers believed that industries with remittances from abroad are at risk of money laundering. Thus, remittances from abroad still seem to be considered less at risk than, for example, cash payments and areas of activity with a lack of regulation. Thus, compliance officers can be expected to pay some attention to the Dubai method; however, this should not be overly weighted.

188. Giuffrida, 2010.

Finally, it should also be mentioned that Dubai has taken massive action against money laundering offences in recent years and sanctions the same with draconian penalties in some cases.[189] In 2015, the police significantly increased their efforts to combat money laundering. However, the responsibility for monitoring the money laundering prevention measures of financial institutions lies with the Central Bank. This may seem sensible from a layman's perspective; however, it should be borne in mind that financial institutions must forward SARs to the Central Bank.[190] This means that financial institutions must report to their own supervisory body as part of the SAR that they have conducted business with potential money launderers. The question of why this business relationship was entered into in the first place is obvious. This means that banks have an incentive not to file a SAR in order not to endanger themselves and their banking licence. Under these conditions, even renowned European banks have apparently become suitable instruments for money launderers and have ultimately been sanctioned. In administrative and mutual assistance proceedings, several parties are always involved. On the one side is the requesting contracting state; on the other side is the requested state party, the accused and the information holder which could be, for instance, a bank. It is obvious that the outcome of such proceedings in Dubai depends on both the authorities there and the information holders.[191]

4.11 SAFE-DEPOSIT BOXES

4.11.1 General Suitability

Safe-deposit boxes were often described as unsuitable for money laundering during the expert interviews. This was justified by the fact that the bearer of value does not change. At this point, the author explicitly points out that this view is a fallacy. Successfully hiding incriminated funds already meets the requirements of the offence of money laundering according to Article 305bis SCC. Safe-deposit boxes are ideally suited for storage and concealment. After all, the contents of safe-deposit boxes are secret. Since safe-deposit boxes are not centrally registered, they are often unknown and inaccessible places. However, the mere storage of incriminated funds in safe-deposit boxes does not mean that they are integrated into the economic cycle. It is therefore purely a (preliminary) part of the placement stage.

In most cases, the money launderer will want to change the medium of value, but this is not always absolutely necessary. If the money launderer can be sure that the incriminated funds will not be found, it may be quite opportune for him to keep it hidden and spend small amounts of it. After all, money launderers also have living expenses to pay for, such as restaurant visits or shopping trips, which can easily be financed with cash. Ultimately, money laundering is usually about preventing the confiscation of the incriminated assets, and safe-deposit boxes are at the top of the list. Having a safe hiding place from which the money launderer can withdraw a certain

189. Financial Times, 2008, pp. 1 ff.
190. Trade Arabia, 2015; Bankers Academy, 2015.
191. Wirtschaftsblatt, 2015; Donatsch et al., 2011.

amount every three months, similar to a current account, is by no means an absurd idea.

In contrast to current accounts, safe-deposit boxes offer an advantage in that no one but the money launderer knows their contents. The custodians of safe-deposit boxes are not allowed to open them. While banks invariably have access to their clients' account data, safe-deposit boxes are surprisingly discreet. This is an aspect that should not be neglected under any circumstances as part of a well-founded analysis, especially in view of ever-weakening banking secrecy.

Nevertheless, it must of course also be mentioned that by merely storing and hiding the assets, there is still no integration into the economic cycle. This means that the money is not invested profitably. However, as long as the funds being stored are in a stable currency, this does not necessarily have to be a significant disadvantage.

Finally, it should be noted that safe-deposit boxes are also suitable for the discreet transfer of assets. Money launderers do not have to travel with large suitcases of money but can deposit their incriminated funds in safe-deposit boxes. Afterwards, they only have to hand over the access code or the corresponding key card to their counterparty. This is particularly relevant with regard to anonymous safe-deposit boxes held at railway stations.

4.11.2 Concrete Procedure

The procedure described below is one of the simplest methods of money laundering and can be implemented by all kinds of criminals. Essentially, all that needs to be done is to seek out private safe-deposit box providers without identification requirements. It is essential that the money launderer does not keep any references to his secret safe-deposit boxes in his environment and takes care that as few people as possible know about his secret storage locations. Furthermore, for the transfer of assets in safe-deposit boxes, care should be taken to ensure that the codes and keys are transferable.

Due to the recent increase in the number of providers of private safe-deposit boxes, setting up a safe-deposit box with a private provider without identification requirements is not a major challenge. This ensures a great deal of anonymity and non-transparency: 'You don't know who's behind it et cetera if it's not declared or if nothing is identified, as with the other financial intermediaries' (Interview partner 2). Banks are less suitable in this context, however, as they are subject to the AMLA. If possible, the safe-deposit box is paid for in cash and for several years in advance. Care is taken to ensure that the provider is reputable so that the money launderer can rely on the safekeeping of his incriminated funds.

The money launderer does not keep any references to his safe-deposit boxes in his environment. This applies in particular to rental contracts and materials advertising the names of safe-deposit box providers. In the event of a search of his residential and business premises, these documents must not be found under any circumstances. Nevertheless, the money launderer should keep the safe-deposit box rental agreement in a safe place.

Furthermore, the money launderer must be meticulous in ensuring that as few people as possible know where he keeps his incriminated funds. While it makes sense for his heirs to know where the funds are stored, this group of people should be kept as small as possible. Essentially, it is only a matter of ensuring that the funds are not lost in the event of the money launderer's death because no one knows where they are kept.

The money launderer could consider not opening the safe-deposit box in his own name and involve trustworthy people instead. Particularly suitable would be the heirs of the money launderer or related third parties with whom no direct connection can be established by the authorities. However, the problem arises here that these persons could have unrestricted access to the safe-deposit box and the money launderer might only find out about a theft months after the fact. For this reason, using frontmen to carry out this method of concealment is particularly delicate and only carried out after thorough consideration.

Insofar as the safe-deposit boxes are also to be used for the transfer of incriminated funds, care is taken to ensure that the access codes or keys are transferable – it would be of limited foresight to work with powers of attorney. Anonymous operations are preferred in this context.

4.11.3 Resources

This method of money laundering requires surprisingly few resources. Essentially, the money launderer only needs to rent a private safe-deposit box from a provider who is not subject to the AMLA. Furthermore, under certain circumstances, a straw man could be helpful to ensure concealment. In addition, the money launderer needs a safe place to store the safe-deposit box rental agreement where it will not be found in a search of his premises.

The safe-deposit box provider must be reputable to ensure the safekeeping of the money launderer's incriminated funds. Since the safe-deposit box provider has privileged access to the safe-deposit boxes in his care, he should inspire confidence.

With regard to ensuring the security of the depository, an obvious first choice would be a leading bank. In this case, maximum security would normally be guaranteed during safekeeping. However, as financial service providers, banks are subject to the AMLA and would have to report to the MLRO if they saw any red flags. Thus, money launderers avoid banks and prefer private safe-deposit box providers: 'The others who simply offer lockers are not subject to the AMLA' (Interview partner 2). It is therefore obvious that money launderers pay close attention to what other services their safe-deposit box provider offers to ensure they are not subject to the AMLA.

Furthermore, the safe-deposit box provider is chosen on the basis of whether it will accept cash payments for safekeeping for several years in advance. This ensures the anonymity of the money launderer. A transfer from the money launderer's bank account for payment would provide the authorities with telltale clues as to the presence of a secret stash in the event of an investigation. It would not be advisable to make a transfer payment from an unofficial account either, as this could also blow the whistle on the presence of a money launderer's unofficial account in the event of the safe-deposit box being discovered and investigated.

Using a straw man would ensure a minimum amount of concealment. Should the safe-deposit box be discovered, the assets found in it would normally be clearly attributable to the money launderer. The use of a straw man reduces the risk of the safe-deposit box being discovered. Furthermore, in the event of discovery, the money launderer would not be associated with it. However, since the straw man has sole power of disposal over the safe-deposit box, he must be chosen extremely carefully to ensure his trustworthiness.

Finally, it should be mentioned that the money launderer needs a safe place to keep the safe-deposit box rental agreement. While it could be argued that the money launderer should destroy the rental agreement and all documents referring to the safe-deposit box, this would leave him with almost no way of proving that he is entitled to the contents of the safe-deposit box. It is therefore important that the money launderer keeps the rental agreement in a place where he could access this document at any time but in a place so secret that the document will not be found in the event of an investigation.

4.11.4 Risks

Each method of money laundering carries specific risks. While the safe-deposit box method is undoubtedly one of the lower-risk methods, as few people are involved and the sector subject to the AMLA is avoided, there are some risk factors to consider here as well. One major risk is inadequate concealment. There is also the risk of a loss of value due to inflation. Furthermore, the safe-deposit box could be searched. This should be considered if the money launderer is under observation.

Inadequate concealment is a serious problem for the money launderer if the safe-deposit box is discovered: 'But the concealment doesn't take place, after all, by me putting it in our safe or in the post office in a box or somewhere' (Interview partner 14). If large amounts of cash are stored in a safe-deposit box in the name of the money launderer, he could struggle to justify it, but this hurdle can be overcome. One possibility is to open the safe-deposit box in the name of a straw man instead. However, as described in section 4.11.3, the straw man could claim the money for himself. Therefore, it is obvious to look for an alternative. One possibility would be to combine the safe-deposit box method with one of the other methods presented in this book. For example, the money launderer could store art objects, jewellery or gold in the safe-deposit box instead of cash. Should the safe-deposit box be discovered, he could declare the goods as hereditary property. This would at least partially solve the problem of concealment.

Furthermore, a possible loss of value due to inflation must be considered: 'Assets tend to decrease in value' (Interview partner 17). This largely depends on the currency and the goods and has to be assessed on a case-by-case basis. The risk can be spread by the money launderer exchanging his foreign currency for different currencies or tangible assets. In this case, he might have to resort to one of the other methods described in this book, namely the exchange office or the purchase of gold. However, a loss of value through inflation is not a specific risk of money laundering.

A search of the safe-deposit box is unlikely unless the safe-deposit box comes into the authorities' sights in the course of an investigation or the money launderer behaves suspiciously enough for the safe-deposit box operator to inform the police: 'If you have a tip-off, there are certain police possibilities. You can go and open any locker' (Interview partner 2). Therefore, care must be taken to establish plausibility. Should the safe-deposit box operator become suspicious, the money launderer could discreetly point out that it contains tax-neutral assets to evade suspicion of money laundering.

However, there is a risk that the money launderer is being observed by the authorities. In this case, making regular visits to a private safe-deposit box provider would presumably be noticed. A location tracker on his mobile phone could also be his undoing. This risk can be reduced by the money launderer not carrying a mobile phone with him when he visits his safe-deposit box. He can also make sure that no one is following him. If the money launderer himself is not in a position to evade surveillance, he can give a trusted person power of attorney for the safe-deposit box and not make any visits to the location himself. However, this again creates a new set of risks, as his authorized representative would have unfettered access to the assets he is concealing.

4.11.5 Overall Assessment

In conclusion, it should be noted that due to its simplicity, this method of money laundering is also suitable for money launderers who do not have in-depth professional or specialized knowledge and access to an extensive infrastructure. Ultimately, this method is just as suitable for hiding illicit funds procured by a minor, corrupt public official as it is for hiding those accumulated by a highly accomplished professional money laundering who devotes himself full-time to the pursuit of organized crime. This alone makes it obvious that anti-money laundering is not a panacea against drug trafficking, human trafficking and arms trafficking and can only marginally help to fight corruption. Unless the money launderer is clumsy or very unlucky, the risks described above will not be of much consequence. He will rent a safe-deposit box from a private provider and deposit the sum of incriminated funds of his choice there. Normally, no one will find out about this safe-deposit box, which he will visit from time to time to collect or add funds. It can thus be stated that this method is inexpensive, simple and relatively low risk.

This method seems to be particularly popular among Italians. In Ticino, for example, safe-deposit boxes are extremely popular.[192] Politicians have tried to introduce stricter rules for safe-deposit boxes, but these efforts have not been successful. Thus, it is currently still the case that money laundering via safe-deposit boxes only becomes known in exceptional circumstances, such as if the tenant of the safe-deposit box does not pay his rent on time.[193]

192. Tagesanzeiger, 2014; Aargauer Zeitung, 2013.
193. Handelszeitung, 2013.

The safe-deposit box method seems to rarely attract the attention of compliance officers. The vast majority of the compliance experts surveyed, namely 80.5 %, stated that they had not come across any cases of money laundering in connection with safe-deposit boxes in the last three years. This figure is unsurprising given that the contents of safe-deposit boxes are not usually checked.

4.12 CASH AGAINST CASH

4.12.1 General Suitability

In the 'cash against cash' method of money laundering, money launderers exchange foreign currency among themselves. This method is essentially a preliminary stage of the placement phase and as such falls within the scope of Article 305ter SCC. It is extremely difficult to prove, as it essentially takes place among criminals who observe a code of silence. However, it does not involve an injection of the incriminated assets into the legal economic or financial cycle.

In certain circumstances, exchanging foreign currency among money launderers is a suitable means of disguising the origins of incriminated funds. For example, if large amounts of Japanese yen were found on a European drug trafficker, it would initially be difficult to prove that these funds originated from trafficking narcotics on the streets of Zurich, Munich or Milan. However, the Japanese yen would still raise some questions. Thus, when describing this method, sufficient concealment does not factor in. Furthermore, it should be mentioned that the incriminated funds do not enter the economic cycle through this method at this stage.

On the positive side, for the money launderer at least, this method is extremely difficult for the authorities to prove because it essentially rests on one of the parties involved testifying to this effect or the perpetrators being caught in the act. In all other conceivable cases, such as the use of registered banknotes, establishing concrete proof of the procedure would still be very difficult.

4.12.2 Concrete Procedure

The concrete approach for this method of money laundering depends on the amounts to be exchanged. While exchanging amounts under CHF 1 million can probably be achieved among drug, arms or human traffickers, corrupt central banks will need to be involved for exchanging amounts over CHF 100 million. For smaller amounts, netting among criminals can also help to overcome logistical problems and related exchange rate fluctuations. Fictitious invoices could be used for this. Even the use of mobile phone apps is conceivable. Larger amounts should also be split into smaller sums.

Ideally, the money launderer already has access to a broad criminal network that connects him to other money launderers. In this case, he only needs to make contact with another money launderer and explain his needs in a personal conversation. If he does not have a solid criminal network, it is possible to make contact with other money launderers through corrupt financial intermediaries. Small private banks could be suitable for this.

While the exchange of smaller amounts is relatively easy to manage via the money launderer's personal network, the challenge with larger amounts is that even drug barons are not necessarily able to exchange hundreds of millions of US dollars. In these cases, it is advisable to go through a central bank: 'I mean, what we're also seeing in part is that ultimately state entities are in part using means of money laundering and ultimately funnelling funds past the official central banking or banking system' (Interview partner 9). Corrupt governments are particularly suitable for this. In this case, contact must be made with central bankers via corrupt members of the government. The advantage of this route is that central banks can easily access large amounts of cash.

Another problem is logistics. Very few money launderers want to move enormous amounts from one place to another. This means that amounts should first be split. It is a good idea to make an initial arrangement to exchange a relatively small amount in order to get to know the counterparty better and to test the efficacy of the exact procedure. Henceforth, the amount being exchanged can increase. However, for security reasons, one should exercise restraint and not overdo it.

The targeted netting of amounts can at least partially solve transport problems: 'You have a Latvian in London who wants to transfer euros home, and then you have someone in Latvia who wants to transfer euros to the UK. There is no physical transaction at all between Latvia and England, not even an electronic one, but only the difference is transferred directly' (Interview partner 17). This variant is particularly interesting if money launderers store the amounts in locations far away from each other or want to avoid a physical meeting of the goods. In this case, a physical exchange does not necessarily take place at one location, but the amounts are handed over at different locations at different times and cleared with each other.

Bogus invoices may be issued for any differences: 'You trigger a transfer with a bogus invoice. Then 2 million are sent from A to B to clear the balance. These are forms of cooperation that we have also seen' (Interview partner 16). However, these bogus invoices inevitably create traces of illegal activity. Thus, from the money launderer's point of view, they are likely to be useful only in certain cases.

In order to find other criminals, money launderers might also use apps. These help to link people who are willing to swap currencies with each other: 'The system is intelligent. It brings people together and says okay, you want euros there and you want euros in another country' (Interview partner 17). However, these apps were primarily developed for small-scale currency exchange to take place among immigrants in order to circumvent common money transfer providers. Since the investigating authorities are also aware of these apps, they are likely to be of only minimal relevance for money launderers.

4.12.3 Resources

To exchange cash against cash, the money launderer needs access to other criminals who have large sums of cash at their disposal and are willing to exchange them unofficially. If the money launderer does not have access to his own network, corrupt financial intermediaries can help. A corrupt government official or professional currency traders could also help to exchange the cash amounts. In the future, apps could play an increasingly important role in finding potential exchange partners.

Gaining access to other reliable criminals is probably the biggest challenge for the money launderer to overcome when using this method. He needs to make connections with criminals who have similar capabilities and, above all, complementary needs: 'I have dollars and you have euros. I need euros, you need dollars. We settle it at the same time' (Interview partner 17). A criminal who also wants to exchange euros for dollars is of little help to a money launderer with incriminated cash amounts in euros. Ideally, the money launderer has access to other criminals through his personal network.

Alternatively, the money launderer needs to know a criminal banker who, for a small commission, can put him in touch with clients with complementary needs: 'If the financial intermediary himself has criminal intents, then he is difficult to catch. The control mechanisms would not work' (Interview partner 2). This variant offers an advantage in that the banker can probably also provide a secure handover location within the bank. If the bank's 'know your customer' (KYC) rules have been applied, then the banker certainly has in-depth knowledge of his customers that will help him establish contacts that inspire trust, insofar as possible.

If the money launderer has very large sums of cash at his disposal, it is a good idea for him to conduct the foreign currency exchange through a professional foreign exchange dealer, a central bank or a corrupt government: 'As a lawyer, I once had a client who lived on foreign exchange' (Interview partner 7). For this, however, the money launderer needs appropriate contacts with unofficial currency traders or corrupt officials. Therefore, in this respect as well, success ultimately depends on the strength of his personal network.

In the future, apps could also play an important role in finding exchange partners: 'They wrote an app for us. You can register there and the system searches for you' (Interview partner 17). However, one would have to split the sums. Immigrants might have an interest in exchanging currencies and avoiding the usual fees and unfavourable exchange rates of mainstream currency exchange providers, meaning that the money launderer could offer them private exchange services. For this, the money launderer would essentially need a mobile phone and the corresponding software. However, this is more of a look into the future.

For exchanges of larger amounts of cash, the money launderer needs access to a secure room and testing equipment to be able to check the authenticity of the foreign currency. When selecting the location, care must be taken to ensure that it protects the money launderer from robbery. This is particularly relevant because in the event of a crime, the help of the police could not be sought without the money launderer incriminating himself. At the same time, the room must be chosen in such a way that the money launderer leaves as few traces as possible. Video-monitored corridors could ultimately make it easier for the investigating authorities to gather any evidence. The vaults of private security companies are therefore suitable, as are banks and hotel rooms. In the latter, additional security precautions should be taken by private security personnel.

When selecting private security personnel, care must be taken to ensure that they possess the necessary qualifications and can guarantee discretion. In any case, the security guards must be armed. At the same time, they should not have access to intimate knowledge regarding the operation being conducted.

4.12.4 Risks

The main risk with this method is certainly the presence of counterfeit banknotes. Undercover investigators posing as exchange partners also pose a risk that should not be underestimated. In addition, the potential risk of being robbed must be taken into account.

Ultimately, when using this method, the money launderer operates within a criminal milieu. Therefore, it must be expected that potential counterparties will behave criminally: 'There are, of course, the big counterfeit notes. Exchange for genuine or contaminated banknotes' (Interview partner 18). Counterfeit money coming into play in this method is almost inevitable. Therefore, the money launderer is dependent on using the latest technology to check the authenticity of the money being exchanged in the transaction. The exact requirements are currency-specific and will not be elaborated on here.

At the same time, there is a risk that undercover investigators might pose as criminals pretending to exchange a certain amount of money. In these cases, a special police task force might also take part in the handover. The only way to mitigate this risk is for the money launderer to work with criminals he has trusted for a long time and who have a solid reputation in the underworld.

Furthermore, the possible risk of being robbed should not be underestimated. Here, too, it should not be forgotten that it may have become known in the criminal milieu which transactions the money launderer is planning on carrying out as a result of his enquiries into exchange partners. It is therefore quite possible that various criminals have knowledge of the large amounts of cash he possesses. The money launderer would not be able to rely on the support of the police without incriminating himself and could not report a robbery. Therefore, he should use private security services.

Finally, it should also be borne in mind that not too many people should be made aware of the money launderer's transactions. All persons who know about the transactions could eventually testify as witnesses against the money launderer. Thus, it is essential that as few people as possible have knowledge of the transactions and their exact circumstances.

4.12.5 Overall Assessment

This section presented a procedure used by criminals operating in the underworld. Nevertheless, the scenarios presented are quite realistic and feasible for people entrenched in the criminal milieu. A known trafficker in humans and weapons probably has less to fear from being robbed than a defenceless public servant who simply wants to exchange currencies for a small bribe.

The *Lapis* case in Italy shows that this method is used in practice. There, money launderers tried to exchange large sums of US dollars for euros. However, through one of the first operations carried out by undercover investigators in the field of financial crime, the investigating authorities succeeded in tracking down the money launderers.[194] Among the suspects were a judge as well as two military police officers.[195] As a result of the raid by the Italian financial police, EUR 11.5 million was promptly seized.[196]

Not surprisingly, the cash-against-cash method very rarely comes into the focus of compliance officers. In fact, 87.3 % of the compliance professionals surveyed said they had not come into contact with money laundering related to unofficial foreign exchange dealers in the last three years. Since unofficial foreign exchange dealers do not need a bank to operate, this figure is not surprising, but it suggests that unofficial foreign exchange dealers are not the focus of compliance officers.

4.13 BUREAUX DE CHANGE

4.13.1 General Suitability

Depending on how they are used by money launderers, bureaux de change are suitable for both the placement and layering of illicit funds. As a widespread and common activity that offers anonymity, bureaux de change operate discreetly and flexibly. However, the increasing standardization of currencies should be seen as a disadvantage. Therefore, money launderers should consider utilizing combinations of virtual currencies and prepaid cards.

If a money launderer uses an exchange office as a customer, it is suitable for the preliminary stage of placement or at most for the placement itself. The mere exchange of foreign currency does not lead to its integration into the economic cycle. However, since a bill of exchange is issued, this could possibly serve as a sufficient explanation for the origins of the cash in the case of inattentive controls. When asked about the origins of any foreign currency a money launderer possesses, he can answer by providing an official document from an exchange office. While this may no longer be sufficient in Switzerland due to increased due diligence measures, offshore banks may still be satisfied with this. In any case, by using the exchange office as a customer, the money launderer succeeds in exchanging his foreign currency for another currency. In

194. Palazzolo, 2011.
195. Pipitone, 2013.
196. Corriere del Mezzogiorno, 2013.

the case of laundering drug money from Zurich, exchanging Swiss francs for US dollars can already help to disguise the illicit origins. Ultimately, the investigating authorities will have trouble proving that the US dollars found on the drug trafficker originated from drug transactions carried out in Zurich.

In certain circumstances, it is much cleverer for the money launderer to actually operate the exchange office. In this way, the money launderer succeeds not only in placing but also in layering his incriminated funds. If the money launderer himself operates a bureau de change, he also circumvents various money laundering prevention mechanisms. The simple reason for this is that he would hardly report himself to the MLRO. Since he not only exchanges foreign currency but also charges high fees and high market exchange rates, he feeds incriminated funds into a completely legal and official business. After deducting his costs, he can show this as profit at the end of the year and invest it as he likes in legal and official business.

The fact that bureaux de change are cash-intensive and anonymous widespread activities is an enormous advantage for the money launderer who runs a bureau de change himself. Compared to banks, it is relatively easy to fake fictitious customers of an exchange office. Furthermore, there are hardly any identification obligations, and at the end of the day, an outsider can only roughly estimate the exchange office's actual turnover.

However, the money launderer who only uses the exchange office as a customer also benefits from the enormous anonymity it offers. When exchanging smaller amounts, there are hardly any identification requirements. Through the use of frontmen, the money launderer would never be forced to identify himself during a random check. Thus, almost complete anonymity can be assumed here.

The increasing standardization of currency poses a slight challenge when using this method but does not really create much of an obstacle. The money launderer can still choose between euros, Swiss francs and US dollars at any train station that houses a bureau de change. These are three relatively stable currencies that are subject to natural fluctuations but unlikely to result in a total loss. Furthermore, they can be used in different regions of the world, which facilitates geographical concealment.

Nevertheless, it can make sense to supplement currency exchange with prepaid cards and virtual currencies. These methods are still in development but ultimately offer the possibility of transporting foreign currency in a compressed form. However, they usually leave an electronic footprint behind.

4.13.2 Concrete Procedure

With regard to the concrete procedure, a distinction must be made between the operation and the mere use of currency exchange offices. Should the money launderer want to operate a bureau de change himself, he must either set up a bureau de change or use existing establishments in the red-light district. Subsequently, he must pretend to have customers to launder his funds, and he should be able to show profits. Transactions between CHF 400 and CHF 800 seem to be particularly unsuspicious. If, on the other hand, the money launderer only wants to use exchange offices as a customer, it is advisable that he use prepaid cards to transport foreign currencies. Possessing exchange vouchers can also be useful in certain circumstances if the origins of the funds need to be proven. Where appropriate, straw men should be used.

Operating his own bureau de change is a good idea if the money launderer regularly wants to change large sums of cash: 'It would probably be much smarter to have an exchange office yourself. Then I could fake money exchanges that didn't even take place and would thus sneak my cash into my completely comprehensible plausible front business' (Interview partner 8). For this purpose, the money launderer establishes or buys a bureau de change with all the necessary licences. Since the establishment of a bureau de change may require obtaining a licence, purchasing an existing licensed bureau de change is likely to be quicker, easier and possibly cheaper for the money launderer.

Corresponding businesses are easy to find: 'Go to the Langstrasse district in Zurich. It's full of small bureaux de change' (Interview partner 15). The money launderer then fakes transactions and brings his own money into the exchange office. In doing so, he generates high exchange fees, which the exchange office can report as income at the end of the year. The remaining part of his money is returned to him in another currency.

If the money launderer only occasionally has incriminated funds at his disposal that need to be exchanged, it is probably too expensive for him to set up his own exchange office. However, it is possible for him to profit from the services offered at existing exchange offices. Here, he can have smaller amounts exchanged at a time while strictly observing the threshold values: 'If a Saudi businessman will change that amount and says he wants to shop at Station Road, that is quite plausible' (Interview partner 15). If this activity is queried, the money launderer is at an advantage if he has used frontmen who are resident in Eastern Europe, Saudi Arabia or Dubai to carry out the transactions, as this makes it difficult for the authorities to follow up on any SARs.

In the case of fictitious transactions and the use of stooges in the context of genuine transactions, amounts between CHF 400 and CHF 800 seem particularly innocuous. While these amounts are substantial enough to justify using the exchange office, they are also too low to trigger more detailed compliance checks. They are also low enough to be entrusted to brokers.

Transporting foreign currencies across national borders is often a problem for money launderers, but prepaid cards can be used for this purpose: 'In this day and age, there are all these prepaid cards, so just also cards that you can top up and if I go for a drive with a card like that, probably no one will check how much money I have with me' (Interview partner 13). The money launderer can load a prepaid card in Germany, for example, and withdraw the money again in Switzerland. Should he encounter a border control on his way from Germany to Switzerland, it will seem as though he is hardly carrying any funds. Customs officials should not be able to read the prepaid cards or know their value.

Bill vouchers can also be used to substantiate the source of funds if required: 'The only thing I have is a bill of exchange receipt, and maybe I can tell a bank that that's my source of funds, but it's not a material source of funds, it's just a receipt for a money exchange. But we have seen that before' (Interview partner 8). This is a tricky one, because on closer inspection it quickly becomes clear that a bill of exchange receipt does not explain where the money originally came from. However, a bill of exchange receipt may still be better than no receipt at all.

4.13.3 Resources

When using this method, the money launderer must have access to forged passports or genuine passports from people on the street. Furthermore, implementing this method in a city with a large tourist population makes the most sense. The use of stooges can also be helpful. Should the money launderer himself operate a bureau de change, he must ensure that he has a physical location that offers credible and official services.

Regardless of the approach chosen, the money launderer must have access to various people's passports. These could be both genuine and forged passports. Should the money launderer decide to operate one or more bureaux de change himself, he must be able to pretend to have customers. Although in this case he will fake the majority of the transactions so that they remain below the thresholds triggering identification requirements, occasional spot checks will lend credibility to his business. However, if the money launderer does not operate his own exchange office, it is essential that he has access to various passports to carry out transactions in existing exchange offices under various names. These existing bureaux de change usually carry out spot checks and report to the MLRO if there are reasonable grounds for suspicion. For that reason, a corrupt public official or a city drug dealer would avoid engaging in exchange transactions in his own name.

If the money launderer decides against using stooges, he must at least have access to other people's real passports or forged passports to present during the exchange transactions: 'You can't expect the person at the counter, whether it's at the train station or the bank, to recognize whether a passport is genuine or not. That would be going a bit too far. That's not a customs officer' (Interview partner 15). In the case of a random check, the money launderer could show another person's passport or present a forged one. In either case, care must be taken to ensure that the money launderer and the photo of the person identified in the passport bear a certain resemblance. In the case of foreign passports, it is probably advisable to use exotic passports. Very few exchange office employees are likely to be familiar with Kazakh passports, for example, making forgeries more difficult to detect. This variant also offers an advantage in that any investigations triggered by the MLRO will most likely end at the border.

Probably the easiest resource to find in order to carry out this method of money laundering is a city with many tourists from countries with a range of currencies: 'In a bigger city, such as Zurich, Geneva, Bern or even in Ticino, there are many tourists from Russia and China' (Interview partner 17). A possible currency exchange looks plausible here because the money launderer or his stooges can pretend that they entered the country as tourists and unfortunately have brought the wrong currency with them. In order to be able to go on extensive shopping sprees in their host city, they are now forced to exchange their cash into the local currency. So if a businessman from the UAE wants to exchange euros for Swiss francs in Zurich, he could argue that he brought euros with him from Dubai for his holiday in Bavaria. At short notice, he had decided to take a day trip to Zurich. When he saw the shops on Bahnhofstrasse, he could not resist the temptation to do some shopping while he was there. This story sounds amusing, but it is ultimately also very plausible and close to reality for many tourists.

When selecting possible straw men, the money launderer should pay attention to their plausibility and trustworthiness. In the story of the businessman from the UAE described above, for example, a well-groomed young man of Arab descent would be a suitable candidate. If possible, he should appear respectable and wealthy. By contrast, asking a homeless person from the station forecourt to fulfil this role would raise red flags and any sensible counter employee would immediately have doubts about the plausibility of the story. Young Russian women pretending to be on a shopping spree are also good candidates as straw men. The plausibility of straw men depends strongly on the city selected. In principle, care should be taken that the invented story corresponds to the stereotypes and prejudices of the general population. At the same time, of course, care must be taken that the straw men do not embezzle the funds entrusted to them. This risk is relatively low because only small amounts are exchanged at a time when using this method.

Should the money launderer himself operate a bureau de change, it is essential that he establishes a physical business location offering actual services: 'It needs a certain official basic activity that is credible ... These are also those businesses that still exist physically, but which can be pumped up almost arbitrarily, to fictitious turnovers, which are then not shown or which are perhaps shown, but do not actually come from the exchange activity at all' (Interview partner 11). Without a physical business, the money launderer would already risk being exposed during the first superficial check done by the tax authorities. Care must be taken to ensure that the physical exchange office meets the needs of the money launderer, however. For example, it should be located in an area where actual transactions will take place. It is also important that it is not under video surveillance, so that if doubts are raised about the business being a front, the actual number of customers going in and out cannot be confirmed or denied. Furthermore, when employing staff, care must be taken to ensure that none of the employees gain too deep an insight into the actual intentions of the business. This can be achieved by employing a large number of part-time and temporary staff so that no single employee spends too much time in the exchange office learning about its inner workings.

At this point, it should be mentioned that the resources can of course also be combined, but this might be risky. For example, a corrupt public official operating a bureau de change on the side would be very conspicuous. Even if the public official himself were not registered as the owner in the commercial register, doubts about this constellation could certainly arise in the case of a possible examination of his person or the bureau de change. Thus, the use of straw men might be more appropriate.

4.13.4 Risks

Using bureaux de change is considered a significant risk, especially since exchanging larger amounts could attract attention. In addition, exceeding certain limits could trigger control mechanisms leading to clarifications of origin. The monitoring of exchange offices makes it more difficult to infiltrate the limits through so-called smurfing. Furthermore, transporting foreign currencies poses a certain risk.

Probably the biggest risk of bureaux de change is that they have long been used for money laundering: 'There is a danger that this is, of course, a recognized risk factor. The bureaux de change are viewed very critically' (Interview partner 5). The authorities are of course also aware that bureaux de change are used for money laundering. This is problematic in that both the authorities and compliance departments might immediately suspect that money laundering is taking place in a bureau de change. This means that operating a bureau de change in one's own name is probably too risky for many money launderers. It is therefore advisable to operate exchange offices under the name of a straw man instead or merely use existing exchange offices owned by other providers.

Exchanging large amounts usually attracts unwanted attention:

> *Someone changes, as you say, 25,000 francs. That is a very high amount, also an extremely high amount for holidays, and you don't do something like that at the exchange counter, but with advantage at the bank. So in this case, you would have to clarify where the money comes from, and then you would have to ask for what purpose you need so much money. If the person does not cooperate, for example, then you would have to check whether you [should] make a report* (Interview partner 15).

In exchange transactions, the money launderer must be meticulous in order not to exceed any limits. This can easily be achieved in three ways. First, he can carry out the exchange transactions in countries with relatively high thresholds, such as the UAE. Furthermore, the individual amounts can be reduced accordingly through a targeted division of the sums to be exchanged. This undermines the threshold values: 'But of course, there is also monitoring of these transactions and the monitoring is to ensure that there is no smurfing (i.e., that the same people do not make several transactions below the threshold and thus actually exceed the threshold)' (Interview partner 15). Although reputable bureaux de change try to make it more difficult to circumvent the thresholds, which is also known as 'smurfing', through their monitoring, this should not be too much of a hurdle for the money launderer to overcome, as he will gain certain experience over time. Moreover, it should not be a problem for the money launderer to find out the threshold values, especially if he operates his own exchange office.

The control mechanisms of exchange offices lead to clarifications of origin: 'Large bureaux de change of have relatively large structures and measures in place to ensure compliance with money laundering obligations' (Interview partner 17). However, reports to the MLRO are triggered by the exchange offices' control mechanisms. If the money launderer has used stooges to carry out the exchange of foreign currency, for example, the Russian tourists mentioned above, then these reports are not very threatening for the money launderer himself since he is not directly identified or affected. Moreover, the MLRO reaches its limits with the SAR. It is not in a position to carry out investigations in Russia, and its jurisdiction ends at Switzerland's borders. Although a report could be made to the Russian authorities, this would probably not affect the money launderer.

Should the money launderer wish to reduce the risk further, he could occasionally change the Russian straw men he uses, although doing so naturally creates numerous potential witnesses over time. However, the money launderer does not have to hire or control the Russians himself. If he also uses a straw man for this purpose, he only has one potential witness at the end. Of course, a trustworthy person should be chosen for this role.

Finally, the transport of currencies must also be mentioned since this represents a considerable risk under certain circumstances: 'To get a foreign currency into the country, you have to travel through somewhere at some point' (Interview partner 13). Although it is supposedly easier to exchange foreign currency in Dubai than in Munich, the money launderer first has to transport the foreign currency into Dubai and back again. In addition to the numerous security risks this poses, customs controls should also be taken into account. It is therefore advisable to avoid unnecessary transport and to act as locally as possible.

4.13.5 Overall Assessment

In summary, it can be said that this method can be implemented in both low-risk and high-risk ways. If the money launderer prefers the low-risk variant, he uses existing exchange offices to exchange larger amounts. In doing so, he fails to integrate his funds into a legal business. However, thanks to the bills of exchange, he at least gives the funds an air of legitimacy. In addition, he interrupts the traceability of their origins since drugs in Zurich are rarely paid for in Japanese yen. If the money launderer wants to take a little more risk, he sets up a bureau de change with straw men and uses it to place incriminated money into a supposedly legal business. However, it must be borne in mind that using and operating bureaux de change is a recognized risk factor.[197]

Despite the fact that bureaux de change are a recognized risk factor for money laundering, 77.8% of the compliance officers surveyed stated that they had not come into contact with this form of money laundering in the last three years. This can at least partly be explained by the fact that bureaux de change have to fulfil the majority of their compliance duties themselves. If irregularities occur, it is not necessarily apparent to compliance officers of other companies. This once again highlights how bureaux de change continue to be well suited for money laundering.

197. Neue Zürcher Zeitung, 2001; Zeit Online, 1994.

4.14 LAW FIRMS

4.14.1 General Suitability

Law firms are perfectly suited for all stages of money laundering. Since it is common in the legal profession to ask for advance payment, even in cash, doing so is suitable for the placement stage of money laundering. However, law firms can also be used for the concealment of asset flows. Finally, many law firms have so-called client money accounts. These are used to receive and pass on assets. Thus, law firms are also suitable for layering. Finally, however, it must be emphasized that law firms can also be used for the integration of incriminated assets into the economic cycle. For example, legal and illegal assets can be combined. By distributing dividends to partners, there is nothing to stop funds from being used in other areas. The legal profession is also characterized by a high degree of discretion, and lawyers' professional secrecy is also protected under criminal law.

4.14.2 Concrete Procedure

With regard to the concrete procedure, a distinction must be made between two basic scenarios. On the one hand, it is conceivable that one or more lawyers knowingly and freely intend to launder money and misuse their law firm for this purpose. On the other hand – and this is likely to be the more common scenario – there is the possibility that law firms are abused by money launderers without lawyers being able to recognize it at all, or at least not in time to prevent it. The present analysis starts with the latter scenario.

A clever money launderer who wants to misuse a law firm for his criminal activities does not necessarily have to disclose this to the law firm concerned. Rather, he approaches a renowned law firm and poses as an internationally active businessman. He explains that he has been very successful abroad and now wants to make investments in Switzerland. He justifies this based on, among other things, the excellent legal security and stability offered by Swiss investments. He then suggests plausible investment scenarios. For example, he would like to acquire and restructure struggling companies. At the same time, he wants to invest in real estate. For all of these types of transactions, he claims to be looking for a plausible partner who can advise him on all legal matters. The investment volume he gives the law firm is based on the amount he wants to launder. He then enquires about the law firm's fees and offers to transfer a generous advance on any subsequent costs.

In the next step, the money launderer concludes a fee agreement with the unsuspecting lawyers. A high hourly rate is agreed upon, which adequately takes into account the high interest value of the matters mentioned by the money launderer. Since the money launderer is not domiciled in Switzerland, he offers to pay a generous advance on costs. For example, an advance on costs in the amount of CHF 100,000 would be conceivable. The lawyer issues a corresponding invoice to the money launderer. The money launderer transfers the advance on costs the same day. The advance on costs is credited to the lawyer's account the same day. The next day, the money launderer writes an e-mail to the lawyer first thing in the morning and informs him that he has slept on the matter and would like to wait a little longer before making any investments in Switzerland for personal reasons. The money launderer politely asks the lawyer not to provide any services for the time being and to confirm receipt of this e-mail. The unsuspecting lawyer replies to his new client that he has received the e-mail and will wait before providing any services. This way, the money launderer does not run the risk of draining his retainer. The skilful money launderer waits a few more days and then informs the lawyer, also by e-mail, that he has decided against investing in Switzerland. He politely asks the lawyer to reimburse him for the advance paid, minus any lawyer's fees, and sends him a different bank account number for the reimbursement. At this point, the lawyer can at best charge for the initial meeting because the money launderer had asked him not to provide any further services for the time being. Depending on the agreed hourly rate and the duration of the initial meeting, it can be assumed that at least 99 % of the advance on costs will have to be reimbursed.

According to the money launderer's instructions, the reimbursement is to be made to a different bank account abroad. Many lawyers are not likely to worry about this at first. After all, they are obliged to reimburse an advance on costs that has been collected and not used up at the end of the mandate at the client's first request. The reimbursement to a new bank account abroad should only lead particularly attentive lawyers to ask any questions. However, the money launderer had posed as an internationally active businessman from the beginning, so there is nothing suspicious about him having bank accounts abroad.

At this point, the lawyer is in a quandary. On the one hand, there should be no doubt that the advance on costs paid and not used up must be refunded. On the other hand, demanding the return of the advance on costs to a bank account abroad is somewhat suspicious. Lawyers acting with particular care will therefore contact their client and politely enquire whether a refund to the account from which the advance on costs was originally transferred is possible. The money launderer will deny this and ask the lawyer again to transfer the refund to the bank account indicated by him. He will give plausible reasons for this. For example, he could state that he had transferred the advance on costs from a euro account to the lawyer's Swiss franc account and that the reimbursement should be made to a Swiss franc account. Unfortunately, he does not have a Swiss franc account with the bank that holds the euro account. In the end, the lawyer has no choice but to have the (former) client confirm in writing with a signature that the payment should be made to the specified account. As a result, the money launderer has used an unsuspecting and respectable lawyer to transfer assets from one account to another. Should queries arise about the transfers, the lawyer could and would initially have to invoke his legal professional privilege. In justifying the use of funds at the time of the transfer to the lawyer's account, the money launderer may invoke the advance on costs. When the advance on costs to be refunded is received in his other account, the money launderer can tell a story of his choosing as to why the lawyer is transferring money to him. On the one hand, he can state that the lawyer returned an advance on costs. On the other hand, he could also claim that he won a case against a third party and that the lawyer claimed the money for him and forwarded it to him. Both versions seem plausible at first glance.

In the above explanations, it was assumed that the money launderer already has bank assets. Should this not be the case, a slightly modified procedure would be conceivable. For example, the money launderer could pay the required advance on costs in cash. In this case, it would make sense to choose a somewhat smaller amount. For example, CHF 80,000 would be reasonable. Here, too, the money launderer requests the reimbursement of his advance on costs by bank transfer at a certain time interval. In this way, the money launderer can conveniently turn cash into bank deposits.

Another way of abusing law firms for the purposes of money laundering is through the use of client money. The money launderer goes to a law firm and pretends to have lent a third party a sum of money in the amount of CHF 1 million. He presents a loan agreement. The loan agreement shows that the loan claim is due. The money launderer informs the lawyer that the borrower, who is in fact an accomplice of the money launderer, has not yet repaid the loan despite several requests to do so. From the point of view of the money launderer, who presents himself as a new and serious client of the lawyer, a strongly worded letter from a law firm is necessary to bring the borrower, who is in default, to his senses. The money launderer patiently lets his new lawyer explain his hourly rates and signs a power of attorney, including a fee agreement. At this point, he urges to write a letter to the borrower first. If this does not lead to the desired result, the lawyer should assert the claim by means of initiating a recovery and subsequent proceedings. The lawyer prepares a letter to the borrower and sends it to his client for review. The money launderer immediately releases the letter. The lawyer writes to the borrower asking him to transfer the debt due plus interest on arrears at 5% from the date of maturity to his client's money account. To the lawyer's astonishment, the amount due plus interest at 5% from the due date is received in his client money account the day after he sent the letter. This is because the borrower is an accomplice of the money launderer. A few days later, the money launderer enquires with the lawyer as to whether the money has been received because the defaulting borrower had informed him that he had paid his debts in the meantime. The honest lawyer confirms with his client that the money has been received in his client money account. The client thanks him for his excellent work and informs the lawyer of his bank details. He politely asks the lawyer to deduct his fee from the amount received and to transfer the balance to his account abroad.

At this point, one could argue that the payment of an advance on costs in the amount of CHF 80,000 would be unusual and therefore attract attention. It may well be that such advances on costs in cash are not the order of the day. Nevertheless, many lawyers are likely to be pleased when a client agrees to pay such a high advance on costs. This is especially true for law firms that otherwise handle less lucrative mandates. If it is not possible to pay the advance in cash, the money launderer can ask for a payment slip. The advance on costs can then be paid in cash at the post office, giving the money launderer an invoice from a lawyer's office. The same applies, of course, to claims made by the lawyer. While a deposit of CHF 1 million is likely to cause a stir, it should be possible to politely contact the lawyer for smaller amounts and ask for a payment slip.

The lawyer was not a criminal in either of the above scenarios. Rather, he was exploited by money launderers for their own criminal gain. In many cases, the lawyer may not have realized that money laundering was taking place. However, lawyers can be criminals, too, and they could try to abuse law firms for the purposes of money laundering.

First of all, this raises a question as to whether lawyers would be prepared to take such a high risk and intentionally misuse their position for money laundering purposes. This is probably unlikely to be the case for the majority of Swiss lawyers. After all, a great deal of money can be earned legally with a licence to practise law in Switzerland. Thus, it cannot be assumed that many Swiss lawyers would be willing to launder incriminated assets through their law firms. This might be more likely in the case of lawyers from other EU countries who have few lucrative earning opportunities. However, under certain conditions, lawyers with a foreign lawyer's licence can also register in Switzerland on the so-called EU/European Free Trade Association (EFTA) list of the cantonal bar association. This enables them to practise as lawyers in Switzerland independently and under their own responsibility. They can then set up a law firm. For tax reasons, it is advisable to set up a so-called Anwalts AG. These are public limited companies that are allowed to provide legal services.

In order to be able to use the newly founded Anwalts AG for the purposes of money laundering, it is imperative to establish an actual presence as a law firm. This includes, among other things, the renting of office space and the creation of an adequate Internet presence. The lawyer who intends to launder money should appear regularly on the legal market. He obtains mandates from real clients and provides actual legal services. At the same time, he issues fictitious invoices and encloses payment slips with them. The invoices are paid in cash at the post office counter. He makes sure that the invoice amounts are not particularly conspicuous, perhaps ranging from CHF 2,000 to CHF 10,000. It quickly becomes clear that the money launderer can easily issue several fictitious invoices per day. If the fictitious turnover is exceeded by what a single lawyer could reasonably expect to achieve, the money launderer either hires employees or opens accounts at different banks. The latter helps to distribute the turnover among different accounts so that it continues to look plausible, at least at first glance.

Furthermore, it is possible for the money launderer to bring cash receipts to the bank. He declares these as advances on costs. In particular, he claims that clients were with him at the law firm. Since the Federal Supreme Court ruled that lawyers cannot collect debt from their clients without an explicit waiver of attorney–client privilege, he claims to be in the habit of collecting an advance on costs as a matter of practice. Some of his clients pay this advance on costs in cash. Thus, cash payments should be expected, within reason.

Law firms are particularly suitable vehicles for money laundering because lawyers can and must always invoke their legal professional privilege when it comes to providing information about their clients. If the bank starts asking questions, lawyers can simply state that they are not permitted to provide that information. Other possible variants or steps that lawyers intending to launder money could take are found in section 4.8, since laundering money through consulting companies is analogous to laundering money through law firms.

4.14.3 Resources

Ideally, the money launderer should hold an EU/EFTA licence to practise law. If the money launderer does not have a licence himself, he should find an accomplice with one. If this is not possible to achieve, then unsuspecting lawyers can be exploited instead.

4.14.4 Risks

This method is particularly low risk, although there may be queries from financial service providers. However, lawyers and their clients can ultimately always invoke their attorney–client privilege. Lawyers themselves can claim that it is not possible for them to divulge more detailed information because of client confidentiality. Their clients can at least state that the matter is strictly confidential and that it is therefore not possible to comment on it in too much detail.

4.14.5 Overall Assessment

This method of money laundering is ultimately an extension of the consulting companies method. It offers the same advantages and disadvantages as the consulting companies do. The main difference, however, is that money launderers who are also lawyers can easily invoke their legal professional privilege when queried regarding the source of the funds. Furthermore, in contrast to the consultancy sector, it is more common in the legal profession to accept cash advances for costs or to process payments via client money accounts. This method is therefore superior to that of consulting companies.

4.15 DEBT COLLECTION

4.15.1 General Suitability

As a method of money laundering, debt collection offices are particularly suitable for the placement of incriminated assets. The method can also be considered for layering.

4.15.2 Concrete Procedure

Money launderers who want to use debt collection offices for their criminal machinations put a fictitious claim in debt collection. They send the debt collection request to the responsible debt collection office and claim that the debtor (an accomplice) owes them a certain amount. As a rule, it is sufficient to state a banal reason for the claim, such as claim according to the contract of 15 May 200X plus 5% interest since 1 January 200Y. The debt collection office serves the debtor with the order for payment. The debtor does not raise a legal objection. The day after the service of the order for payment, the debtor appears at the debt collection office. He states that he owes the amount and would like to pay it immediately in cash. When asked whether a bank transfer is out of the question, he states that he does not have a bank account. He insists that he would like to pay the amount in cash at the debt collection office.

The employees of the debt collection office will most likely accept the amount. They will then deposit it at the bank and transfer it to the creditor's account. It is possible that the bank will ask questions about the origins of the cash, but the employees of the debt collection office are not permitted to provide more detailed information due to their professional secrecy obligations.

Alternatively, the debtor transfers the amount owed to the debt collection office. The debt collection office then forwards the amount to the creditor, and the origins of the funds are thus concealed.

4.15.3 Resources

For this method to be successful, the money launderer needs accomplices who are willing to risk being prosecuted. Their actions lead to being entered into the debt collection register. However, it should not be difficult to find suitable people to act as a front for the money launderer.

4.15.4 Risks

This method is low risk. However, clever money launderers take care not to process exorbitantly high amounts through debt collection and then have them paid in cash since this would lead the debt collection office to ask questions. Rather, money launderers use a multitude of straw men to make smaller transactions (so-called smurfing) which ultimately lead to achieving the desired aim.

4.15.5 Overall Assessment

This approach is simple but effective. It can help money launderers place smaller amounts without having to answer too many questions. If bank balances are already available, the method can also help to transfer bank balances from Switzerland and abroad to the account of a Swiss debt collection office and then to that of the creditor without being queried.

4.16 DEPOSITS AT THE POST OFFICE COUNTER

4.16.1 General Suitability

Depositing cash at the post office counter is a method that is primarily suitable for the placement of assets. On the one hand, this can be used to settle the money launderer's bills. On the other hand, this method can also be used to create bank deposits from cash reserves.

4.16.2 Concrete Procedure

As already explained in section 4.11 regarding the safe-deposit box method, money launderers who either do not take in large sums of money or have only taken in a large sum once do not necessarily need complex structures to launder their incriminated assets. A corrupt public official who has received a one-time bribe of CHF 1 million does not necessarily need to set up consulting companies or open an antique shop to launder his money. Rather, this person needs to be able to use his incriminated assets to finance his everyday life. Switzerland offers the ideal conditions for this because of the widespread practice of paying bills using payment slips at the post office counter.

A money launderer who has received assets in the amount of CHF 1 million from a criminal predicate offence cannot easily take the funds to the bank. Depositing such a large amount of cash into his bank account would lead to considerable queries at the bank. In addition, he would also have to declare such a bank balance in his tax return and could not justify it. After all, he has not declared any legal income in the same amount.

However, the above-mentioned problem can easily be solved. The money launderer asks for a payment slip for all invoices owed. He then goes to the post office counter with these payment slips. There, he pays his bills in cash. The payment slip is stamped and the money launderer receives a receipt for his files.

If the money launderer wanted to use this method for larger or recurring bills, he could combine it with other methods mentioned in this book. He could set up seemingly legitimate art or antique shops and purchase goods from himself using deposit slips and fictitious invoices.

4.16.3 Resources

No special resources are needed to use this method, although having a residence in Switzerland is certainly beneficial, since making payments at the post office counter is not common in all countries.

4.16.4 Risks

This method is extraordinarily low risk. Postal payments are widespread in Switzerland. It is a customary and local practice that many bills are accompanied by a payment slip. Numerous legitimate payments are made at the post office counter every day. It should hardly be possible for the post office to distinguish legitimate payments from those made by money launderers.

4.16.5 Overall Assessment

The explanation of this method was deliberately kept brief because the method is characterized by its extraordinary simplicity; as such, it does not require much explanation. The procedure is banal but nevertheless very effective. Money launderers who want to integrate their incriminated assets into the legal economy can resort to payment slips to pay their bills quite easily without attracting unwanted attention.

4.17 TAX RETURNS

4.17.1 General Suitability

Tax returns are suitable for different stages of money laundering. On the one hand, they are suitable for placement. In particular, the origins of the funds can be plausibly proven. At the same time, however, they can also be used for concealment (layering) and integration into the economic cycle. The primary goal is usually to prove the origins of the assets. The secondary objective is to create evidence that can serve to exonerate defendants if they face criminal proceedings.

4.17.2 Concrete Procedure

Money launderers can particularly benefit from the Swiss wealth tax to help plausibly prove the origins of funds. For example, an EU national moves to Switzerland for the first time. If the said EU national intends to launder money in the near future, he takes advantage of the transfer of his main residence to Switzerland. Although he would initially be taxed at the source, he contacts the Swiss tax office responsible for him and states that he has considerable assets as well as income of more than CHF 120,000. Taxation at the source is therefore out of the question. The EU national in our example is subject to regular taxation.

As part of the regular assessment, all income and assets must be declared in the tax return. While people who do not want to launder money would generally try to value their assets as low as possible in order to pay as little wealth tax as possible, the EU citizen in our example declares significantly more assets than he actually owns. For example, he claims to have gold coins worth CHF 10 million. He also declares holdings in companies abroad. How much wealth the money launderer actually declares depends on his future plans. The EU citizen in our example submits this tax declaration to the competent tax office. Since this is a first-time assessment in Switzerland, and most countries do not charge a wealth tax, any discrepancies between this claim and any tax declarations from previous years are not noticeable. If the EU citizen was resident in Germany, for example, he did not have to declare his assets. The German tax authorities therefore do not have a list of them. The Swiss tax authorities therefore have no possibility whatsoever to confirm the information provided by the taxpayer. Furthermore, they are unlikely to have any motivation to examine the information more closely – after all, the person in our example seems to be particularly honest. He even declared gold coins worth CHF 10 million that he could have easily concealed. It can therefore be assumed with a very high degree of probability that the assets declared by the taxpayer will be accepted by the tax office as genuine and that a definitive tax assessment will be made based on the information provided in the tax return. Naturally, the money laundering taxpayer is unlikely to have any interest in appealing against his tax assessment.

As a result, the taxpayer receives a tax assessment notice listing numerous assets. According to this tax assessment, the taxpayer possesses, among other things, gold coins worth CHF 10 million and shares in various companies abroad. The taxpayer thus appears to be very wealthy. This tax assessment is great benefit to the money launderer.

In the next step, the money launderer opens a bank account. He contacts several leading banks in Switzerland and asks for an appointment with the private banking department. Among other things, the money launderer brings his tax assessment with him to the initial meeting. According to this tax assessment, the money launderer has considerable assets. The money launderer suggests that the bank employee makes a copy of the tax assessment in order to verify the origins of his funds. As a rule, the bank employee will gratefully accept this offer. The tax assessment (including all the false information provided) ends up in the bank's KYC files.

The money launderer has thus created the ideal conditions for laundering money through Swiss banks. Insofar as he wants to sell gold coins in the future, he can even offer them for sale to the bank itself without raising suspicion. A sale to a third party would also be possible at any time. An influx of funds into his bank account would have to be plausibly explained, but if the money launderer is asked why he received a transfer of CHF 1 million, he can always state that he sold some gold coins. At this point, he can discreetly refer to his tax return. In his tax return, he declared gold coins worth CHF 10 million. The money launderer can thus argue that he has only sold 10 % of his gold hoard. Of course, the money launderer will send a copy of his tax return to his bank at the first request.

Selling off shares could also help the money launderer plausibly justify the origins of certain funds. For example, the money launderer could state that he has sold his shares in a foreign company. In this regard, too, he can always refer to his tax return as well as the definitive tax assessments.

In general, it can be said that a money launderer who is in fact not wealthy is able to suddenly appear extremely wealthy on paper by declaring fictitious assets on his tax return. Based on the tax return and the final tax assessment, his bank will most likely assume that the client is actually wealthy. Accordingly, high incoming funds, which would be critically questioned in the case of a non-wealthy client, will hardly be noticed in the case of the 'wealthy' money launderer in this example.

This method also works for people who have been resident in Switzerland for a long time. However, they must proceed slightly differently because a discrepancy between their previous years' tax returns and the current year's tax return would raise suspicion at the tax office. For those who have been resident in Switzerland for a long time, a declaration of non-existent assets is therefore generally not possible without making a few detours. However, these obstacles can easily be overcome by submitting a (first-time and thus penalty-free) voluntary declaration to the tax authorities.

In the voluntary disclosure, the taxpayer declares that thirty years ago, he inherited gold coins worth CHF 10 million from a deceased relative. Unfortunately, he had failed to declare this inheritance. The inheritance tax is now statute barred. However, the wealth tax for the last ten tax periods would still be owed. The tax authorities would be allowed to make a retrospective tax assessment. The taxpayer accepts the corresponding tax assessment. Afterwards, the money launderer can comfortably sell his gold coins. If he has to justify the origins of the funds to the bank, which is likely to be the case, he can enclose a copy of the voluntary declaration and the corresponding tax assessment. It is highly likely that the bank will consider the source of funds plausible under these circumstances. The bank is likely to assume (wrongly) that the tax authorities have verified the facts. However, this is not the case; after all, the tax authorities are unlikely to have any way of actually verifying the accuracy of the taxpayer's statements. They will most likely assume that the taxpayer would not declare any assets that are not his property.

4.17.3 Resources

The money launderer needs few to no resources to use tax returns to launder money. He only needs to be able to fill out a tax return correctly or to file a voluntary declaration completely and correctly. If necessary, he could call in specialized advisors, such as lawyers or tax experts, for this purpose, and they would be easy to find. The money launderer does not have to disclose to his advisors that he does not actually possess the assets he wants to declare – he can simply claim that he owns these assets and wants to declare them on his tax return.

4.17.4 Risks

This method is extraordinarily low risk. As long as the money launderer does not falsify any other documents, it should hardly be possible for anyone to prove that he has made false statements in his tax return. For example, he may declare that he has gold coins worth CHF 10 million. The likelihood that the tax authorities will verify whether the taxpayer actually has these assets is extraordinarily low. This is especially true for an EU citizen who has recently moved to Switzerland. If the tax authorities nevertheless have doubts about the taxpayer's statements, it is unlikely that they will be able to prove that he does not have the gold treasure he declared. Even in the case of a voluntary declaration, the risk of discovery should be low. The only thing to note is that the information provided should be reasonably plausible. Admittedly, the authorities are unlikely to have records for anyone who died thirty years ago and allegedly left the money launderer an inheritance. Nevertheless, it would be wise to declare having received an inheritance from an actual wealthy person and not from a person from a socially deprived milieu.

4.17.5 Overall Assessment

The present method is extraordinarily low risk. It can help to establish the plausibility of the origin of funds. It can be combined with other methods as desired. In particular, it can be combined with the gold method outlined in section 4.2.

4.18 SUMMARY OF THE DISCUSSION OF THE EMPIRICAL RESULTS

When reading this chapter, it quickly becomes clear to the reader that there are a variety of methods that can be used to circumvent the existing money laundering prevention measures that are in place. Some of these methods, such as the establishment of a consulting company or the restructuring of companies, are complex and require sound business and legal expertise. Other methods, such as buying and renovating real estate, trading in jewellery or exchanging foreign currency among money launderers or in exchange offices, are much less complex and can easily be carried out by laymen. While some methods require access to sound infrastructure, others are available on demand and without initial investment. This means that using the procedures described, both the needs of the civil servant who has to launder CHF 50,000 once and the requirements of someone involved in organized crime – who may want to launder more than CHF 500,000 every month – are met. Therefore, it is not true that only 'little fish' or 'big fish' can use the methods presented to their advantage.

It should also be mentioned that the approaches explained in this chapter can be combined almost arbitrarily and still be effective. However, it should be kept in mind that in terms of risk diversification, while the risk is distributed by using different methods, the money launderer also runs the risk of being noticed in at least one of the different areas, which can then shine a light on their illicit activities in the other areas. Thus, risk diversification only makes sense for the money launderer under certain conditions.

Furthermore, the author would like to rebut any criticism that individual aspects of the methods presented above may need to be adapted in individual cases or may not work in certain situations. The purpose of this book is not to provide money launderers with professional guidance on their activities. Rather, by outlining these methods of money laundering, the author aims to demonstrate the ease with which the very costly existing compliance measures of certain sectors can be circumvented. Unless fundamental changes are made to the methods, making small adjustments – as would certainly be necessary in individual cases from the perspective of the money launderer – is irrelevant in terms of the validity of the arguments presented.

The quantitative survey largely confirmed the results of the qualitative evaluation of the expert interviews. In particular, 74.5% of the compliance officers interviewed were of the opinion that money launderers will increasingly switch to less-regulated industries due to the high compliance standards of financial service providers. Industries accepting cash payments and with little or no regulation are seen as particularly critical in this regard. This suggests that the money laundering methods developed in this book are likely to become increasingly relevant in practice.

At the same time, the quantitative survey revealed that compliance officers have so far only had very marginal exposure to the methods developed here. There may be two reasons for this. On the one hand, it can be argued that these methods are simply not yet in common use and therefore compliance officers rarely come into contact with them. However, in view of the ease of implementation and the compliance officers' assumption that money launderers are increasingly switching to less-regulated industries, this argument is only partially convincing. Thus, it can be assumed that the methods developed in this book are applied but are often not recognized because compliance officers are simply lacking in certain places, such as in the retail sector. On the other hand, it can be assumed that the industries mentioned in this book have so far only attracted the attention of compliance officers to a limited extent, as state regulation is still focused on the financial sector, and thus there are few if any compliance obligations in other areas.

Nonetheless, it can be confirmed that the methods of money laundering developed here do occur in practice but only attract the attention of compliance officers in exceptional cases. It cannot be conclusively determined whether compliance officers overlook many cases or whether the methods are rarely used. This cannot be determined by a survey due to the naturally high number of unreported cases in this area.

Finally, it should be mentioned that the methods presented are merely samples taken from the broad spectrum of possible money laundering methods. A fully comprehensive study of all the possibilities would not be realistic due to the multitude of variants and options for modification. Rather, various examples and variants have been presented and combined to show the reader that there are many possibilities. Since it is true that even more variants are possible, this book does not claim to be exhaustive.

CHAPTER 5

Recommendations

It is necessary to put oneself in the mindset of the perpetrator in order to understand how intelligent and educated criminals act. In the quest to combat money laundering, it would be disastrous to assume that only simple-minded criminals launder money since the vast majority of criminals are intelligent and educated. Furthermore, the perpetrators have numerous possibilities to buy in expertise. The starting point for any analysis should therefore be to understand the perspective of an intelligent and educated offender.

A complex phenomenon like money laundering can only be effectively combated if it is also understood from the perpetrator's perspective. It would not be expedient to make comprehensive theoretical statements on complex compliance mechanisms without having adequately presented the perpetrator's perspective. First, the following question should be asked: how would one proceed oneself if one wanted to launder money?

Of course, the answer to this question cannot be generalized. Rather, the answer is likely to depend on the individual's situation. There is a difference between a perpetrator who wants to launder cash from drug transactions and one who wants to launder embezzled bank deposits. The volume of the money to be laundered also plays a significant role. While complex money laundering methods are probably not necessary for incriminated assets of up to CHF 1 million, as one could quite easily deposit these assets in a safe-deposit box, the starting position is different when it comes to accounting for income of CHF 5 million per year. However, this is not a major obstacle to overcome when analysing the behaviour of possible perpetrators. After all, both banks and law enforcement agencies usually require evidence to initiate an investigation, such as suspicious transactions in a bank account or the discovery of large sums of cash.

In the next step, one should basically ask what one would do if one wanted to launder money. After all, it can be assumed that intelligent and educated perpetrators would proceed similarly to readers of this book. A bank client who crafts a story about real estate transactions in Russia would most probably not appear at the bank without plausible notarial deeds to show. Consequently, such deeds should always be critically scrutinized. The simple fact that a client presents plausible deeds to support his story does not necessarily mean that the story is true.

In this context, one should also ask oneself what stories one would tell if one wanted to launder money. Particular attention should be paid to supposedly plausible background stories. Intelligent and educated perpetrators are likely to embed their actual construct within a plausible context. Here, too, it is important to avoid blindly trusting what someone claims. The findings are summarized in Tables 5.1 to 5.7.

Table 5.1 Recommendations for Practitioners

Recommendations for Practitioners
- Put yourself in the role of the perpetrator. - Consider how would one go about laundering money. - Ask what documents would one prepare. - Think about what stories would one tell. - Consider which constructs would one choose.

5.1 COMPLIANCE OFFICER

Compliance officers regularly struggle with the fact that, unlike investigating authorities, they only get to see a small part of a larger picture and yet are supposed to judge whether assets are incriminated or not based on this sliver of information. Consequently, when assessing any information, they must remember that it was provided out of context.

Another challenge for compliance officers arises from the fact that they often have to base their analysis on the KYC profiles prepared by client advisors. In doing so, an obvious conflict of interest must be considered. Client advisors usually have certain goals to achieve. For example, they often have to acquire a certain amount of new client money each year. It is not uncommon for relationship managers who fail to meet these goals to face termination of employment. Compliance activities, on the other hand, are generally not remunerated. Client advisors therefore have a considerable interest in acquiring new client funds, and compliance actions often stand in the way of them achieving those goals. Thus, compliance activities do not benefit them. At the same time, it is precisely these client advisors who write KYC profiles. It is obvious that relationship managers have an interest in writing KYC profiles in such a way that the compliance department approves the opening of accounts.

It is reasonable to assume that client advisors write KYC profiles in such a way that it ensures that the new clients they have painstakingly acquired can actually open an account with their bank. It would therefore be downright naïve to assume that relationship managers write objective KYC profiles. Rather, it is reasonable to assume that relationship managers embellish facts or present them as favourably and plausibly as possible. They are most likely pursuing their own interests. For compliance officers, this leads to the conclusion that the KYC profiles written by client advisors cannot be relied upon. Rather, they must be critically scrutinized.

The ultimate goal of a compliance officer must be to determine the true source of the funds. In doing so, compliance officers must reasonably assume that there is an intention to deceive them, and they must scrutinize all documents to check whether the people who issued them actually verified the facts. Court rulings are a good example of this. Compliance officers often assume that the facts recorded in a court judgment are true. However, this is a fallacy. Especially in civil law proceedings, the disposition maxim usually applies. Thus, the court will base its decision on the facts of the case as presented by the parties. If two parties present the same facts, the court will generally not review them. Thus, facts can be constructed and, based on them, court rulings can be obtained. This illustrates once again how critically compliance officers should examine the documents available to them.

In this context, a question always arises as to whether facts seem contrived. As a rule, this question cannot be conclusively answered. However, compliance officers have the opportunity to ask critical questions to tease out the truth. If the dossier shows that all documents - even court rulings - were critically examined, then compliance officers should rarely face reproach, even in the event that they were nevertheless deceived.

Table 5.2 Recommendations for Practitioners

Recommendations for Practitioners
- Do not blindly trust legal documents or those produced by the authorities. - Confirm the actual sources of funds. - Ask whether the facts seem contrived.

5.2 PRIVATE BANKERS

Private bankers should also ask themselves whether the facts they are presented with appear contrived. In particular, they should not blindly trust client documents. Rather, the actual origins of funds must be critically questioned. The following question must always be asked: how plausible do the client's stories seem?

It goes without saying that as an account manager, one's primary interest is to successfully open accounts for new clients. Nevertheless, it is advisable to exercise caution when writing the KYC profile. In particular, one should refrain from giving clients tips on how to justify the sources of funds as plausibly as possible. Otherwise, the account manager risks being accused of aiding and abetting money laundering. However, this is always a balancing act. After all, it is not possible to demand that the client brings all the documents needed for the creation of a solid KYC profile if doing so is not an actual requirement to open an account. By asking clients to provide certain documents, account managers inadvertently give money launderers insight into the forms they need to provide in order to evade detection. To protect themselves, private bankers should have all statements from their clients supported with documentation.

If there are doubts about the truth of the client's story, private bankers have options that go beyond those of compliance officers. In particular, private bankers often have personal networks they can consult. New client money is often acquired through personal recommendations. The acquisition of large clients via the Internet or other anonymous sources, on the other hand, is extremely rare. This personal network allows private bankers to check the plausibility of their clients' statements. People who have been known to be reputable for many years and have been recommended through various common contacts may be less suspicious than new clients who have only recently appeared in the banker's personal network.

Ultimately, a question also arises as to the extent to which combating money laundering is the responsibility of private bankers. There are voices in favour of a clear division between private bankers and compliance departments. In this context, it is argued that it is the task of private banker to acquire client funds. On the other hand, it is the task of the compliance departments to check the origins of funds. However, this division of tasks must be strongly contrasted. Compliance departments can only fulfil their responsibilities if private bankers do the corresponding preliminary work. In particular, it is the private banker who conducts all discussions with the client. It is therefore of crucial importance that private bankers document all processes properly. This ensures the best possible protection for financial service providers. The work of the compliance departments ultimately builds on the information collected and provided by the private bankers.

Table 5.3 Recommendations for Practitioners

Recommendations for Practitioners
- Consider how plausible the client's stories seem. - Exercise caution when writing the KYC profile. - Ensure all statements made by the client are supported by documents. - Do not inadvertently give the client tips on how to circumvent money laundering prevention measures. - Monitor clients using one's personal network.

5.3 ASSET MANAGERS

External asset managers are a mixture of private bankers and compliance officers. They must therefore perform the functions of both professional groups described in sections 5.1 and 5.2. On the one hand, asset managers – similar to private bankers – have a vested interest in attracting new clients and retaining existing clients. On the other hand, in many jurisdictions, they also assume the function of a compliance officer and would have to independently file a money laundering report if they suspect that it is occurring. Thus, they regulate themselves, especially in smaller businesses owned and operated by one person.

At this point, the question of the plausibility of the client's stories naturally arises. Wealth managers should ensure that their clients' stories appear plausible and logically comprehensible. In particular, caution should be exercised when writing KYC profiles. Similar to private bankers, asset managers should obtain documentary evidence to support all statements made by their clients. However, they must go further than private bankers. In particular, asset managers should critically scrutinize the documents submitted by their clients. They should not blindly rely on documents from courts or authorities. Civil law contracts should be examined all the more critically.

Asset managers should also be encouraged to continuously monitor their client relationships. However, they often have less sophisticated technology than banks. It is therefore all the more important that they also use their personal network for monitoring purposes and stay alert to the presence of even small discrepancies. Ultimately, everything that applies to compliance officers also applies to asset managers. Critical questions must be asked as to whether the facts seem contrived and whether the actual sources of funds can be fully traced.

Table 5.4 Recommendations for Practitioners

Recommendations for Practitioners
- Fulfil the function of both a private banker and a compliance officer. - Consider how plausible the client's stories seem. - Exercise caution when writing the KYC profile. - Have all statements made by the client supported by documents. - Do not give tips on how to circumvent money laundering prevention measures. - Monitor clients using one's personal network. - Engage in continuous monitoring. - Do not blindly trust documents from courts or authorities. - Confirm the actual source of funds. - Ask whether facts seem contrived. - Do a press analysis.

5.4 PUBLIC PROSECUTORS

Public prosecutors are frequently confronted with money laundering proceedings. These proceedings are often based on reports from the MLRO. Financial service providers have to forward their suspicions to the responsible MLRO. These suspicions are often based on the principles of the Egmont Group, which is an international association of national FIUs that facilitates cooperation and the exchange of information or expertise between these FIUs. This means that they analyse the information transmitted by the financial service providers and, if necessary, supplement it with further information. However, they do not check the accuracy of the information. If the suspicion of money laundering cannot be eliminated, the MLRO forwards the information to the competent public prosecutor's office. It follows that it is the task of the public prosecutor's office to critically assess and verify the information. In particular, it must be verified whether there is sufficient suspicion to initiate proceedings.

In practice, it can often be observed that public prosecutors act almost blindly on the facts reported to them by the MLRO. This regularly leads to serious errors that can hardly be completely corrected in later proceedings. Neither financial service providers nor the MLRO has a duty to check the facts. They merely report suspicions. One can think of articles in foreign newspapers as an example. If reports about a client of a bank appear in less reputable Russian or Ukrainian online media outlets suggesting that the client has committed certain crimes, the bank will detect this, thanks to its sophisticated IT systems. The question then arises as to whether the proceeds of the crime mentioned in the articles could have ended up at the bank. If this cannot be ruled out, the bank will send a report to the MLRO. The latter will investigate and, if necessary, add further information to support the facts.

MLROs, however, are not usually law enforcement agencies. This means that MLROs are just as unlikely as financial service providers to be capable of identifying whether the contents of foreign newspaper articles are fictitious. This scenario is not far-fetched since it is possible to plant fake newspaper articles and spread damaging content in order to harm competitors and other enemies, especially in countries rife with corruption. The approaches taken by the banks and the MLROs are not unreasonable considering this context.

The bank monitors the activities of its clients and submits a report to the MLRO if it identifies suspicious circumstances. This reflects solid monitoring practices. The MLRO verifies the information provided by the bank and supplements it with its own research. This procedure is in no way objectionable. It is then also proper that the MLRO forwards the matter to the public prosecutor's office, unless the suspicion proves to be unfounded. The public prosecutor's office, on the other hand, is responsible for examining the facts described by the financial services provider and the MLRO as critically as possible.

It can hardly be assumed that public prosecutors would seize major assets entirely based on some damning newspaper articles – after all, there is always the risk that the journalists' investigations are misinformed or even entirely fictitious. It is therefore important to critically examine the facts that are transmitted by the MLRO.

Furthermore, the connection between the alleged predicate offence and the assets to be seized must be critically examined. It is not uncommon for prosecutors to discover in the course of their investigations that the assets have been with Bank Y since year X, but that the alleged predicate offence was only committed in year X + 1. In this case, a connection between the alleged predicate offence and the assets on which the report to the MLRO was based would have to be denied.

In addition, the connection between the accused, the alleged predicate offence and the beneficial owners of the assets must also be examined. It is natural that financial service providers might report to the MLRO even if they are uncertain. It then also makes sense that it should not ultimately be left to the financial service providers to conclusively assess whether assets are incriminated or not. Frequently, however, reports are also filed if there is a more distant connection to suspected criminal offences. For example, consider a wealthy couple. Both spouses have accounts with Bank Y. The husband faces accusations abroad of having embezzled assets to the tune of CHF 50 million.

In such a context, it is quite possible that the bank will also file a SAR concerning the man's wife. At the same time, however, it is conceivable that the wife knows nothing about the (alleged) criminal activities of her husband. Thus, within the framework of a critical examination, the possibility must also be considered that the husband's assets could possibly be incriminated but those of his wife could originate from legal sources.

Furthermore, a trend towards politically motivated proceedings has been observed in recent years. Therefore, in the context of money laundering proceedings, prosecutors should always ask themselves whether the allegations could be politically motivated. This is especially true in proceedings concerning very large assets. If there are indications of a possible political motivation, further clarifications should be made. In this context, proceedings before foreign authorities should also be critically examined. If there are indications of serious criminal procedural errors here, special restraint should be exercised in applying coercive measures at home. In particular, one should avoid inadvertently facilitating politically motivated proceedings for the benefit of foreign entities.

Table 5.5 Recommendations for Practitioners

Recommendations for Practitioners
- Investigate suspicions – do not simply accept the validity of foreign facts or press articles. - Check the connections between assets and predicate offences – do not seize hastily. - Examine the connection between the accused and the criminal predicate offence. - Exclude politically motivated procedures. - Check procedures of other authorities for errors in criminal procedure.

5.5 DEFENCE LAWYERS

Criminal defence lawyers are usually called in once significant assets have been seized. Clients usually have two concerns: on the one hand, they fear the loss of their freedom; on the other hand, they fear the loss of their assets. Therefore, whether the existing suspicions can justify the measures taken by the public prosecutor's office must first be examined, and all suspicions must be questioned. If this is successful, the criminal proceedings often end at this point. Without confirmed suspicions, a continuation of the criminal proceedings can hardly be justified. Any assets seized must be released immediately.

If there are sufficient grounds for suspicion to justify the measures taken by the public prosecutor's office, the predicate offence must first be questioned. As is well known, the public prosecutor's office is obliged to prove the predicate offence. From the point of view of a defence lawyer, it is therefore worthwhile to seriously question the alleged criminal predicate offence. In doing so, the defence must argue that the client had no motive. In many cases, it is obvious that very wealthy clients are unlikely to have a financial motive. A person who has legal assets of more than CHF 100 million is unlikely to be interested in embezzling CHF 1 million and thus jeopardizing not only his own wealth but also his own freedom.

If raising questions surrounding the predicate offence is insufficient to end the investigation, any connections between the predicate offence and the assets must be critically examined and disproven. Ideally, the assets seized by the public prosecutor's office were already invested in the bank when the alleged predicate offence was committed.

Furthermore, any connections between the accused and the predicate offence must also be explained or disproven. Criminal proceedings for money laundering are regularly conducted against individuals who are merely associated with other individuals who have been accused of committing a predicate offence, like spouses, for example. However, criminal behaviour by a husband does not necessarily mean that the wife's assets must also be incriminated.

If neither the connection between the accused person and the predicate offence nor that between the predicate offence and the assets can be disproven, it must be examined whether alternative explanations – such as a political motivation – could be offered as a defence. In this context, it is important to point out any procedural weaknesses in foreign proceedings. It is often the case, for example, that proceedings abroad were conducted in absentia.

Finally, a so-called source-of-funds analysis can help to prove the legitimate origins of the accused's assets. Thus, it is up to the public prosecutor to prove that the assets are incriminated and originated from a criminal predicate offence. However, if there are some suspicious circumstances surrounding the accused that would justify maintaining the seizure of their assets, it may be in their best interest for their defence lawyer to make an effort to prove the legal origin of the funds. This way, the client can dispose of the assets again sooner than he would otherwise be able to. As an interim solution, it is also possible to ask the public prosecutor's office for its consent to the continued (active) management of the assets.

Table 5.6 Recommendations for Practitioners

Recommendations for Practitioners
- Question probable cause. - Question the predicate offence. - Question the connection between the predicate offence and the assets. - Question the connection between the accused and the predicate offence. - Offer alternative explanations (political motivation, etc.). - Express doubts about predicate offences abroad. - Rebuke criminal procedural weaknesses of foreign procedures. - Carry out a source-of-funds analysis.

5.6 JUDGES

From the perspective of the court, it must first be examined whether the existing suspicious facts justify the measures requested by the public prosecutor's office. In particular, it must be critically examined whether the public prosecutor's office has sufficiently checked and analysed the information provided by the MLRO. If this is not the case, the prerequisites for coercive measures should not be met in the vast majority of cases.

Furthermore, the court should also examine from which alleged predicate offence the assets under discussion originate. In addition to the connection between the criminal predicate offence and the assets, the connection between the accused and the criminal predicate offence must of course also be examined. In particular, foreign criminal proceedings must be critically scrutinized. Finally, it must be examined whether the source-of-funds analysis is plausible.

Table 5.7 Recommendations for Practitioners

Recommendations for Practitioners
- Investigate suspicions; in particular, check whether the prosecution has sufficiently checked and analysed information from the MLRO/FIU. - Check criminal predicate offences. - Check the connection between predicate offences and assets. - Examine the connection between the accused and the criminal predicate offence. - Take a critical look at foreign procedures. - Consider whether the source-of-funds analysis is plausible.

CHAPTER 6

Summary, Limitations and Conclusions

The starting point for this book was Article 305bis of the SCC. In particular, the aim was to examine whether the existing money laundering prevention measures are suitable for effectively combating money laundering. It was shown that the existing money laundering prevention measures can be circumvented with relatively little effort by money launderers who have either some specialist knowledge or at least competent advisors. This was achieved by explaining the concrete methods of money laundering since ultimately, this is one of the best ways to demonstrate that circumvention is possible. Moreover, this suggested that gaps have to be closed by the legislator in order to fight effectively against money laundering. At the same time, however, whether it is at all possible to close the existing loopholes to such an extent that money laundering is at least made considerably more difficult should also be questioned. Furthermore, the methods presented should help to give investigators and compliance officers insight into the intelligent money launderer's perspective so they can hone their ability to identify possible offences, which are often not immediately recognizable.

The explorative approach used in this study, namely the interviewing of experts and an evaluation by means of a qualitative content analysis according to Mayring,[198] had certain methodological limits and was influenced by the author's discretion. However, this played only a very minor role in the context of this book. The book does not claim to present all methods of money laundering. Rather, the aim of this book is to point out some loopholes that can be exploited and concrete approaches that can be employed by money launderers in order to support the argument that the existing prevention measures are expensive but clearly insufficient. Therefore, the exploratory approach was appropriate. Moreover, the validity of the results was not significantly limited by the choice of methods. The quantitative verification of the results of the qualitative investigation further contributed to strengthening the validity of the empirical results of this study.

---

198. Mayring, 2010.

The author has deliberately refrained from estimating the volume of money laundering in general and its distribution among the respective methods in particular. This is due to the fact that a precise estimate is almost impossible. First of all, it should be noted that predicate offences to money laundering are not defined uniformly at the international level. This already massively limits the comparability of the data. This obstacle could be overcome through adjustments. However, this only makes sense if the estimates on which these adjustments are based are accurate. So far, however, the assumptions regarding the scope of possible predicate offences vary significantly. In addition, the scope of money laundering is not particularly relevant in terms of answering the research question. After all, this book is primarily concerned with demonstrating methods of money laundering. Therefore, the author continues to hold the view that it makes more sense to dispense with estimates than to reproduce mindless values without engaging in a critical appraisal. It should also be noted at this point that the numerous existing estimates of the extent of money laundering are rarely (if ever) sufficiently substantiated. It is simply unknown, and one would first have to find out what turnover is achieved with the predicate offences to begin to shine a light into the depths of money laundering. However, this is difficult to do, as it can be assumed that only a fraction of the offences committed are ever actually detected.

The empirical results of this study should also be briefly acknowledged. While some of the methods presented have been known about for a long time and have merely been proven in the context of this book to still be applicable to money laundering, new methods, which have hardly been considered in the literature so far, have also been developed in some cases. The methods related to the trade in tangible assets, namely gold, jewellery, rough diamonds, antiques, art and real estate, as well as banks in Dubai, bureaux de change and safe-deposit boxes, have already been known about for several years but were further developed and refined within the scope of this book. In particular, it should be noted that in the past, the literature has primarily dealt with the fact that money laundering exists, but very few authors have thought about the concrete methods used by money launderers. The methods of using consulting companies and corporate restructuring to launder money, on the other hand, have only been marginally considered in the literature to date and have been largely developed anew in the context of this book. This makes it clear that money launderers are continuously developing their methods and are usually one step ahead of legislators and investigating authorities.

In particular, it should be reiterated that compliance officers also believe that money launderers will increasingly switch to less-regulated industries due to the high compliance standards of banks. In particular, industries that take cash payments and are fairly unregulated seem to be particularly at risk of being exploited for money laundering purposes. All the methods presented in this book seem to occur in practice, albeit to varying extents. Nonetheless, they rarely come into the focus of compliance officers.

Furthermore, the author would like to emphasize that he is fundamentally in favour of combating and consistently prosecuting money laundering within the meaning of Article 305bis SCC. At the same time, however, he would like to point out that expensive preventive measures, such as those currently expected of banks, insurance companies and other financial intermediaries, only make sense if they can actually prevent incriminated assets from being laundered. Due to the increasingly demanding fight against money laundering, costs have to be borne which, with regard to the circumvention methods presented in this book, are increasingly disproportionate to their potential benefit. This affects private financial service providers in particular. Accepting costs in the multimillion figures only makes sense if money laundering can actually be prevented. If, however, the only effect is that money laundering is shifted away from certain areas but ultimately takes place in others anyway, the benefit of these costs should be questioned.

If one really wants to combat money laundering, a drastic tightening of the measures would be necessary. It should be mentioned at this point that the methods described in this book barely scratch the surface of what is possible and that any regulation would have to be much more far-reaching. Ultimately, money can even be laundered at the checkout in the supermarket. The measures to be taken to prevent money laundering would only be effective if they could be implemented globally. Otherwise, they would lead money launderers to shift from one country to another.

The alternative is to admit that money laundering – similar to other crimes like murder, manslaughter or assault – cannot be prevented, only identified, prosecuted and consistently punished. If one were to take this perspective, one would have to effectively relieve the financial service providers of their current reporting obligations and reduce the compliance requirements in the area of money laundering. After all, it makes no sense to fight money laundering in one sector and tolerate it in all others.

The author does not want to presume to make recommendations for action here. He has presented both options, namely a tightening as well as a loosening of money laundering prevention measures, and leaves the final decision as to the best approach to take to the powers that be. However, it is obvious that the status quo, namely a combination of high anti-money laundering compliance costs and a lack of effectiveness in combating money laundering, is becoming increasingly unsustainable.

Finally, the author would like to emphasize that the methods described in this book are obviously only applicable to criminals with larger turnovers and corresponding competences. A petty criminal who has made a modest profit of CHF 10,000 in the course of committing a crime does not normally need access to companies with subsidiaries abroad in order to launder this small amount. At most, the safe-deposit box method would apply to storing the incriminated assets, although this also seems rather disproportionate for such a small amount that could otherwise be used to fund the criminal's daily expenses.

The methods presented in this book show how criminals with large turnovers can launder their incriminated assets, which makes sense considering money laundering prevention measures also ultimately focus on criminals with larger turnovers. These prevention measures are not concerned with petty criminals. The focus of the fight against money laundering seems to be more on seizing the profits of international (organized) crime than on catching petty criminals.[199]

199. Graber, 1990.

However, it is questionable whether criminals with substantial assets also have the skills to launder money professionally, as outlined in this book. Apart from the safe-deposit box method, all the approaches outlined here require considerable expertise. It could be argued that these methods are only accessible to a minority of criminals with the requisite skills, which most criminals do not possess. On the other hand, it should be considered that criminals with significant assets could buy in expertise. Finally, criminals could seek advice from money laundering experts and thus easily overcome this obstacle.

Nevertheless, it should be noted that competent advisors are expensive. Very few lawyers who have the necessary expertise are admitted to the bar for a one-time fee of CHF 100,000. These advisors are therefore unlikely to have much interest in helping criminals with middling incomes. However, if a criminal launders several million francs per year, then charging high fees might make giving them advice worthwhile. Thus, it should be noted that the methods presented in this book are approaches that are usually reserved for criminals with substantial assets and access to certain skills. While petty criminals often use their earnings to finance their daily lives, the problem of money laundering primarily arises for criminals who have substantial amounts of incriminated assets at their disposal.

Ultimately, this book deals with several unknowns while showing how intelligent criminals and their accomplices would have to act in order to launder large sums of incriminated assets. This should help legislators and compliance officers to anticipate the behaviour of these criminals and take appropriate measures to combat money laundering. It is not currently possible to offer a reliable estimate of the sums actually being laundered at present using the methods described in this book because the extent of money laundering in Switzerland is simply unknown. Thus, the volume of incriminated assets that are laundered annually can only be speculated.

APPENDIX

Qualitative Content Analysis of the Expert Interviews[200]

Generalization	Quote
Banks screen ownership positions/beneficiaries	Which is not always easy, because with the areas where it's about trusteeships, about indirect, uh, uh, ownership positions, because that has to be determined first. It has to be shareholder structure and so on. That is done, and it is taken very seriously. At least at the banks I work for.
Fictitious hotel guests	Of course they're clean, there are, they have a few people there, there's someone like me, for example, I got hired from Berlin and I regularly go to Berlin or just show it off and stay in this hotel, yes, it costs 150 euros a night and I'm really there 150 days a year. And there are a thousand people like me. Of course, I'm never in Berlin, well not in the hotel either, and I don't pay 150 euros or anything like that. Everything is completely legal – my identity card, my personal details – everything is there; everything is known.
Betting shops	But that also works for betting shops, for example. So all such gambling halls, betting shops, exchange offices, that can all be used for laundering money; yes, everywhere where cash is [it is] relatively common.
Creating paper trails	Straw men, there doesn't always have to be a perpetrator, the perpetrators don't always have to appear themselves. The perpetrators are not money launderers in the legal sense, yet. Uh, even money laundering does not yet exist as a criminal offence in our country, and, uh, others always have to step in and they build themselves; they can also create paper trails for themselves.

200. Please note that some of the quotes have been translated from German into English.

Generalization	Quote
Form chains	Of course, you always have to form a chain somehow.
Select cash-intensive areas	So, where a lot of cash can flow. Jewellers and car dealers. The same thing; the same questions arise with casinos on the one hand and slot machine halls on the other. You have to say okay; you don't have enough resources; concentrate on these and these and these.
Use limited monitoring capacities in municipalities	Municipalities, counties, states, you name it, have very limited capacity for supervision in the non-financial sector.
Taking advantage of the lack of centralization of supervision	In Germany, we have a very fragmented landscape of supervisory responsibilities in the non-financial sector, and this must also be seen as a weak point, although it cannot be eliminated altogether in the federalist Germany.
Investing cash in cars	Uh, or even if it's cash, that can be in the hundreds of thousands at least, something with expensive motor vehicles, the stage of money laundering.
Making use of the lack of awareness of those affected	There are areas where the supervision and the actual information, and for all I care, the sensitivity of the people concerned is not yet so well developed.
Straw men and fragmentation	This is definitely a modus operandi, that money is always divided.
Letterbox companies with trustees across several countries	If the sums involved are larger, then it would be the classic principle with some shell companies or something, i.e., some letterbox companies with a few trustees over three or four borders, and that's it.
Non-financial sector suitable for small amounts	The non-financial sector might be considered for amounts below 1 million. Above that, it might be a bit difficult in the non-financial sector to really accommodate the money.
Seek out the non-financial sector	The so-called non-financial sector, which results from the Money Laundering Act, is still somewhat 'behind', I would say in non-technical terms in inverted commas.
Banks are familiar with money laundering	Because in the banks, in the financial institutions, which are also centrally supervised by the German BaFIN, people have been familiar with the topic for a long time, and it is regulated more intensively there.
Seek out the non-financial sector	If you want to launder money in Germany and try to find loopholes, you should choose the so-called non-financial sector.
Money laundering costs	Sure, so you always have to pay something for money laundering.

Generalization	Quote
Use gaming salons	Um, yes, I mean, it's a bit, I mean, I'm thinking of Frankfurt, I just think, if I have contact or want to make contact somehow, I would go to one of the gambling dens at the station, hire an unemployed person who throws my money into machines all day. Then I'd pay proper tax on it and what's left over would be my laundered money.
Straw men	Or you use straw men, uh, straw, uh, straw men.
Bank with weak compliance	Which bank is suitable here? A small bank that is under a lot of customer pressure might be suitable. Because here, you might be more likely to accept transactions without questioning them.
Client details must match transactions	Is the client's information coherent with the transactions that have been made? Yes or no? So actually, we look at, is the story plausible? And do the transactions match it?
Detailed contracts	Yes, detailed contracts quite simply, perhaps even with product lists to go with them, that don't even exist.
History must be plausible	If I have a small operating business and I have millions to launder, my story is not plausible.
Different jurisdictions	I would also send it in circles for a long time and make it as complicated as possible, because I believe that the law enforcement agencies really have huge problems with it, not only because at some point you can hardly see through it, but also because it is international and our law enforcement agencies are not international, they are national. And they very quickly reach their limits, I think.
Bank with weak compliance	I think you also have to choose the banks well; you have to decide in which destinations I can do that. Where people are more likely to look the other way, where they have more understanding of such constructs. You have to think carefully about which destinations you work with and which banks you work with.
Use offshore companies	If, for example, I were to be very corrupt and receive a lot of consultancy fees, and it was not in cash, then I would probably set up an extremely complex offshore company network.
History must be plausible	I think the important thing in money laundering is, my story just has to be plausible.
Operate fast-food chain with supply chain	Officially, he runs a fast-food chain, which really exists, and he really sells his fast food. He even has his own chicken farm and offices and so on and employees.
Open a legitimate business	One method for me would be to open a quite legitimate, um, business actually, um.
Method depending on volume to be laundered	I think it comes down to, always, how much money do I have to launder?

Generalization	Quote
Transfer money via fictitious transactions	But I wouldn't transfer my money in cash. So there are ways to do it through financial transactions. Be it through foreign exchange transactions, speculation or business, certain transactions, uh, that are then done as a business, so to speak, to really make the money look legal and to do it within the framework of a (fiat money?) transaction. So I wouldn't, uh, I wouldn't bring it across in the case, quite honestly.
Money faster than regulators	I think the regulators and the places are always running behind. So if yesterday it was Lichtenstein and Switzerland, then today it might be Dubai and then tomorrow it will be, I don't know, Panama, uh, well, I think my money would always be faster.
Tangible assets with non-transparent pricing	So I, the easiest and the quickest way you would do it is just alternative investments that are not, uh, that are not subject to the Money Laundering Act. So now, uh, real estate is a big topic. Uh, precious metals, uh, [it is a] whole topic, uh, also valuable art objects that ultimately have no regular market price.
Traders only need to appoint auditors	Um, but it is also a fact that these traders will not have to submit to any supervision, uh, no similar supervision as with the financial intermediaries; they only have to appoint an auditor.
Using fiscal motivation as justification	Um, that will also change, but that leads to the fact that, of course, one can say in certain cases [that it is] tax-motivated, [so] no money laundering conviction. Uh, that (unintelligible) cannot apply here.
Money Laundering Reporting Office Switzerland cannot respond to reports from private traders	That means that if a private person reports something to us about the, uh, art trade business, uh, we simply can't respond to it. Uh, that is, then all, uh, has to be done on the side of the police, uh. This is also the case, but it is correspondingly difficult to analyse systematically on the one hand, and on the other hand, of course, this information is much more incomplete than the reports, which provides a very good picture about the system in Switzerland and the risks. But of course, uh, within the framework of the ... the law, the legal obligations.
Hardly any reports from art or antiques dealers	Which take place outside the market that is regulated by the Restriction of Competition Act, I would say, it's all still a bit in the process of being worked through, I would say. Uh, of course, for certain elements certain things have already been done, real estate, art trade, things like that, there are certain studies, uh, there is a certain attention, et cetera. Nevertheless, in principle, we do not receive any reports from these sectors because there are no financial intermediaries. So we cannot process these reports, because there is no legal basis.

Generalization	Quote
Limited reach of the Money Laundering Reporting Office	But we're still in the process of establishing a bit of an overall picture; we're trying to link everything a bit. But there are many areas where there are still many question marks. That's a fact, and of course the MLRO, Money Laundering Reporting Office Switzerland, has limited reach.
Use asset managers for transfers	The asset manager had, uh, good contacts to a drug ring, you can say, abroad, uh, and made combination payments with the client's money and, uh, was able to launder this drug money accordingly. Especially by [clearing throat] paying out the client's money across the border. Er, via cash transactions, that is, the money did not flow at all; it remained in the country of origin as drugs, er [jewellery] (unintelligible), and was paid out to the customers there and then booked in Switzerland, er, and laundered accordingly.
Operate restaurants	Certain companies that operate catering establishments, for example.
Do not involve a financial intermediary	If you don't go through a financial intermediary, you can, uh, launder your money relatively easily in Switzerland, just like abroad.
Areas not subject to the AMLA	I think, um, there are certain areas in Switzerland that are not subject to the Money Laundering Act.
Transaction must fit the customer	With us, we only look at the money first, whether the input fits the customer. If the transaction matches the customer 'yes/no', then it's good.
Distribute money to straw men	It's a huge effort, but let's say, if I were the one who had something to say, I would always distribute the money here to several straw men, so to speak.
Refuge in tangible assets	I would always take refuge in tangible assets. So I would try to take refuge in tangible assets.
Avoid the scope of application of the AMLA	All the institutions that are covered by the Money Laundering Act, with whom it is really becoming more and more difficult to place criminal money.
Involve several countries	As soon as one, two, three countries are involved, it becomes difficult.
Choose international models	It is simply the case that when such constructs go through several countries, the execution of sentences and criminal investigations often fail due to legal assistance.
Consider overall assessment of the contract (language)	And the contract is then also in a bad German or bad English and that's how you end up on the bank's radar, rather than if you present a nice, supposedly healthy business model.
Renewable energies as the subject matter of the contract	Often the keyword is renewable energies. It is a well-known pattern that if there is no operational background, but there is money, then they say that it will come from the project in Slovenia anyway, I'll say now, and we want to promote renewable energies there.

Generalization	Quote
Design fictitious contracts professionally	Often the perpetrators make the mistake of making up their own contracts to justify these payments, which is what I'm saying now in the field of white-collar crime. But the contracts look totally weird at first glance. And then you look again and see that it's a fictitious contract for a service that wasn't provided.
Establish plausibility	It always depends; you can probably say that in general, it always depends on the whole set. If it's all clever and plausible, it's much less noticeable.
Gift tax not relevant for bank	I think so, and I would assume that the bank does not care whether they have paid the gift tax.
Gift from aunt	Of course, I can go to the bank and say that my aunt gave me this 20,000 as a gift, and then, if I have confirmation like that. They probably won't believe it without further ado.
Limited regulatory options	Ultimately, you will never be able to make the network so finely meshed that you, well, as it is in criminal law, but, um, that you can no longer, um, bring illegal money into circulation.
Stupid money launderers get caught	I remember from my time that we caught the stupid money launderers who were simply too stupid to set up their system in a reasonably intelligent way.
Taxation as a seal of approval	Quasi the seal of approval, or when you say, okay, I have even been taxed on these assets. So you can't show them more legally or when the tax authorities do the math.
Never launder through the banking system	I would never go through a banking system like that, not at all.
Shift assets away from the banking sector	There are alternative ways to move assets outside the very heavily regulated banking sector.
Select non-regulated areas	So basically, I would just go to areas that are not regulated.
Avoid state pressure	If this state pressure is not there, is not present, then nothing will be done by the actors.
Select poorly regulated or non-regulated channels	I would rather go through channels that are less regulated or even not regulated at all, because, uh, there is no government pressure that you have to do something.
Consider databases with names of people involved	There is a relatively high chance that this is the name of one of the persons involved, who is listed in these databases (unintelligible), which can be purchased, so to speak, the world check, world compliance, the OFAC lists and the UN sanctions lists.
Danger of getting caught in nets	I think the chances are relatively high that you will get caught somewhere in these networks if you are criminally active.
A lot gets stuck in the banks' networks	Let's say we go through a bank, the simplest example, or they have such, let's say, tightly meshed nets cast nowadays, a relatively large amount gets caught.

Generalization	Quote
Avoid conventional channels	Rather less via the traditional channels.
Mixing black money with white money	Or I run a business and, uh, have regular income from the customer and mix that up now and then with a little bit of money that I somehow still have on the side.
Mixing incriminated money with official income	In our country, at least, it has been the prevailing doctrine for years, as soon as it is mixed with legal assets and you can no longer prove exactly that the EUR 3 is criminal money and the EUR 3 is legally acquired money. That's when you get out.
Mixing incriminated money with official income	And I have to say, if I were a money launderer, I would just, uh, make sure that I always mix the money with regular income or with normal legal money, um, on occasion.
Split cash	A yes, so first and foremost, still the cash, because I can split it, I can divide it into small amounts, I can give it to different people, I can bring it together again and so on.
Special knowledge as an obstacle	The regular money launderer is more likely to be someone who needs a safe way to convert their assets quickly without a lot of risk, and these won't usually be things where you really need specialist knowledge.
Special knowledge associated with effort	So there you have to, wherever special knowledge is required on the part of the money launderer, the question is again, does one really go to this trouble?
Buy tangible assets with a long track record of value	Yes, it is a difficult topic in the area of money laundering because monitoring is also very difficult. So, mm, I can invest as a money launderer in pretty much anything. I can buy jewellery; I can buy gold, I can buy real estate and, if possible, everything that has a long lasting value.
Disguise the link to the beneficial owner	I would simply exhaust as many of the possibilities as possible in order to actually be sure that the, um, that the reference to me is veiled, so to speak, and that of course the reference before is also veiled there.
Use offshore companies	I would use offshore companies, uh.
Use stooges	I would take a straw man.
Distinction between cash and book money	The difference between having the money, the dirty money, in cash or whether I receive it in some other way, for example, because I do forms of commission on the Internet and thus actually receive the money already transferred.
Professional vs personal money launderers	Of course, you also have to differentiate, um, do I have a money launderer who really, uh, offers his services full time, so to speak, in the area of, um, white-collar crime, for example, or just really advanced forms of crime, or do I have, uh, money launderers who launder their own money, for example, and are often perpetrators themselves?

Generalization	Quote
Consider the environment and resources of the money launderer	So it simply depends on the environment in which the money launderer operates and which methods are available to him.
Different circles use different methods	Well, basically, I would say that there are very many methods, which are also used in very different ways in different circles.
Involve experienced money launderers	Then I would have to get people who have been doing this for many years and can tell me how I can plausibly present it to the bank official in a trial and who will take it off my hands.
Establish plausibility	If I were a money launderer, I would try to establish plausibility.
Credible representation through pooling of funds and investments in tangible assets	That would be a possibility, of course, but as soon as the source of funds can be somehow distributed in a credible way, it is also difficult. But I think this pooling of allegedly small turnovers, uh, is a, is a certain risk, and I think mobile material assets have a role or play a big role there.
Procedure depends on the origin of the money	Typical lawyer's answer: it depends, and it depends on where, or money, where the money comes from that I want to launder.
Offshore construction with over/underinvoicing	Of course, with offshore construction, overfactoring/underfactoring, these are the two big issues that come up again and again in practice.
Alternative payment methods	With all the payment methods, technologies, rechargeable prepaid cards. So everything where the physical presence, I say, on one side of the pie is going down, on the other side where it's rechargeable.
Virtual currencies	That's all the virtual currencies.
Fake higher turnover	Anyone can do that, the higher turnover. I mean, any business can do that. Restaurants can do it because I'm simply pushing the daily lottery.
Offshore companies use	Whether then different jurisdictions that have jurisdiction, companies log into the Offshore Destination 1, there are executive offices under Offshore Destination 2 [and] the account is in Offshore Destination 3. Very often, these offshore companies are another offshore company.
Money laundering is expensive	So if you're making money from drug trafficking and you're needing to launder that money, it now costs you more than it did in the days before anti-money laundering to launder that money because you've probably got to set up some companies and pay it through the bank and pay some tax on it maybe, all those kind of things.
Different banks' monitoring not networked	You have to comply with a threshold of 100,000 per client relationship. That applies, we are talking about client relationships within the framework of the Anti-money Laundering Act. You can't network monitoring from different banks; that's not possible at all.

Generalization	Quote
Observe threshold values	For example, the entire public law sector, i.e., the debt collection and bankruptcy offices or, as we mentioned, the art trade, the real estate trade and so on and so forth. And within the scope of money laundering, there is of course the area where there is a duty of due diligence above a certain threshold value. Threshold values are foreseen, for example, for motor vehicle transactions. Uh, in the area of bill of exchange transactions.
Unmarked prepaid cards for transport across borders	Because when I drive my car across the German border, the customs officer won't even know what this single card is. If he asks, I say, yes, that's my parking garage. They are neutral. There's nothing on it. Um, the customs would surely have a reader and somehow get a hint that there's actually cash on it. Um, they are always in the known, common products, the amount is limited.
Preparation for queries from the bank	Then to have a story in hand that says, well, he always has to reckon with the bank saying today, where did the money come from, why are you doing it this way and not another way? And a good money launderer is prepared for this situation.
Many transactions	He makes a lot of transactions; the money doesn't stay there for long; it's not invested sensibly.
Money laundering costs	The money launderer is in itself acting economically irrationally.
Countries with high inflation	They have in the countries with high inflation, so I said, you can't leave the money in the bank at all, because then it won't be worth anything in a year, but I have to spend it, I keep it in cash.
Countries with weak banking systems	Countries where the banking system is weak, where people have no alternative to cash.
Choose cash-intensive jurisdictions	Relocate to jurisdictions where cash is simply part of everyday life.
Use existing structures	Um, he makes use of already existing, um, structures, so to speak.
Retailers as straw men	There are quite a few retailers in the city who are having a hard time. I go to them and say, look, um, I bring you a few thousand in cash every day, you enter it in your bookkeeping, everything is even taxed, VAT is paid on it, um, you bring it to your bank in a box every evening.
Cash-sensitive industries	And then we see somewhere in the used car, used car trade, um, um, retail, um, casino, um, something where, I say, the occurrence of cash is the rule rather than the exception. So cash. I'm in a cash-sensitive industry and then I'm probably not an unknown person to the bank with 5 million, where all the alarm bells go off, but I'm the successful owner of a chain of snack bars that don't accept credit cards for cost reasons, but only cash.

Generalization	Quote
Create structures as justification for cash	Create a structure that justifies the large cash traffic then.
Merge via payment transactions	Um, and I just distribute it, even in different places, and then I bring it together via payment transactions.
Denomination to max. CHF 100,000 for placement	I can break it down into reasonable sizes, I'll say 100,000, because I can still place 100,000.
Cash only with a plausible story	If cash, then I must have a good story about where it came from.
Tax evasion an obsolete justification	You just had to list the story, that's just untaxed money. So it's also illegal, but you don't have a predicate offence to money laundering and then you can place cash relatively easily in many places, even in large sums. That has only changed in recent years.
Own bank	A bank with which I myself have a close relationship, so ideally it belongs to me.
Bank with economic difficulties	A bank that is in economic difficulties is probably less willing to throw out a lot of money blindly to customers.
Bank with weak compliance	It is very helpful to choose the right bank because there are different types. Um, a bank that has a weak compliance is likely to be more vulnerable.
Bank necessary	Sooner or later in the process, they need a bank
Mixing legal and illegal funds	What we are increasingly seeing is a mixing – a blending – of illegal commodities of assets with legal.
Interruptions and nesting	So to make as many, many interruptions and nestings as possible.
Obfuscation	The main issue in tracing the assets, i.e., if they are found at all, is that it is impossible to draw a connection to the crime from which they originate.
Different jurisdictions	So never everything in one country, but always distribute assets according to as many investments as possible and have as many cash flows as possible through different transactions/jurisdictions.
Concealment by means of stooges	Straw people, um, yes, that should be about what is still strategy 1, to conceal one's identity.
Social structures for layering	Interpose social structures.
Separate legal ownership and economic use	In other words, always establish a separation of legal ownership from the economic use of the assets.
Use foreign identities	So on the one hand, uh, playing with identities. So never having assets in one's own name or too obviously in the name of a spouse or children, for example.

Generalization	Quote
Strategy with different elements	Currently, I would recommend every money launderer to always make a multi-strategy, a graduated strategy, which includes very different elements.
Investigators' burden of proof	So the Achilles' heel, I would say, of the investigators is the burden of proof.
Establish plausibility	Whereas today, also due to the measures, money launderers must of course already reckon with the fact that the funds can certainly be found and identified somewhere, but thereby already anticipate that one can find a credible, um, scattering method that plausibly or somewhat plausibly shows where the funds come from and where it is then very difficult to prove the opposite.
Interrupt proof of origin	I want to prevent people from being able to prove that the expenses came from crimes.
Hide the primary target	Primary objective, I don't want the funds to be able to be traced that came from the offence.
Value and turnover difficult to measure	Or a company that sold jeans, you can also measure how much a pair of jeans costs that had a turnover every day, as if it had sold a hundred jeans. A hundred jeans, that's ... So even big department stores will probably not be able to sell that amount a day, yes, and that's one thing where I have to say that people thought it was too stupid, so you really have to choose sectors where the money can't be measured approximately, where you can say, okay.
Antiques market records high turnover	So some kind of trade where they say that's okay. Let's assume that it's best to trade in art and antiques; I would almost suggest that, because antiques are sometimes sold for higher amounts.
Antiques market not regulated	That they don't have to be organized in self-regulatory organizations either.
Antiques market not regulated	So, uh, the big, um, issue is that they have no duties.
Observe threshold values	There is no upper limit of an amount where you say if it exceeds the cash sum by so-and-so much, it is no longer permissible or something.
Antiques market not regulated	Yes, it is just that ... that these traders are not financial intermediaries and have no obligations.
Antiques market not regulated	It is not regulated at all.
Collectors' prices	That's a lover's price if you, I personally never have a problem with, I don't do anything with it. Some painting or whatever, it probably wouldn't be worth anything to me. It's worth a lot to somebody else, so I can certainly accommodate a lot through that.

Generalization	Quote
Value difficult to measure	The attraction for me as a money launderer is actually that an object can be moved at a value that I determine myself.
Expertise	And, uh, for that they would first have to, um, learn different languages, learn to read cuneiform. So different languages were simply written in cuneiform, so they would then have to um actually acquire specialist knowledge, which is what you actually do at university.
Restorers	So if they are very fragile things, let's say metal objects are often very fragile, they are often already very corroded, for example through storage in the ground, and they would then actually have to be restored in order to be secured, so that the corrosion process does not continue.
Volatile prices	Between private companies, the prices are extremely volatile.
Non-transparent market	But, of course, it is also a very intransparent market and everything that is intransparent is, of course, pleasing to the money launderer, because it becomes difficult again to recognize whether a transaction is plausible or no longer plausible.
Traceability through serial numbers	You have photos of things that have serial numbers, which were then taken up again.
Smuggled goods recognizable on the basis of soil adhesions	If it is so obvious that there is still soil on them, then they are freshly looted and freshly smuggled.
Well-trained customs officers	Yes, that depends again, I would think, on how good these controls are and how well trained the customs officer is.
Antiques trafficking and terrorist financing	One of the five or six ways of financing, uh, ISIL is effectively through antiquities trading. They destroy some stuff, but only stuff they can't really sell.
Increased attention due to ISIS	As far as antiquities are concerned, an important issue at the moment is of course the financing of ISIL, the Islamic State, where Switzerland is relatively well positioned in terms of control mechanisms.
Financial loss	Then there is the threat of a quasi-financial loss.
Counterfeits	Counterfeits there too.
Customs controls and documents	Once again, you have to make sure that you declare them properly, don't you?
Counterfeits	And the risk that I get the wrong antique or (unintelligible) is huge.
Antique tracing not a priority of the authorities	The antiquities search. An international area is not top priority.
Lack of expertise or confidence	It needs knowledge, an antique, that it really is – you have to have trust. The highest good is trust, simply certificates of testimonies, also of persons, also of experts.

Generalization	Quote
Lack of liquidity in the market	The unfortunate thing, at least for a big money launderer, is simply the lack of liquidity in the market.
Select previously unknown objects	They should actually be things that come fresh from the earth, so to speak. In other words, things that are not yet known to science. If you were to find a life-size Roman bronze statue somewhere in the Mediterranean and put it on the market, it would be worth millions, um, of course, uh, people would immediately say that this is disreputable, it can't be right, it must have been collected illegally somehow.
Choose robust clay vessels or jewellery made of semi-precious stones	Other things, for example clay vessels or even jewellery made from semi-precious stone, from this gemstone and so on, are a bit more robust.
Hiding goods in larger loads of modern art	So if, for example, you actually let the whole thing get lost in a whole load of modern handicrafts, then these customs officers would actually have to be archaeologists or art historians in order to be able to scoop out really suspicious pieces.
Make goods unrecognizable	For example, he smuggled things out of Egypt and made them very ugly beforehand. For example, he covered them with, uh, masses, uh, real sculpture with, uh, mouldable mass and then painted them very garishly, colourfully, so that they looked like bazaar kitsch and every customs officer who looked at something like that immediately said, no, that's bazaar kitsch, that's terrible, and that's how he brought them to Great Britain.
Have expert reports prepared and published by renowned archaeologists	But this well-known axiologist had no reservations whatsoever and examined everything that was shown to him, published the things and through this, through publishing, one has a little bit of an entry point as a layperson to be able to judge whether the things are rare?
Declare it 'property of a private gentleman'	And, um, yes X have, so since X has, the whole thing has, uh, put on the market under the heading 'property of a private gentleman', in principle.
Auctions	Then offered them for sale at X in London.
Have false papers issued	This actually happens at these places of freedom, so to speak. Um, that the corresponding papers are issued, um, with which, for example, the origin is named in such a way that it no longer falls under certain laws.
Define the origin of the goods	Sometimes it is also very difficult to really define the origin there.
Worthless goods in the shop window	So, let's put it this way, I would really choose antiques, because, um, I would put a few night, old art objects, even if they have no value, in the shop window, decorate them with an insane price, where every idiot says, 'how can you ask EUR 5,000 for an old chamber pot?' But we said, that was the old chamber pot that Hitler used back then, yes.

Generalization	Quote
Shop with overpriced antiques	The tenant has his shop, and in this shop, they hang a few worthless pictures or put up a few figurines or a few chamber pots, the antique selections, and then, when you look in, you only see, aha, he's actually selling something.
Declare money at the house bank as cash turnover	So if we had an antique customer, we wouldn't find out how much he actually gets for his Madonna figures or pictures, normally. And then I pay in a lot of money, and then it's just not noticeable, a good deal has been made.
Price formation non-transparent	You can sell Madonnas there, you can sell a painting there, and whether you then make a discount or a surcharge, no one can assess that.
Not registered	And there is also a registry, like now, for example, when buying a car, where you have to say, here a car is recorded with a chassis number. I would suggest antiques.
Plausible sales	Yes, and if you check the plausibility of the turnover there.
Regularly handle antique business	If that's one deal a year and otherwise he's just selling weird little things, he probably won't get away with it.
Build up actual activity to fill the bank's dossier	The bank has probably already compiled a whole dossier on the client's usual course of business, if this is within the bounds of the usual and the bank considers this client to be serious. Then he may get away with it.
Auctions	I'm thinking more along the lines of auctions.
Tradable in other countries	It's wonderful when you buy things like this, which, by the way, you can also sell again in other countries.
Objective price determination difficult	There is the price setting or that is a market, yes, supply and demand, but who determines now how much value something has.
Acquire expertise	But I think that what you have to bear in mind is that as a money launderer, you have to be just as [much an] expert in the field.
Choose non-transparent markets	So, some other antique piece, and the middleman buys it from me accordingly, where I develop my own market. Because the market is probably not transparent. Transparent continuation would mean the same number of sellers and buyers and then there would be an equilibrium price.
Managing supply and demand	Of course, there is also supply and demand [laughs], which you can of course control.
Mixing legal with illegal goods	They also mix them with legal goods and illegal assets, so that it becomes even more difficult to determine what is illegal.
Cash problematic	Nevertheless, there is always the problem of splitting up this cash, which comes from somewhere at some point.
Avoid regulated areas	There is also the whole financial advisor area in a financial advisory area, still a lot of unregulated things that are not subject to FINMA regulation, for example, and, uh, um, there are probably still some grey areas, yes.

Generalization	Quote
Hardly any controls	That is hardly controlled. At the end of the month, one would simply show the number of customers, whether they were there or not, no problem, the money was then (unintelligible) integrated into the financial tract in a dignified way.
Quantity difficult to measure	But if you now start an ice cream parlour or a sushi stall, the problem is that you can of course always measure the quantity.
Legal entity recognized in Switzerland	So, the background idea is to establish a legal entity that is recognized in Switzerland.
Disguise the beneficial owner	This can have a legal and useful purpose, but it can also serve to conceal the beneficial owner. So that, there is no need to make a secret of it.
Credibility of the sums	With smaller sums, I can do it, as I said, via some, uh, fictitious restaurants or something. With large sums, it's no longer credible.
Non-transparent pricing	With goods you have prices, so let's work hard to verify performance, consideration, what else is one - yes, financial engineering or whatever - where it is more difficult to verify performance against performance. So, commodities I would rather push over to this intellectual area, consulting.
High-quality Internet presence	So if I'm a private consulting firm in Switzerland, I expect a high-quality website with contacts and maybe contact persons and ... so, do you know what I mean? If you Google a company and then, if I only find a page with three sentences on it, that's what I would look at, yes.
Serious Internet presence	It needs a good website. We've had websites before. A page where you can't click on anything, where you think, well, this is a joke page.
Banks with correspondent banks	You just have to find institutions where you will eventually work as a correspondent bank or where, with whom, you now work with the financial institution.
Few people, especially accountants	A few backers, well not backers, but accounting activities, uh, uh, so that can easily be done with a few people.
First stage (placement) decisive	The first stage is really crucial. The money has to come into circulation somewhere.
Cash must come into circulation	But the cash has to enter the cycle somewhere.
Establish a company with cash sales	That is, I would set up a company that sells something, where cash can flow like that.

Generalization	Quote
Competent advisors	But the Russian didn't know, um, that you don't need the whole million and simply told the trustee to find him a corporation – he took the whole million as share capital and there it was in the company. And then he distributed it there, and so the Russian was of the opinion that he still had a lot of money somehow that he could simply take out of the company again, and the substance is not that simple. So to sell the share capital back again. So he almost didn't get his money back.
Good reputation	Probably still helps if you have a good name. If you are somehow well acquainted with the local conditions. So here, let's say, on the train, um, a trustee you know and so on.
Letterbox companies with bank accounts in Dubai	Letterbox companies in Dubai; they then have bank accounts in Dubai, and that is just really difficult.
Offshore companies	An offshore company, without any name appearing there.
Bearer companies	Then there are the owner-operated companies, where you never really know who owns them and so on.
Select credible states	I have, when I set up a foreign company, which is my alleged client, who opens an account, the question is of course, for what or whether that is in a regulated, um, state or a state with a regulated, um, financial sector.
Account or contacts abroad	So I either have to have people there or I have to maintain an account myself so that this, uh, that this, uh, with an origin, in Switzerland, is somehow, uh, possible at all.
Companies abroad for deposits	So I need certain outposts abroad, which I control and which are in my power of disposal, so that I can actually deposit the money.
Societies in reputable countries	Um, as a money launderer, I would rather invest a bit more money and, yes, a German GmbH or an Austrian AG. So somewhere, or an Italian company where nobody suspects that money could be laundered.
Directors	Then certainly the possibility to have, um (unintelligible) directors, so that I really also have an offer that someone makes himself available to then also appear directly there.
Low taxes	Taxation that is not too high is an advantage.
Low taxes	Um, then taxation is of course an advantage, as a money launderer, I am very happy to pay a price for the money laundering process, and it can and often does include tax, but I don't want to hand over 50% to the state now.
Non-transparent participation structures	It certainly plays a role, how transparent the participation structures are. So, how much, how well do I get data that also tell me who is involved in the company, i.e., who is entitled.

Generalization	Quote
Take seasonal fluctuations into account	So, we reported the cases when an ice cream company came, an ice cream parlour, which brought EUR 5,000 every day in the beginning. Then we thought about whether the EUR 5,000 were actually real for the company. In summer, you can say, well, if they have a lot of customers and sell cool ice cream for EUR 1.00, it has to be very high, but it could work. Only the sales were still as high when it was winter. Of course, it was a bit conspicuous to sell ice cream for EUR 5,000 in winter.
Bank might notice that turnover is too high	And yes, and this company then handles the turnover that is later deposited with the bank, and if the bank didn't have the brightest head at the top, it wouldn't notice that the turnover of this company is much too high.
Consulting firms have no cash turnover	With a turnover that is as cash intensive as possible, i.e., not a company that only, I mean, I wouldn't set up a marketing company, because of course it doesn't have any cash turnover.
Consulting company for Eastern European clientele could already raise suspicion	If you don't already get on a special radar with the ... with the reference to consulting company for Eastern European, er, clientele.
Banks' know your customer requirements	A, you probably have to be able to take on this hurdle; it depends on the amounts and the bank's know your customer requirements.
Banks want to identify beneficial owners	So with us, um, if they push someone forward, then they still have the name somewhere. At the bank, at least, you have to state who the beneficial owner is.
Reduce risk through involvement of various jurisdictions	So the more countries are involved, the more difficult it becomes in terms of mutual legal assistance.
Attention through unusual cash fees	But in a consultancy, where it is paid in cash, that is rather unusual, and I think, um, there is a risk that the whole thing will get stuck.
Cash payments not normal for consulting firms	Even if they can be documented with an invoice, I find that cash payments for consultancies are not standard at all.
House bank could get suspicious about cash deposits	I think that the consulting firm's bank might become suspicious if amounts are repeatedly paid in cash.
Place the company under the control of a non-beneficial owner	If this company itself is not subordinate to the person, I don't know how one could, uh, reprimand this company, so to speak, yes, uh, as long as it is done properly.
Cash fees unusual	I find it very unusual, to be quite honest, if fees are paid in cash. I wouldn't be comfortable with that as a company.
Bank could become suspicious	I think that if (unintelligible) causes a stir, it is more likely to be at the bank.

Generalization	Quote
Anonymity of the beneficial owner no longer preserved	So that the beneficial owner can keep his anonymity, which he no longer has now anyway, but it used to be that way.
Traces must not get lost	If the traces get lost there then, then the risk.
Swiss clients must be traceable when audited	And if anyone gets the idea to check my books and sees that I actually, yes, to whom I, to whom, I bill, and where that comes from. There is also the question, how credible is that? If I am active in Switzerland and abroad, at least the Swiss accounts should be somehow traceable. I always say this from a tax perspective or from the perspective of a tax audit.
Appearance of credibility	I think the risk is, uh, the appearance of credibility, to build up the appearance of credibility, uh, in the first place, and then to maintain it.
Lack of Internet presence unusual	Er, only in a trade register entry. One wonders, what does she really do? That's, uh, conspicuous. When I, uh, present myself on the net with certain services, one soon asks oneself, yes, how is that judged? And, uh, how does she expose herself, uh, how does she present herself? How, uh, uh, with which persons does it appear? And then I have to build up a credible image.
Inactive companies stand out	Well, as soon as I show my company on the market somehow, everyone asks how it's actually doing, how does it stand there? How is it judged? It's a bit strange when I have a service company that is completely silent. You can't find it anywhere, not even on the web.
Banks demand proof of the origin of the money	And, uh, the thing is simple. As soon as I involve banks, they wonder, if they are regulated, where does the money come from? And then I have to show proof.
Plausibility check of cash amounts	And why cash?
Verifiable origin of the money	Uh. They ask, where does the money come from?
Invoice recipients should be verifiable	It's a bit awkward if I, uh, just produce a paper with some billing address on it, give the impression that I've sent it out, and then a deposit comes from somewhere. And, uh, from the –there should be the invoice recipient, should be somehow known or known, should be somehow verifiable that there is at least such a company.
Examination by public prosecutors and tax authorities often stops at the border	If anyone, be it the tax authorities or the public prosecutor's office, wants to check a company, it stops very quickly at the border.

Generalization	Quote
Administrative assistance	There anyway, so within the framework of administrative assistance. In the EU and with Double Tax Agreements and so on, we pass on bank data, bank information to EU countries and third countries. And for - and the next step now is, if the tax authorities examine Austrian entrepreneurs, then they have to - then Austrian banking secrecy no longer applies, and then they have to disclose more or less all accounts, bank details, in general.
Administrative assistance	And because of these grey lists, we have had to take a number of measures, including administrative assistance, i.e., not legal assistance.
Motivated and attentive investigators	The problem is that the colleagues firstly have to be motivated, and secondly, from the training point of view, it takes a bit, and there are not so many colleagues who are so motivated and who look over there and use the instruments of the authorities.
Bank must not accept black money	Yes, but not the bank, so today, it would be like this - the bank would not be allowed to accept the black money.
Bank must create customer profiles via companies	It also has to create a customer profile via the AG, and if the transactions then, uh, lead to there being, uh, doubts or deviations in the customer profile.
Commission payments	The concrete classic in corruption, Mr Teichmann, is commission. Somebody is told that you are entitled to a commission, and he also invoices you, not just an advisor, so somehow the commission taker invoices you and then gets at least part of the money. Or he is part of a money laundering chain and passes on part of it. So the commission is more for me, that's really factual knowledge now, in foreign corruption.
Pay taxes	Pays taxes on it and then gets to keep the money legally, yes? That is, as in all areas, you can also do that in the counselling sector.
Fake invoices	That you can do, you can fake consultancy fees - that's like all fake invoices, Mr Teichmann. That's a way to launder illegal money, so to speak, by showing consultancy fees in your, what do I know, in your annual overview.
Intra-group transactions	It's also, of course, the normal thing, uh, for the large amounts, they just make these dummy companies that do business with each other and everywhere there's some legal person behind it. And the (unintelligible) owner is incredibly difficult or even impossible to find out.
Website	Well, then I would ask myself, well, okay, there is, so that's something, if I saw such a test case, then I would probably first Google the consultancy company and look at it - does it exist at all?

Generalization	Quote
Use complex structures	So the more complex the matter becomes, the more financial centres are involved and the more complex the structures are, be they social structures or whatever, the more suitable the whole thing is, of course.
Amounts of the totals must be plausible	Um, of course, the whole thing has to be in – for the various sums involved, there have to be relations. You can't buy a property and make a restaurant out of it if you have scarce assets to launder. But if you have enough, you can build a restaurant in the best location and [clearing throat], uh, is not dependent on the actual success of the business.
Deposit money abroad	Always through the foreign criminals or those who deposit money, who also face a certain monitoring problem at the banks there, where the money comes in.
Found a company	Best to start a company.
Trade in goods of all kinds	Trade in goods of all kinds.
Transfer from Russia to Switzerland	If you pay it into a bank account there, and the Russian bank sends it to the Swiss bank, and the Swiss bank puts it into the blocked account for the foundation capital, and then you have (unintelligible) done it.
Transfer from Latvia to Switzerland	And the capital is delivered in cash, and then it's not immediately obvious that it's coming in cash. So no, it is transferred. It was transferred from Latvia to Switzerland.
Incorporate in Switzerland	Another good option is to set up a Swiss public limited company. Let's say someone from Latvia, that's what I'm saying, I'll just take it up now, someone from Latvia has a million in cash. And he then transfers it to a trustee in Zug and says, so that's what happened, uh, set me up a limited company.
Establish plausibility	So you have to explain what exactly your business activity is, and if it doesn't look plausible, then you have to expect that the bank will report it.
Concealment of the beneficial owner	With an international connection, where the beneficial owner can be kept under wraps as far as possible.
Subsidiaries abroad	So you have to have, um, sometimes [laughing], sisters abroad.
Involve companies abroad	Social structures. The more abroad the better.
Involve companies abroad	These are the many companies that are interconnected and that then also quickly go abroad and have other companies there, and so on.
Daily turnover must stand up to industry comparison	I'm convinced that you can also make industry comparisons and say, okay, for a clothing boutique, this order of magnitude, for this location, for this product, uh, are our empirical values that the daily turnover is in this range.

Generalization	Quote
Walk-in customers increase cash plausibility	So with walk-in business, yes, that is, with a restaurant or a garage or any other business where walk-in customers come and pay cash for products, as I said, products and you can say that is normal.
Establish plausibility	The question is always about the circumstances. So how plausible does the whole explanation actually seem?
Holding structure with trustee	Of course, in a holding structure, it can make perfect sense to involve a tax advisor or trustee to manage structures here and, for example, perfect tax issues and DTAs.
Include verifiable contracting parties	If the (unintelligible) then cares, yes who has, who is the recipient, who has paid, who has invoiced, who has been paid? And that must be a contractual party that is also verifiable.
Not only advertised through word of mouth	There is, I think just, with service companies, it is rather untypical that they are very discreetly (unintelligible), er, clientele accessible. I can of course specialize in, uh, I'll say art consultancy, for people who want to invest in art, and that's such a limited market that I could probably make a living from word of mouth.
Use capital contributions	From capital contribution or whatnot.
Include multiple levels of obfuscation	I let it run through several stages so that it doesn't actually show up directly with my alleged client as a receipt or as a cash deposit but is already transferred to him from some source or another.
Establish a legal entity abroad	This means, of course, that I would have to set up some kind of legal entity abroad, which would then receive the invoices.
Set up an actual consulting company	So a service is also provided in Switzerland, for example, then also fictitious services for which payment is then made in order to launder the money. And then I would hire a few people, set up an actual consulting company and invoice the services and then charge the services to fictitious recipients abroad and then collect the money from there.
Actually provide part of the services	It is important to ensure that if you make it so open or supposedly so open, that some part of it is actually provided.
Offer services at home and abroad	But, uh, it, on a very simplified structure, uh, then of course in Switzerland, a company can officially offer services at home and abroad.
Service abroad to ensure lack of verifiability	And that is already the case, foreign services abroad, for which a fee is then earned in Switzerland, is, uh, would be feasible, if the service cannot be verified, right.
Allow fees to land abroad	My experience is that services to foreign clients are typically controlled in the same way as the money ends up abroad and not in Switzerland at all. At least officially with a foreign legal entity. Because in Switzerland, a legal entity is more likely to attract attention, and you then ask yourself – who is it?

Generalization	Quote
Fictitious suppliers in a network of companies	I need a fictitious supplier. So I can't avoid building a network of different entrepreneurial activities, companies or something, in order to make the money look real.
Feign effort through acquisitions	And then, of course, uh, you can't just have turnover and no effort. So you have to get, uh, material, because of course I don't really want to buy the money for me, for me or the goods for a restaurant, and then throw it in the rubbish; uh, I buy that without really buying it.
Non-verifiable services	To build up a network of activities, services by name, i.e., services that cannot be physically verified, in order to make the money that flows back and forth look like income for it.
Different companies with fictitious service relationships with each other	Uh, uh, by incorporating various companies that maintain service relationships/officially service relationships with each other and feed these funds into them, even if these services do not exist.
Working with neighbouring countries	So that the path of money laundering is not far, and ultimately the requirement for this other service comes from an EU neighbouring country and (unintelligible) that then comes from a bad, grey or black-light-afflicted country.
Charge for market analyses	In terms of sales tax, they invoice other services or market analyses and so on in order to raise money from a neighbouring country and then pass it on to offshore areas, and these offshore areas then have a bank account in Switzerland, Vienna and Lake Zurich, and so on.
Transfer funds via offshore centres and loans	The money ends up, ultimately, at an offshore centre, a model, just then worth the loans to the civilized world ultimately (unintelligible, quietly) to have a comfortable standard of living.
Offshore companies with accounts in different jurisdictions	Because the company is an offshore company and the account is somewhere else.
Fake business expenses	A correspondingly huge turnover, yes, you need a certain percentage to reduce operating expenses, to invest or to transfer abroad.
Always accept tax assessment notices	So even if I reduce the tax burden, of course I will accept the payments I have to make.
Society in Switzerland	And then, for example, a company in Switzerland, with which one can then move throughout Europe.
Representative business address with forwarding order	I would also look at where I can buy additional services, such as representative business addresses, where I only have a forwarding order, address lists and so on. So that's how I would structure it.
Choose destinations without an equity check	Might want to select a destination where equity is not verified, but there would be high equity.

Generalization	Quote
Involve existing societies	So one, perhaps I would preferably buy a stock that was founded years ago. Of course, that can also document a certain history, that this company has been around for a while.
Organized crime	I mean, we are then very quickly in the realm of organized crime, and organized criminals do business with each other, of course.
Not yet in circulation	So in the end, yes, he hasn't really brought it into the economic cycle yet. Actually, it only brings him half a step further.
Difficult to detect	So you really won't be able to determine that as a rule.
Deep milieu	But that is very, everything they are talking about, in a very deep milieu, really in criminal, deep narcotics area and so on. But the, let's say, with the tax, you should then already in the (unintelligible) because it is, after all, inter-corruption and laundering these funds. The over-factorization serves the factorization and that is, of course, a big issue. But of course, yes, that – the narcotics traffickers need that.
Bitcoin transactions can be traced	We have a big project with Bitcoin, so Austria and Germany, and, yes, Bitcoin is just as much a possibility, but if you adapt the software, if you manage that, that you then ultimately recognize, because the Bitcoin, you can trace the transactions, for example.
Corrupt government	So when you have government corruptors who are now in the oil and gas business, yes, there are relatively many and large sums going out – in and out.
Financial intermediary with criminal intent	If the financial intermediary himself brings criminal intent to light, then it is difficult to grasp. Because it is not because the control mechanisms would not be effective.
Professional foreign exchange traders	I'm a lawyer and once had a client who lived from cash currency trading, i.e., currency exchange.
App searches for money launderers	Um, and they say okay, um, we would like to transfer money even more cheaply, they have written an app for us, you can register and the system searches for it, so to speak.
Costs	It works, not always favourably, but it works.
New technologies	New technologies that exist to send assets from A to B.
Two money launderers with different currencies	Okay, I have dollars and you have euros. I need euros, you need dollars, we settle it at the same time.
Counterfeit banknotes	Now, of course, there are the big counterfeit notes, trade-in for real, yes, or illegal, contaminated with addiction, narcotics, certainly contaminated.
Settle cash via central banks	I mean, what we also see in part is that, uh, ultimately, yes, state authorities also make use of money laundering means in part and, and ultimately channel funds past the official, uh, central banking or banking system.

Generalization	Quote
Use app to bring money launderers together	So the system is so intelligent; so it brings people together and says okay, you want to have euros there and you want to have euros in another country, and sometimes that it is just quasi-transferred from country to country – it is just calculated, and the transaction only takes place within the, uh, state and the destination country and no longer across borders.
Settle differences electronically via app	But you have a Latvian in London who wants to transfer euros home, but then you have someone in Latvia who wants to transfer euros to the UK and there is no transaction at all, let alone a physical transaction between Latvia and England, but not even an electronic one, but only the, only the difference is transferred, so to speak.
Avoid financial intermediaries	They do not go through a regular financial intermediary, i.e., one, just one filter point that has leaked and the [laughing] other, a fishnet – contaminated water leaks out, because, um, they say we don't even go into this area or where one, where we have to go through a regular financial intermediary.
Bogus invoices as a tool	Um, we do current account accounting; we create so much high cash volume, then the balance is drawn in the month and then some fictitious transfer is triggered, i.e., with some fictitious invoice, the transfer is triggered, um, when 2 million are then sent from A to B in order to balance the account. So these are forms of cooperation that we have already seen.
Netting between criminals	Um, probably it goes in the direction of, um, transfer business. Yes, so, um, we have for example, in a city in the south of the country, they have forgotten a high, um, a high, a high generation. For example, there are street drug dealers. In every city, they produce a lot of cash, and in another city, they have a high demand for cash because, for example, many American tourists come ashore on cruise ships and buy all the euros at the port in the exchange office. They need a lot of cash. And instead of shipping the money from one city to the other for each transaction, we do a combination business between the two, don't we?
Trust in correspondent banks	Theoretically, these banks should have fulfilled their money laundering obligations there and then they are correspondent banks and transfer the money here to Germany. Then it is not problematic from a German point of view, because it comes from a reliable correspondent bank.
Free trade zones	I would do it through one of these free trade zones in Dubai and, um, uh, maybe consult a relevant bank there [laughs].
Offshore banking	But these, so these stories can be relatively well alternated throughout some Central African countries and banks at the moment. Um, I wouldn't do that, but there are only, I think, very stable offshore banking places, uh, be it the Channel Islands, but also Singapore or Dubai. So in Dubai, we see quite a lot at the moment where that's still quite possible.

Generalization	Quote
Standards theoretically exist, but implementation is unclear	Um, that is, they more or less meet the standards. But the question is certainly justified, or are they also effectively implemented?
Dubai, Singapore and Hong Kong are popular	Dubai, Singapore, Hong Kong – these are destinations that are very much on the rise.
No longer exotic	Dubai is no longer so exotic.
Dubai not on the grey list	There are still Dubai and Co., and until today, there are no, uh, I haven't seen these countries on any grey list of FADs.
Cash-sensitive society	I mean, it's a cash-based society. It's easy to get rid of cash. It's easy to deal in cash, er, because you've got a lot of money exchanges there as well.
Dubai does not take anti-money laundering seriously	But I would, the problem with Dubai is that whereas in some financial centres, anti-money laundering is treated a bit more seriously, in my view, it's not treated very seriously in the UAE, and there's no enforcement by the regulator.
Banks get in trouble when you report money laundering suspicions	Erm, when they do have a suspicious activity report and they make it, the, the Financial Intelligence Unit in the UAE sits within the Central Bank, which is the wrong place for it to sit. It ought to sit with law enforcement, and, erm, as a consequence, every time the bank makes a compliance, er, a suspicious activity report, the Central Bank then comes and, and, and, erm, hits the bank, because they opened the account in the first place.
Banks have no incentive to make money laundering suspicious activity reports	Erm, so, the poor old banks are very reluctant to make suspicious activity reports. There's no, no encouragement to make them, because if they do, they know they're going to get told off by the Central Bank for opening the account in the first place.
Incompetent or inattentive compliance departments	I now have someone sitting there in the area of compliance who really only adheres to the prescribed rules and perhaps has relatively little foresight as far as the phenomenon as a whole is concerned, then a money launderer probably wouldn't recognize it either if it said money laundering in the subject line.
Very secretive banks	If they want to have ID from the customer or something and it cannot be transmitted to them by the bank.
Few cooperative banks	The credit institutions in the European area do not have the ability to obtain certain information.
Restricted freedom of the press	Um, I think the free press factor plays a big role, because often cases are not discovered by investigators but by the media or at least spread [by them].
Unsuspicious environment	Apart from that, you need an unsuspicious environment – you need a highly professional financial centre that offers you everything they want.

Generalization	Quote
Correspondent banks are partly no longer accepted	If, of course, they don't do this de facto, or there are also some indications that some banks are no longer accepted as correspondent banks. Because it is known that they do not do this and do not fulfil their obligations.
Police dogs at the airport sniff out cash	Yes, and if they have larger quantities in the suitcase, the dogs sniff that out. That can be the same in Dubai.
Foreign jurisdiction	The foreign legal system; I don't know if that's probably a bit unpredictable.
Foreign jurisdiction	It is subject to a completely different legal system, which is probably a risk. I mean, the risk for the money launderer.
Message based on few plausible explanations	And then he made a strange declaration – first, none at all, and then a not entirely plausible declaration. And then they made a suspicious activity report to the Money Laundering Reporting Office.
Queries from the bank in Switzerland	When a Swiss bank is involved, that is now the case with us, that was the case. The money came from Dubai to a bank account in Switzerland, and Switzerland, the bank inquired with the accused and with its client where the money came from.
Money laundering reporting by the bank	This can, of course, come to light via a money laundering report from a bank.
Information is sold	Hm, and there is certainly also a leak sometimes, and information is sold.
Dependence on compliance officers	So I think that especially in the money laundering compliance area, a lot really depends on the action and people.
Increased due diligence of the bank	The question is rather what standards of due diligence do our banks apply? That is, how do European banks deal with the fact that they have a counterpart in Dubai or somewhere else?
Hidden controls due to sanctions against Iran	For us, the banks in the [United] Arab Emirates are not (unintelligible) high-risk banks because we suspect that money laundering is being carried out there, which would also be possible, of course, but rather, as European banks, we have the problem that sanctions with Iran, where one notices in a few isolated cases, however, that the sanctions can be used as a substitute.
Dubai unobtrusive	But Dubai is, uh, already like that [laughing], just no longer unusual or noticeable.
Residence or place of business in Dubai no longer exceptional	It's kind of within reach, it's well known, it's nothing special, so it's ALREADY, but for rich people, it's not necessarily like that. Uh (...) unbelievable or unusual to reside or do business there, and that's why I can list this destination as, uh, as a business place without seeming exotic.
Correspondent banks could pose queries	We also know today that the reason for this is that the correspondent banks are unable to track transactions and to evaluate this information.

Generalization	Quote
Correspondent bank	There is the famous keyword: correspondence bank.
Complex uses	With such large companies, it's a bit more complex. There is a concrete reference to invoices, to projects. It simply looks different.
Consider transaction analyses of the financial intermediaries	Everything must always be seen in the context of the entire business activity, of course. Um, the transaction analysis, which of course has to be set up per client, per activity, etc. So if the client receives a certain monthly amount from Dubai due to his activity, and this is accordingly plausible - so, the financial intermediary could plausibilize this accordingly - then this is of course unproblematic.
Use straw men for companies in free trade zones	You know, the Filipino maid or somebody will give you their passport too, you know, so it's pretty easy.
Establish a company in a free trade zone	Well, it's pretty easy to establish companies. There's 32 or 33 free zones in the UAE, most of them in Dubai and other smaller emirates. And you can set up a company there very quickly and easily for a bit of cash, erm, and then just - and then get a bank account and hide behind it.
Document processes and justify legal background	A clarification also includes documenting the processes and then you also have to weigh up the legal background.
Direct transfers	That is, if I make a payment instead of, I'll say some example now from Portugal to Switzerland, I make the diversions via Mexico, Singapore and I don't know where to, uh, then of course I have to clarify that, and I have to say, why did they make this diversion, why no direct bank connection to Switzerland?
Avoid detours when transferring money	So if, for example, instead of making a direct transfer to a destination country, I make it via detours with several correspondent bank relationships and so on, then that is very unusual, and I have to justify that, don't I?
Pay straw men well	People I give a lot of money to for their job. So, if someone shows up as an account holder and gets enough money for it, then I have to think ten times, um, if they go against the trustor, as long as they get enough money for it every year.
Use professional secrecy holders as stooges	So it's a question of those who are themselves subject to professional secrecy; for example, lawyers are increasingly at risk because even if they are the subject of an investigation, they are not allowed to testify, and those who are subject to professional secrecy [obligations] are suitable for such functions.
Use straw men from the same island	People from the same island tend to stick together, don't talk about each other with people from outside the island. Um, then that helps me, so certainly one person who/with whom I have absolute trust, so that's one variant.

Generalization	Quote
Avoid banks with good risk systems	I would go where it is not noticeable and [where] I know that a bank has a good risk system; it will not control payments from Germany as intensively as those from Lichtenstein or Russia or Afghanistan or Canada.
Avoid countries that give authorities access to financial transaction data	As a money launderer, avoid countries where the authorities have relatively direct access to financial transaction data.
Suitable paper trail	That would be a good paper trail to create, for example.
Ideal value of the companies	So, this is of course a general problem concerning companies, goodwill ... ideal value, and so on and so forth.
Flexible assessor	That is, of course, a question of how receptive someone is to writing a fake expert opinion.
Fake typical industry sales to pass balance sheet exam	Because you can also see from the balance sheet roughly how the company's business (unintelligible) is going, whether it is also typical for the sector, what they do. Or a kiosk owner who has a raw cash turnover, but a marketing company does not have a high cash turnover, and so you can also see how the stocks are, the cash balances, do they have high accounts? Account balances? Do they have high deposits? 'Yes/no'.
Find companies in need of investment	Yes, you also have to find such companies where you can make such investments.
Company conglomerate able to write off losses	Yes, you can deduct it again for tax purposes; so, if you have a conglomerate where you say, okay, I'm investing in a new company or in an ailing company and I'm now making a loss, can I then offset it against a part of the business that is run according to business principles but that I can write off for tax purposes?
Nobody asks questions	So that no one asks questions.
Nobody wants to know where money comes from	I want to know where that comes from, but you probably don't make yourself very popular if you then ask all-too-critical questions during company restructuring.
Willingness to lose money	Because the money launderers are willing to spend a certain percentage, um, apparently, to make their assets look legal.
No critical questions	And because there is no critical questioning.
Distressed society with many jobs at risk	Um, where I can say, um, listen, it's maybe suffering, maybe even distressed, um, and there are a lot of jobs at stake.
Maintain actual activity	It is important here that there really is an activity that can then also be, um, that can then also be, um, put back into shoes.
Use reputable appraisers	Certain plausibility checks take place and I mean, if some backyard auditor comes in with an expert on the valuation, I would be rather suspicious.

Generalization	Quote
Involved authorities not specialized in the AMLA	In the case of company restructurings, authorities are involved, of course, which basically have more to do with the Anti-money Laundering Act, if at all. Um, you might have to look at that; I don't think that this was and is an issue in the international area.
Traders without credit stand out	There are hardly any tradespeople today who don't need a loan. If a company opens an account and doesn't need a loan but has a high turnover, you'd be surprised.
Balance sheet must be submitted with loan application	And for that they need a balance sheet first. But in Germany, they only get the balance sheet if they also give the company a loan. If the company doesn't need a loan, it is also suspected.
Banks/tax authorities want balance sheet	That's why we have to take a look; with companies, we feel sorry when we have a balance sheet from the company.
Financial loss	Financial risk, so if you invest in a distressed company that is trying to be restructured, then there is a great risk that it will not be successful. So to speak, that you have to write off the investment.
Investment risk	The focus is on rescuing the ailing company and that an investor accepts the risk, so to speak, of making an investment, of making a rescue, and that the chance of selection is relatively high after all.
Questions about the origin of the assets	And whether one then asks oneself the question, where do these assets come from?
Financial loss	On the contrary, one is glad that there is an investor who is willing to take a financial risk, uh, and inject assets and accept a loss.
Trade register entries	And then the question will probably arise with the new entry in the company register or with any other, let's say, actions, which in turn require a lawyer or a notary.
Involvement of groups subject to reporting requirements	Again, if there, if the transacting person falls under the reportable occupation, then they have to look.
Credible representation	I think the question here is how do I credibly demonstrate that I and an investor want to invest 10 million, or 50 million, in an ailing production company?
Company reorganizations difficult to follow in practice	Company reorganizations themselves, practical cases where we cannot pursue [them] to the end, would also be conceivable.
Consider balance sheet and valuation methods	The question of course is always what we have on the [balance sheet], and if you see restructuring now, what the valuation actually looks like.

Generalization	Quote
Take out a loan to avoid attracting attention	So I would always take out a loan as a company, of course at the risk of being asked for more balance sheets. But I would somehow take it out on credit, but only to the extent that I could pay it back again gradually. But simply so that the company wouldn't notice it so much.
Check plausibility	You have to go to a lot of trouble to present it as well as possible.
Gratitude for new capital prevails	Many people, at least the employees of the company, perhaps also the management or existing shareholders, will be very grateful when an investor comes in and injects fresh capital.
Searching for distressed companies with analysts and specialists	Then I look for this from an analyst or specialist environment, there are distressed companies and they say they are trying to get in there as an investor and save this company, so to speak.
Companies in need of redevelopment abound	I would look for companies that are in need of renovation, and in this day and age, there are probably plenty to choose from.
No control over the origin of the rescuer	No one cares where the saviour comes from when he brings assets.
Company renovations exciting	In the field of corporate restructuring, I find it incredibly exciting.
Credibly demonstrate origin	To declare smaller transactions or to actually pretend to have more in order to then credibly present a large fortune. And then I can invest it where I want. The origin is then, um, credibly presented and is not significantly less questioned.
Disguise true investor through many small investors	Then I, uh, pretend to have many, many small, smaller investments, uh, [to] bring together a large amount and invest it as a single investor behind whom there are supposedly many different ones. That way I can present it in a more or less credible way.
Business angels group	Especially if it's a group, and I think that if you put it into a kind of investment and, uh, it doesn't have to be an investment fund, but maybe also a private, uh, grouping, a private company, which brings together business angels, then not individuals, but a group and says, we'll each bring 5 million, and with this money, we'll invest in an industry that interests us.
Foreign investors less critical	Or that someone brings money into it, but when I come with foreign investors, sooner or later the questions just stop.
Hidden reserves as justification	[Invest in] real estate or in a somewhat ailing enterprise and then officially bring it up to scratch and realize the hidden reserves and the potential, the performance potential. And with both, the question arises, how credible is it that I am putting money into this?
Assume a price fantasy	So one assumes a corresponding price fantasy then. The buyers then all sell and resell the company shares accordingly.

Generalization	Quote
Observe retractability of replacement gold	But if I now have black money and I buy gold with it, then the money is gone and I can no longer confiscate it, but I have a substitute asset, and according to the Criminal Code, I can then assert a claim for substitution and confiscate this gold. That means it's not so safe if I just change the medium of exchange.
Change of value carrier and traceability	And then I have actually already taken the next step of money laundering and have actually already laundered the money. The value carrier changes, if you are right, the, uh, the traceability changes and thus also the, um, the proof of collectability.
Pure asset swap	And when I now, when I buy gold for this money, for the black money, I ask myself, first of all, with whom and how do I get to buy this at all? Through pure active exchange. In other words, an exchange of assets. You are right to say that the bearer of value changes, but the value remains.
Inference of origin through remelting impossible	Um, the nice thing is, I can remelt it, so I can avoid any inference of origin.
Documentation of origin	Gold, I will have to document where I bought it.
Gold dealers are subject to Art. 2, para. 3 AMLA	Uh, and these businesses are, according to Art. 2, para. 3 GWB, subject to the Money Laundering Act. Accordingly, we receive a few reports again and again from these gold traders, etc.
Quantities easily traceable due to standardized prices	With gold, on the other hand, every buyer or seller wants to know the approximate price of gold at the moment. No, so if they bring 50,000 to the bank here on one day, because they say, I sold so-and-so many gold pieces, you know exactly, aha, it must have been so-and-so many goods or so-and-so many kilograms to generate that, and then the customer has to prove again out of embarrassment, where did I get the others, where did I buy them, I would have to be able to produce receipts. So, that is difficult to manipulate, I think.
Fixed price	Well, there is also a fixed price for gold.
Acquisition is registered	Gold has to be acquired somewhere, so it has to be registered again.
Several people involved	It is also noticeable, there are many people involved when it comes to larger amounts.
Theft at the airport	That they are then stolen at the airport.
Theft during transport	There is a danger that it will also get lost on the way.
Difficult to transport	But otherwise, gold is of course, uh, yes, it already has a specific weight. So, a kilo of gold is a kilo of gold and, uh, yes, it's not so easy to transport.

Generalization	Quote
Purchase is registered	In itself, it is of course also a problem; theoretically, it is registered with Redflex of the FADs. So if you now buy a gold bar at the bank or at the big gold dealers, then you still have to declare it, because above the threshold of 15,000 et cetera, et cetera – he will say 'where [is it] from?'
Fraud with bullion gold	We personally have big, um, frauds with gold, with gold bullion.
High volatility	The disadvantage is that it is highly volatile, so if you invested everything in gold as a money launderer three years ago, you have also lost a lot in the meantime.
Profit-taking in the event of positive price development	Yes, you can also see it as an investment, and when the price goes up, it's, uh, usual to sell it again, profit taking.
Easily transferable	And that is much easier to transfer, to transfer to physical gold.
Leave in the safe and transfer only the property rights	So, I wouldn't move that around too much, that gold, but probably leave that in a, uh, safe and really just transfer the ownership rights.
Transfer ownership rights in the bonded warehouse	Um, they don't even have to move it; they can leave it in there and transfer the ownership there.
Duty-free warehouse	I would leave it in the duty-free warehouse. But no one looks in there.
Storage in a bonded warehouse	And I think the bonded warehouses are also a problem. And, uh, that, uh, because I think you could read a lot about that recently. It's also well known. Uh, there is already a, a big problem, that, uh, value, such mobile material assets are stored somewhere in an international area and never leave it. They leave, they change the owner maybe, maybe not even that, they stay there and nobody has any, really no knowledge about it. There, uh, is certainly a risk there. But here, I'm not sure how far the inventory obligation of the, uh, warehouse keepers goes. Whether they really know what, whether they have to record or know what exactly is in there.
Proof of black money already broken through purchase	If I place money in a broad anonymous mass in order to buy up something that is of value, that is correct, then I am actually already interrupting the proof of black money there.
Buy gold together and recast	Of course, I can also buy gold and such together with my black money somewhere and then melt it down and sell it to a gold dealer, a licensed gold dealer, and say, yes, I bought this family heirloom.

Generalization	Quote
Consider the assets and tax returns of the deceased in order to remain credible	And of course, the wealthier someone is, the more there is in it, so to speak. I can come along with ten pictures, with, uh, 20 kilos of gold as a family inheritance, that's more credible than if I, as a simple wage earner, suddenly come along with 20 kilos, with 20 kilos of gold, which I supposedly inherited and, uh, which my relatives – if you look at the tax returns, that's actually, uh, that doesn't appear anywhere.
Present as an inheritance	Although I had just bought it with black money a short time before, I present it as an old inheritance that I have discovered somewhere.
Gold is VAT free	We have said that these transactions are free of VAT and (unintelligible), and a number of EU states already have this sol–, this solution, because ultimately, gold is a problem in the VAT area.
Wholesalers turn granules/jewellery into bullion	There are big gold dealers who buy the – like a, like, yes, granules, who buy jewellery and so on, and from these, from these purchases, again [turn it] into gold bullion.
Gold bullion is VAT free in the EU	In the EU, gold bullion is in itself VAT free, VAT exempt, because investment gold is the fraud method, and if you then change to the re-taxation and through the taxation you end up in (Carousel) fraud.
Lawyers' and notaries' duty of confidentiality	The lawyers, the notaries, do not report. There is also the legal problem of the conflict with the legal obligation to maintain secrecy.
Suitable for purchase and redevelopment	Whether you spend the money on renovation or on buying directly, it remains the same in principle.
Market volatility	Well, I mean, there are prominent examples of properties on Lake Geneva that cost 3 million yesterday and go for over 10 million the next day.
Awareness not given	So the people who are employed in the respective occupational areas, um, they simply don't perceive the risk at all.
Awareness not given	And that's also because the awareness is simply not there at all, so to speak.
Potential danger and suspicious activity reports are disproportionate	The disproportion between the alleged potential danger and the actual suspicious activity reports is simply great.
Possibilities for concealment exist	That means there would be enough lending opportunities and it is a really safe investment.
Stable investment	So it's like this. On the one hand, it is always clear to everyone that, especially in the area of real estate trading, it is a stable investment, which means that I have few losses in normal cases.
Neglected area	I think that's, uh, I think I can really speak for the whole of Europe when I say that this is a very neglected area.

Generalization	Quote
Properties in distant countries to conceal	That means I can always legitimize a relatively large amount of money with the sale of a plot of land. Who goes to these Caribbean islands and measures how big the property is and how much it was really worth? So I can already buy, um, in, um, I say, um, lottery properties and then apparently sell them at a high price and thus legitimize a high flow of money.
Suitable for legitimizing funds	What is very nice about real estate is that when you have to legitimize money somewhere, when you have to legitimize the receipt of money vis-à-vis a bank that asks a question, for example, or vis-à-vis the authorities, there is almost nothing nicer than saying, 'here, I have sold a property'.
Last stage in the process	Um, real estate certainly comes at the very end of the process, when it comes to the fact that pre-laundered money is simply also invested.
Inattentive notaries and estate agents	If I now make such a purchase, then both the notary and the broker would have to register and record this purchase price and the brokerage contract accordingly. Now an idiot comes along with good German who overpays and there you would have a trace of the money launderer again.
Vendor accepts cash	First, you have to find someone who will sell you the property for cash.
Lawyers and notaries act in good faith	Well, and then of course you go, then of course you go to the notary, to the lawyer, et cetera. Well, and then they think the bank reports it, or the lawyer, or the notary, et cetera, et cetera. Everyone believes that the other person is making a suspicious activity report.
Liquid real estate market	And if I am such a reasonably liquid real estate agent, where I know I can buy and sell and don't have to accept large losses in value, um, then of course I can take advantage of that by bringing large funds into circulation.
Queries from the bank	The bank would have to ask where the money came from and if the estate agent says he got it from a house sale, then he would have to say 'Aha, who gave you that in cash?'
Tax authorities could question the origin of money for refurbishments	That the real estate sector is certainly problematic, that the monitoring is there, that both the tax authorities are not very cooperative.
Notary part of the anti-money laundering system	That is, the example of real estate, or when you buy real estate, uh, it is very difficult not to get somewhere through a bank or through a notary or whatever. Uh, and this, uh, is then at best part of the, uh, the anti-money laundering system.
Notary involved	A notary is also involved in principle. Under certain circumstances, he is also subject to the law.
Various persons involved who are subject to the AMLA	On the one hand, there are various persons involved who are subject to the Money Laundering Act and usually, um, the financial flows go through a bank.

Generalization	Quote
Real estate transfer tax	He has to pay the high land transfer tax; he has to pay notary fees, and he makes a loss on top of that. That could be noticeable.
Notary must register contract	If you are now a real estate buyer, of course you might get the idea, the notary has to register the whole thing, of course.
Value loss	People don't care about the loss, the money launderers.
Shoppers who do not look serious stand out	Yes, depending on the case, this can lead to a report if the buyer leaves the impression that something is not good afterwards. So it really depends on who the buyer was, doesn't it?
Traceable cash flow	If the purchase contract stated that the money would be transferred from a bank account, that it would be transferred from the bank, and that it would still be paid in cash, one would find out later, at least to some extent, that this flow of money did not take place in this way, but in a different way.
Documented property payment	Maybe afterwards, when you see, um, if something happens, everything is on record, how the property was paid for. Then of course you can trace it back.
Notary could raise suspicion	The first person who might notice would be the notary. I don't know, he won't take care of it, at least he has no legal obligation to do so. Yes, it's not very risky, I think.
Risk of detection low	I consider the risk of criminal assets that are being moved being discovered to be rather low.
Unpredictable fluctuations in value	That you can't sell it for as much money as you would have liked.
Value loss	That, uh, the market corrects towards the bottom.
Business risk	There is an economic risk, but I think people are happy to accept that.
Little criticism of property redevelopment	When redeveloping a property, I don't think there are too many critical voices.
Little resistance to redevelopment of dilapidated properties	But on the other hand, if an old dilapidated property is turned into a chic residential property, um, probably few protests, uh, voices will appear.
Critical questions about value enhancement	So the only critical questions that could come up is, so to speak, if the cheap housing is then subsequently converted into expensive housing, so that can lead to questions.
Few critical questions	There are no critical questions asked, but people are happy that an investor comes and invests in a property and upgrades it.
Media attention	The media love it when you say, especially in the real estate business, 'Ah, the daughter of a Central Asian ruler has bought a villa for 75 million in the Lake Geneva area'.
Attention of law enforcement	Um, because if you stand out, then there are always people from the law enforcement scene, police officers and maybe even public prosecutors, who take a look at something.

Generalization	Quote
Strong regulation through land registry and public notarization	That may not be as easy as one imagines or because the real estate market is relatively highly regulated with the land registry and notarized contracts and so on.
Lawyers and notaries could report	Then we usually have lawyers and notaries who are responsible for signing the contracts. And I believe that there is already a bit of a safety net. So if a situation were really totally suspicious, I believe that one of the people involved would report it.
Various companies involved	So you don't just have the seller and the buyer, but you also have a real estate agent, or, in the case of redevelopment, a company that takes care of the whole thing.
Involvement of groups subject to reporting requirements	Yes, so you have, you have of course, um, let me say, in a real estate business there are usually relatively many professional groups involved that have to report [suspicious activity].
Real estate agent could trigger SAR	Whether it's really an estate agent in the sense that we get a suspicious activity report from someone like that, it hasn't really happened, to my knowledge.
Secure investment opportunity	A much safer investment opportunity almost doesn't exist.
Offshore structures are not accepted	But we do not accept offshore [structures].
Provide evidence of the origin of the funds	Then my customer will have to prove to me who is sending me this money. Otherwise, I will send it back, or, if there is any suspicion, a report must be filed.
Origin of the money is questioned	Of course, especially with real estate, I have to ask myself where the money comes from.
Source of funds is controlled	This means, of course, that more attention should be paid to the source of funds than to the use of funds.
Foreigners less transparent and thus privileged	This means that if I come from abroad, I have a significantly lower risk than if I am Swiss. And they know everything about me here. Then I can, then I can, I can rehabilitate relatively well from abroad. But from Switzerland, it's relatively difficult.
Comparison of financial performance	The comparison of the, uh, the, uh, the financial performance has to work out.
Assessment by tax authorities for untaxed rehabilitation funds	And then, uh … that's a, that's a real risk, as an investor I have to be able to prove that I actually earned the money myself from somewhere, and if I didn't declare it or can't prove a corresponding source, then my income will be included in the next assessment or in the previous, new assessment. And I can accept this risk, then I pay taxes on it, but, um, that is not impossible, uh, that the suspicion of money laundering arises here.

Generalization	Quote
Tax authorities could question origin of money for refurbishments	At some point the tax authorities will ask themselves, where did this investor get so much money? That he can redevelop a property complex for 10 million? Where does the money come from?
Official tracks dangerous	Not with the seller, but with the, uh, with regard to the buyer. But, um, that's why pure, the purchases, everything that leaves, uh, official traces, I consider critical.
Questions from the bank when cash is deposited by sellers	And then maybe the seller's bank wonders, when he receives his 1.5 million in a small case and wants to bring it to the bank, where he got it from. And then he says he got it from his buyer, anyway, and then that raises concerns.
Notaries and banks in Switzerland critical	I think purchases in Switzerland are, um, critical. Because here, the notaries, and then also the banks, would have to ask themselves, where is the money coming from?
Banks attentive	The banks are on their way, the legal professions still have deficits.
Low sanctions for missing SAR by notary public	So, it, it is missing, and that is perhaps the message to them, or in general, the sanction mechanism is missing. If the notary gets EUR 3 million from me and the Eastern Bloc and buys real estate with it, and he doesn't raise suspicions or doesn't question the matter. Then, in my opinion, he must reckon with the withdrawal of his licence. He must have the consequence. Then much more will start rolling.
Buy properties in need of renovation	That very strange houses are being bought that are completely rundown and where there is a considerable need for renovation, sometimes at a relatively high price, which is also being done relatively quickly.
Appoint own notaries	If it's criminals who behave directly like that, it's, there's a scene that also has its own 'notaries', in inverted commas. Who, of course, wouldn't do a damn thing to report anything then. There are involved notaries and lawyers for every purpose, also with the OK.
Fake rental agreements	And then you can also fake rental agreements, produce rental income, which then turns the illegal assets into legal assets, so to speak. Because rental inflows come in that were not there in reality.
Fake credits	The one who, so to speak, finances himself externally with a fictitious loan, then he has bought the property without now, uh, and even his money perhaps from the origin – provided that the external financing is accepted, uh, that is then okay and it is paid for.
Disguised granting of credit from the buyer's capital	One acts as a buyer and gets that, the real estate financed by some other or by a banking institution; however, it then comes about, that and that, this granting of credit is basically disguised from the actual incriminated capital of the buyer.

Generalization	Quote
Form a team	But you can now work in the real estate sector, but that's not something you have to reveal now, so if someone, of course, you also need people to help you. Not one person can do it alone.
Avoid transactions from offshore destinations	Now the question is, where does the money come from? Maybe it was transferred for the purchase of real estate. The bank is satisfied with that because it is also plausible with the story that the client told me in Austria. The question is, where does the money come from beforehand, if it keeps coming from the Cayman Islands? So I would question that again.
Declare the wrong purchase price	However, the residual risk remains, of course, as it is known that the amounts here are not all always declared as they should be and, uh, probably, uh, cash amounts also flow.
Sell at a loss if necessary	Then you get the flat. Like this. Even though it might only be worth 500,000 or 480,000. Then you have a flat, and even if you sell it later at a loss, let's say EUR 400,000, you have at least laundered a large part of the money.
Excessive prices to secure surcharges	So if I say I have a flat here in Munich, for example, with a nominal value of, let's say, EUR 500,000, and now an estate agent advertises this price and says to you 'Yes, I already have three other interested parties'. So you say to him, 'I'll give you EUR 600,000'.
Use subsidiaries in offshore centres	Let's say the company in Zug, they buy a property, it's then paid for by their subsidiary from the Cayman Islands or something.
Choose inconspicuous names and persons	So anyway, yes, so, I don't know or with, just with a name that doesn't stand out so much or just with an, um, business background that can be explained, or, yes. That's how it is somehow. The whole environment makes the decisive impression.
Do not choose unusual activities	So, if possible, not to attract attention and to do something where no critical questions are asked.
Properties in need of renovation in neighbourhoods with a high proportion of foreigners	These are usually not the properties in the best locations, but I go to neighbourhoods with a high proportion of foreigners, uh, properties that are in need of renovation, um, I buy the whole property plus the building, renovate it or sell it again afterwards, uh, on a condominium basis, um, individually and make a nice profit.
Avoid attention	Um, that's attention, so I want to avoid that, but I look for objects where I can see that it's also worth buying and investing there.
Do not stand out	Yes, I would; so, I think the top device is, uh, that I don't stand out as a money launderer.
No great demand	Nevertheless, it is a good way to at least invest assets without there being much demand for them.
Real estate suitable	Real estate is an area I like.

Generalization	Quote
Use straw men and companies	I can invest really well, can also buy, um, as a company, can use straw men.
Credible origin of the money	But it is of course, if I have the origin and the money is not incriminated, then I lack the foreshadowing, then the use per se, is also relatively difficult to recognize as money laundering.
Luxury refurbishment of existing properties	If, on the other hand, I have an existing property and simply renovate it in luxury with a lot of money, then it looks a bit different. Even if the, um, if the companies all invoice properly and account for it and book it themselves. But they are not obliged to report anything.
Find a tolerant notary to avoid queries in case of cash payment	Of course, I could look for a notary who doesn't ask so many questions and then pay for everything in cash.
Charge excessive rents	Then it's on the Internet. It is then rented out so expensively that unfortunately no customers come.
Acquisition of real estate and leasing as the purpose of the company	Has the intention, must have it, yes, to carry out the property acquisition or the intention to rent it out.
Cypriot shell companies as intermediaries	So it is then, I think, rather owners who buy a Cypriot, uh, yes Cyprus; if now a buyer who owns shell companies buys a Cypriot company, they know.
Control market value via easement agreements	So before certain encumbrances flow in, or encumbrance and sale prohibitions, rights of use that are registered, whether the right is there or not, that of course has an effect on the market value. And accordingly, I think I can also control it.
Acquire real estate through companies	So it will be done through companies; the owner is then the company. I then sell the shares of the company. And so the new owner of the company shares is also the owner of the property.
Sub-securitizations	There may be cash in hand payments, which are cash, yes.
Payments under CHF 100,000 cash	So you never pay for real estate in cash. The most you can do is make a down payment in cash, and the money laundering law restricts payments over CHF 100,000, so it has to be processed through a financial intermediary.
Select problematic properties	Because the municipality where this property is located is somehow happy that someone has finally come and bought this property. The notary has no obligation whatsoever to make any effort to find out whether it was really worth that much. The bank, which perhaps still insures a loan for the property, is very happy that someone finally came and paid off this loan.
Choose large cities with liquid real estate markets	But in big cities, for example, there are certainly liquid real estate markets where you know exactly – in London or New York – how much the property will still be worth in half a year.

Generalization	Quote
Value not transparently determinable	Unlike gold or silver or jewellery, for example, where the precious metal has a market value, the value of art is always in the eye of the beholder, and ultimately, who is to say whether this painting by Picasso is really worth a million or 5 million?
Value not transparently determinable	The value of a picture, for example, is very difficult to grasp, on the one hand.
Lack of comparability of art objects	And so you could imagine that, and there's no one, there's no market where you can say, I can compare that, that this image, that's worth it for others.
The art scene successfully defends itself against regulation and AMLA subordination	For years now, the art scene has been very successfully fighting against being quasi-regulated, in Switzerland at least, under the Money Laundering Act.
Lack of regulation in the art market	This market is very peculiar, [it] is also not regulated or that; yes, there are no regulations.
No risk of disclosure, no critical questions	But apart from that, I see less of a risk of being exposed because there are no critical questions.
Secure bearings	But I think in Germany, too, somehow at the airport or something – these huge storage things there, they're relatively new, where you can store things duty free, i.e., in a no-man's land, like this. So works of art and other things, and I think even cars and so on, can be stored in these things.
Contacts with dubious art dealers	Well, I would first have to have contacts in the dubious art dealer circles.
Brief expert opinions	In a half-page report from an expert or so.
Civil law purchase contracts	Often civil law contracts are sufficient.
Tradable consideration	So, there must be a countervalue that I can get rid of again.
Small assets without substance are suitable	Well, if we say that it's now worth CHF 4 million, that's a different story. There has to be something available right off the bat, but even with amounts of several tens of thousands of francs, you can move a lot of assets from A to B.
Actual value difficult to determine	Very difficult to determine what the actual value of an art object is.
Cash helps gain access	It's easy to get in if you pay with cash.
Professionals for correct value estimation	Again, I need a special, special professional. I need one, I have to buy their trust, otherwise, and – yes, and if it's really good-quality art, the vis-à-vis will probably be questioned more.
Fraud in the art market	Who would be well advised to take a closer look at what it is and where it comes from. There is also a lot of fraud in the classical sense.
Vanity of the persons involved	The vanity of the people involved, that is also a risk that actually exists there.

Generalization	Quote
Lack of self-assessment	The fascinating thing about fine art is that many people don't want to admit that they don't understand anything about the subject and let themselves be blinded by it.
Fraudsters and dishonest experts	Because there are people who know a lot more about it or who pretend that it has some value.
Fraud	If you are active in this market as a layman, then I think there is a risk that you will be ripped off.
Lack of authenticity of the artwork	It is just insanely difficult to determine or have confirmed that the artwork is genuine or not.
Loss of value due to counterfeiting	Loss of value, so I've had experts tell me that 60% or 70% of the art objects on the market are fakes.
Price formation non-transparent	The pricing is not terribly transparent.
Corrupt formation of opinions by the experts	This is not a, uh, scientific market, but, uh, yes, these are personal opinions that are flexible and that can also be influenced and are also influenced.
Lack of determinability of the actual value	There are already auctions where this is done, you can have it appraised, but if, yes, you ask two appraisers how much a work of art should be [worth], then you get three opinions.
Fraud in the art market	Because otherwise it can happen that I think, yay, I have 5 million, I want to launder it now, and I have to spend it somewhere, and I invest it in a painting, and then it could happen just as much afterwards that the painting is in reality, let's say, not worth EUR 100.
Lack of determinability of the actual value	Yes, it is certainly also, let me say, especially with art, it is quite difficult to say whether something is worth something or whether something is worth nothing.
Buyer is screened	Then the person who buys it, if it doesn't come from a private account, will have to be screened again.
Art trade (especially offshore) rejected by banks due to lack of traceability	We have had several requests for offshore to be used for the art trade, or for Swiss AGs or Austrian GmbHs. We have always refused, because for us, art is difficult to understand.
Prove possession of the goods	I have to prove that I have it; otherwise, I won't get the money. Of course, I could also build it fictitiously and then collect money. Um, but if – again, if that leads to controls, yes, the question is, was I as the seller entitled to sell this work of art in the first place?
Documentation of the origin of the goods	If it's really not about services, but about the actual art trade, then there's always the question, 'Where are the goods'?
Notification by reputable art dealers	Art dealers who are reputable pay very close attention to who else is appearing on the market.
Contact archaeologists at museums or universities	So there are, um, just enough art dealers, but also private individuals, who then turn, for example, to an archaeologist in a, in a museum, or in a university.

Generalization	Quote
Have old heirlooms appraised	And say 'Oh I have this, I bought this now on holiday or I got this from my grandfather, can you take a look at it and tell me what it is'?
Locate art dealers via Google	Hm, yes, uh, I think I would actually, um, ask around, try to find out, um, if one then, so there are, uh, I think, um, about quite normal, I know Google search or so, the possibilities to just Google antiques dealers in the vicinity, be it in Switzerland, for example, and contact the people and say 'You know, I have [this] here, I would be interested in selling this'. Do you see possibilities there?
Specify flea market as the origin	We have already seen cases where someone really bought a book at a flea market and then sold it on for 10 million because it was supposedly a rare work of art or a rare collector's item.
Use duty-free warehouse for storage	Then there are these possibilities via duty-free warehouses to store the things for years.
Do not declare	Here, too, many things are not declared; many things probably go under the table.
Freedom of contract in private law	Secondly, because it is always more a matter of private law. You can pay as much as you want for something.
Cash payment usual at auctions	At auctions, for historical reasons, it is still somehow accepted that you pay cash.
Legal entities (domiciliary companies) as owners of the painting	Especially when it is in the area of fine art, i.e., really paintings by great masters, etc., that is not done in cash; these art objects usually belong to legal entities, i.e., a separate domiciliary company is set up, which then owns the painting.
Art world interesting	So it can be in the art world.
Specify flea market as the origin	Or bought from a flea market or whatever.
Build a good relationship with the bank	If we had a client whom we had known for a long time, whom we knew well, and who said that he had a work of art that he would sell, and we were not talking about sales in the millions, but about medium amounts, then that would probably be possible.
Transport problem	And then I have a, uh, transport or a [laughing] physical problem, because I have to show somehow, have to transport.
Seek private are lovers	If there is a certain size of a market, I can also develop an activity as a free rider with people who are perhaps also shy of light. And then I can, uh, let this run alongside without actually entering this market.
Good value	With a rough diamond, you also have a good value.
Origin of rough diamonds difficult to determine	They also don't see where they come from or the rough diamonds.
Easy to transport	It's relatively easy to get across the border.

Generalization	Quote
Origin of cut diamonds difficult to determine	That's a bit more difficult to determine, as with other raw materials. Um, whereas once they are cut, it becomes much more difficult.
Diamond expert	That's why it's always more difficult when I now have a rough diamond, do I have a glass bead or a rough diamond? That means I am always dependent on some expert.
Professionals	The right professionals have to be there.
Document purchase	With gemstones, I will have to document where I bought it at some point.
High-risk industry due to corruption and black-market trade	In the diamond trade, I don't see the problem in money laundering itself, but rather in, well, diamonds are extremely susceptible to black market trade and corruption. So for me, this is definitely a very, very strong high-risk sector.
High comparability	With diamonds, you have a fixed value again. If I had a high cash turnover, you would say, aha, he must have sold so-and-so many diamonds per day to launder the money like that.
Transaction must fit the trader	When a nobody like that comes along with a rough diamond worth half a million, questions are probably already being asked.
Documents in question	That is the great danger of relying too firmly on certificates and not questioning them critically, isn't it?
Kimberley Process	YES, we have, that is part of the Kimberley Process.
Banks often reject rough diamonds	It's not our field of business. I would also not accept any company that is active in the rough diamond trade. I have already received several requests, but we refuse because - hm, hm, we don't know, we can't judge, we don't know how it works.
Attention for sale or exchange	Uh, I would like to use the money somehow then. I can do that of course - otherwise, I always stay on the black side. How can I officialize these values so that I can invest them in a property in Switzerland, for example? I can't do that if I pay the seller of the property with rough diamonds.
Convertibility into cash	But the question is, how available is that? Even if I keep rough diamonds in bonded warehouses, how do I make them convertible?
Dependence on specialists	I personally would not do it. Being dependent on a specialist who can tell the difference between a glass bead and a rough diamond is something that I would involve some people with the knowledge to do, and this seems too risky to me.
Fake certificates	Perfect certificates for fraud. That is, where you have given a higher value than you actually sold your bling [for].
Lack of expertise	This is an area where a lot of people don't really know.

Generalization	Quote
Use duty-free warehouses in Switzerland	I know that many of these trade transactions or trade activities, let's say, go through duty-free warehouses in Switzerland.
Diamond traders to plausibilize origin	He would have to prove that he knows diamond dealers in Amsterdam, for example, and that he gets diamonds from there.
Import in suitcase	But it was common practice in the past to have the diamonds somewhere in a small case.
Import in your pocket	You could virtually import rough diamonds in your trouser pocket.
Buy certificates of origin	Certificates of origin, and I've also been to Africa on business a few times, and I know you can get anything for the money.
Transporting rough diamonds in trouser pockets	They put that stuff in their pocket; it doesn't go off on any metal detector, um, and uh, they can transport it really easily.
Storage in bonded warehouses	Of course, you can also smuggle things in there that are not obvious. I declare, 'I rent a compartment here in the bonded warehouse to store my antiques, and here is the list'. I don't say that the Chinese vase is full of rough diamonds. And uh, then, uh, I have the stuff in there. So it's like that; I can smuggle stuff, uh, goods in there that are not inventoried and maybe won't be discovered. That's also how it is here, uh, one part is officially public and something is floating behind it.
Justify non-transparent pricing through cutting	Um, so still a price range, so I can play with the price, I can say that's a much bigger cut and then worth more.
Storage only conditionally helpful for concealment	Uh, just storage, uh, that basically, well that's more of a philosophical aspect, well, basically, um, it's useful for concealing assets, but you can argue about that.
Good placement opportunity	This would be a possibility to at least place the assets, so to speak.
Unknown and inaccessible place	So the big risk is already mobile assets, uh, which are stored in inaccessible and unknown places.
Only conditionally suitable for money laundering	It does not help them, does not launder their money.
Contents of the safe-deposit boxes secret	Because she does not know what is in the locker and cannot control it.
Maximum safety with minimum risk	Yes, lockers are good. Maximum security with minimum risk.

Generalization	Quote
Safe-deposit box provider who is not subject to the AMLA	Safe deposit boxes are certainly also a topic that is relatively topical at the moment. Um, as I said, uh ... within the framework of a certain financial intermediary activity, the storage of assets is subject to the safe deposit boxes. So the one who offers this service is subject to the AMLA; the others who simply offer safe deposit boxes are not subject to the AMLA.
Safe-deposit box can be opened	If nobody knows, uh, clearly thwarted, if you have a clue, there are certain police possibilities; you can go open any locker.
Decrease in value of assets over time	On the contrary, or the assets tend to decrease in value.
Not sufficient concealment	But the concealment, the concealment does not take place, or the (unintelligible) does not take place, by putting it in our safe or in the post office in a box or somewhere.
Contents of the safe-deposit box cannot be checked	So, of course, I can never rule out the possibility that someone, but the bank safe, yes, that is nothing other than a storage facility from my point of view.
Store and hide	So what you can do, I would rather have thought, is to deposit the money once in EUR 6, 10 million and then pick it up again at some point. It's like you say, I don't want the money to be found.
Visit safe-deposit box providers without identification requirements	But it's true that you don't know who is behind it, etc., if it's not declared or if nothing is identified, just like with the other financial intermediaries.
Handing over safe-deposit boxes and their contents by passing on the codes	That's not the general problem, whether they rent it, but the problem is that there is no one who has the right to pass it on, right? So they rent it, regardless of whether they are people from Switzerland. They can also articulate themselves accordingly and then always, I don't know, code or somewhere else and so on. And I'm the one who can enter the locker at any time.
Choose private custodians	Even better are those that are now springing up like mushrooms - private repositories.
Value retention	They can let the jewellery circulate for all I care, and then at some point someone will offer it again. Or you go to a jeweller who knows about it and sells it again in his shop. It doesn't make the jewellery any worse.
No fixed market prices	Jewellery would be conceivable because you don't have fixed market prices there either.
Universal means of payment	It is, of course, a universal means of payment.
Anonymous and unverifiable	That is simply not verifiable. It's completely anonymous, but I - somehow, I have to perform and actually do that.

Generalization	Quote
Origin of family silver non-transparent	Yes, it's so, uh, jewellery from estate gold, uh, precious stones, uh, you can build up, uh, relatively a lot, because no one knows where it comes from, and if it's bought or sold in small quantities widely spread out, um, it's almost not, uh, verifiable, whether it's really true or not. Because everyone has some somewhere, [laughing] family silver.
Processing knowledge	Um, yes, if you can then also judge, uh, whether the manufacturing method, whether it looks antique or not.
Mineralogical knowledge	There are different starting points for jewellery. On the one hand, it is of course good if you have mineralogical knowledge, i.e., if you can easily recognize what the original materials are.
Product with a lack of comparability	As I said, with jewellery or antiques, a piece of jewellery can have any price. A piece of jewellery can cost EUR 1,000 and you can sell it for EUR 10,000. That already exists in the same way.
Pawnshops already in the sights of working groups	We've heard about it through this working group, money laundering prevention, because pawnshops are on the radar.
The identity of the buyer is often not verified	So, if someone comes and buys a piece of jewellery, then you have to establish their identity even at certain price points, but yes, there is a reporting obligation to the national authorities, but whether that is actually done, I now doubt very much.
Value objectively determinable	Gemstones are involved. You can have the value estimated by various experts, there are professional, objective criteria with, I think, 4 Cs for gemstones, carat and clarity and so on.
Estimation risks	Yes, with antique jewellery, one might have a hard time estimating.
Common possibility	But the jewellery thing, you are absolutely right, as in your example, is a common possibility.
Jewellery is traded everywhere and can be given in payment	So of course you can make payments or trade in a product with jewellery or components of jewellery anywhere in the world, because that is traded everywhere.
Note in the estate register	Then it would have to have come up in – how do we say in our country? In probate proceedings.
Bolster the jewellery trade in the shopping centre	And that's probably where people come and, uh, sell it, and of course you can, could, bolster this business with black money. Who knows how much I really bought and sold this weekend?
Distribute leaflets for jewellery purchases in a shopping centre	I have to perform somehow. But, uh, that's not, that's not great art, that's, uh, relatively easy and, uh, without foisting something on someone, but you surely know the flyers. Uh, next weekend, XY will be in the, somewhere in the shopping centre, and he'll buy your old jewellery.
Boost jewellery trading volumes with black money	Then I can pump up the volume with, uh, with black money. But just like that, without any actual activity, it's a bit difficult, because this activity is very much aimed at the general public.

Generalization	Quote
Establish actual activity in the jewellery trade	If such jewellery purchases are faked in order to launder money, this also requires certain actual activity.
No regulations for donations	We have 15, uh, 10, yes, the 10,000 regulations cash control entry and exit, but for donations, we have no single (unintelligible) with the source of funds.
Origin of funds not checked in cases of donations	I am now giving you a million – no one asks me about my source of funds as part of the gift.
Buy jewellery in holiday destinations	Here are cases where people say why they buy so much jewellery in holiday destinations with cash and so on, because they want to avoid creating a paper trail. Officially, they say, well, the jewellery is from a friend.
Good opportunity	A good way to launder money, of course.
Replace exchange office with prepaid card	These prepaid cards usually have either a Visa or a Mastercard function. That means they can withdraw money from any ATM, they can go shopping everywhere. And it doesn't matter in which currency they pay for it.
Prepaid cards for transport	In our case, they can be topped up with up to EUR 5,000. And yes, they are transferable, which was also the inventor's intention, so to speak, that they are transferable and anonymous. And yes, they can be loaded with all kinds of currencies. Partly also with Bitcoin and virtual currencies.
Currency unification as a disadvantage	I think that essentially these exchange offices are really increasingly taking a back seat in times of currency unification.
Anonymous mass activity is suitable as a basis	Because I can use an anonymous mass activity as a basis for building something up or just pumping it up.
Bitcoin owners' identities are traceable	Without a router, so, as a tool, then they need Bitcoin. But you can trace these Bitcoins, the owner identity.
Units of account on the Internet	But the economy demands it because ATM fees, credit card fees are too high. So there will be a clearing unit on the Internet, where people trust it, so to speak.
Bitcoin will not prevail	Exchange office and then comes, that belongs with the plane to serious countries [laughs]. Bitcoin itself, yes, Bitcoin, I don't know if it will catch on, but the idea of Bitcoin is good, that is a country, I think also the economy. It will become an Internet clearing currency, but it is not a currency in the classical sense, because ... yes, maybe some third country will say at some point, well, uh, it will be recognized as a currency, but I don't think so.
Exchange office a classic	Was always the classic exchange office.

Generalization	Quote
Exchange office a classic	When I go to one of these money exchange houses, either at the airport or in, or in Dubai itself, er, I can buy – I, I think the most I've bought is EUR 5,000 in cash in one go, and, er, nobody asked for anything, no identification at all.
Self-regulation	So it starts with every financial intermediary. If an asset manager, a bank, a fiduciary dealer, whatever, wants to actively launder money himself, and there are a few examples, then it is effectively the case that this will hardly lead to anything for the prosecution authorities under the ARC, because this financial intermediary, who is the trigger for the whole thing, will not become active by reporting it to the MLRO.
Self-regulation	Um, as part of the whole Kimberley Process, these diamonds are basically certified, so you already know something about it, uh, as far as the origin is concerned, et cetera, but the mechanisms are, um ... as far as I understand, uh, not necessarily as mature everywhere as they should be.
City with tourists	In a bigger city, or like Zurich now, for example, also in Geneva or in Bern or in Ticino, where there are tourists from Russia, for example, or from China or wherever.
Credible official basic activity	But again, it needs a certain, uh, official basic activity that is credible.
Physical business must exist	Yes, indeed. These are, uh, these are also businesses that still exist physically but which can be pumped up almost arbitrarily to fictitious turnovers, uh, which are then, uh, not shown, or which are perhaps shown but do not actually come from the exchange activity.
Fake passport	The problem here is that when I change over 5,000 and have to identify myself, you can't expect the person at the counter, whether it's at the train station or at the bank, to recognize whether a passport is genuine or not. That would be going a bit too far, he's not a customs officer.
Transactions in the same currency are suspicious	Um, the only suspicious things are when, for example, uh, Swiss money is exchanged for Swiss money for unknown reasons.
Larger amounts stand out	Hm, larger amounts are noticed relatively quickly here.
Relatively low risk of detection	However, it is often, um, difficult to uncover a real illegal background, um, because it is simply not forbidden to change small pieces into large ones or vice versa, and there can also be other reasons.
Splitting amounts could attract attention	Uh, or larger amounts are, uh, split, in order to perhaps, uh, and that is then an indication that one wants to circumvent certain thresholds, uh, for one, certain clarification obligations would, uh, take effect.

Generalization	Quote
Exchange offices a recognized risk factor	There is already the danger that this is of course a recognized risk factor, the bureaux de change, and that is of course seen very critically. So it wasn't like that in the past, but today, we as a bank – if we as a bank had a customer like that, we would make sure that the turnover is real.
Clarification of the origin of the funds	And they have earned it with really, um, clean investigations of the origin of these funds.
Operators of bureaux de change are financial intermediaries with due diligence obligations	Of course, the operator of a bureau de change is also a financial intermediary, and he also has his due diligence obligations.
Straw men too often from the same country of domicile	Whether there is an accumulation of the same contractual partners, regular customers, or whether there is an increase of persons from the same country of domicile and so on, that one tries to take countermeasures.
Limit value for message is exceeded	Amount XX standard is prescribed that the client is identified, and then this is recorded in the system, and then I would expect the financial intermediary to then check for these transactions that require identification.
Straw men too often from the same cultural background	The ladies and gentlemen at the counters say at some point, okay, we do notice that there are always people from a certain cultural group who change amounts, but that is relatively difficult to recognize.
Large SBB and PostFinance exchange offices have control mechanisms	Large exchange offices of SBB, PostFinance, um, they have relatively large structures and measures to ensure compliance with money laundering obligations.
Transport of foreign currencies	That means that a foreign currency has to be introduced somehow at some point. And there we already have a certain grid.
Transport of foreign currencies	And it is, um, there we also have again, I say, to get a foreign currency into the country again, you have to travel through somewhere.
Amount must match the appearance of the person	It would then be unusual if the information about the person raises doubts, if the person does not give the impression that he or she is here as a tourist – it depends on many factors.
Larger amounts stand out	Someone changes, um, as you say, CHF 25,000 and looks, that is a very high amount, also for the holidays an extremely high amount, and you don't do something like that at the exchange counter but with advantage at the bank. So in this case, you would have to clarify where the money comes from, and then you would have to ask for the purpose for which you need so much money. If the person does not cooperate, for example, then one would have to check whether one makes a report.

Generalization	Quote
Smurfing made more difficult by monitoring	But of course, there is also a monitoring of these transactions, and the monitoring is to ensure that no smurfing takes place, i.e., that the same person does not make several transactions below the threshold value and thus actually exceeds the threshold value.
Fake customers	So it's hard to control how many were there and then you can show quite legal profits with the margins.
Fake customers	Yes, for example, they simply say that someone came and somehow put down EUR 10,000 in cash and somehow got something in return. Sure.
Establish a bureau de change	It would probably be much smarter to have a bureau de change myself, because then I could fake money exchanges that didn't even take place and would thus smuggle my cash into my completely comprehensible plausible front business.
Use bill of exchange document as a source of funds	If I were a customer, I could change money as if I had dollars before and euros afterwards. But I still have cash. The only thing I have is a bill of exchange receipt, and maybe I can tell a bank, yes, that is my source of funds, but that is not a material source of funds, that is only a receipt for an exchange of money. But we have already seen that.
Transactions under EUR 15,000	At a bureau de change, most transactions under EUR 15,000 are likely to take place.
Establish a bureau de change	Let's put it this way, the Swiss system is fundamentally based on a duty of cooperation, an active duty of cooperation on the part of the financial intermediary, more so than abroad. If the money launderer himself is a financial intermediary and brings criminal intent to light, then this is generally difficult to grasp.
Interrupt the paper trail	Because as soon as you have to deal with cash, the paper trail is of course extremely interrupted.
Operations in the red-light district	Who are, uh, yes, who are perhaps based in the red-light district, that's just the way it is. Go to the Langstrasse district in Zurich; it's full of small exchange offices and travel agencies that are being set up at the same time.
Search for microenterprises	I would look for the problems or the problematic games where they are micro-enterprises.
Use prepaid cards for transporting foreign currencies	In this day and age, all these prepaid cards, well, they're just cards that you can top up, and if I go for a drive with a card like that, probably no one will check how much money I have with me.
Show profits	And then the question is, if I really want to launder, do I really have to show and report these turnovers, the profits on them?
Amount must match the external appearance of the client	Um, to report a tourist who, to put it a little exaggeratedly, is well dressed, who changes CHF 25,000 because he wants to go shopping, uh, seems a bit reckless to me.

Generalization	Quote
Present plausible justification	If a Saudi businessman will, uh, now, uh, change this amount and says he wants to shop at Bahnhofstrasse, that is quite plausible.
Transactions between CHF 400 and CHF 800	But there is a threshold for special clarifications, which is CHF 5,000. And most transactions are carried out below this threshold, i.e., most transactions are between CHF 400 and CHF 800.
Subvert thresholds	There, of course, the, uh, amounts below the threshold, uh, can be exploited to launder, uh, money.
Financial sector disproportionately burdened	So a bank, without receiving money from anyone, has to make a big effort, run systems and do everything possible to prevent money laundering and financing terrorism. But for a private locking company, as far as I know, there are no such regulations. Yes, but I go further with the same issue. If I'm a flat landlord and I see that someone is renting here with me who doesn't have a job but still has more money, uh, and despite, and knows that, uh, uh, he's taking flying lessons … if the suspicion arises, so maybe it's a terrorist sleeper. Yes? I don't have to report that to anyone.

Bibliography

ACC. *Federal Act of 23 January 1974 on Acts Punishable by Law (Criminal Code – StGB)* (2015). http://www.ris.bka.gv.at/GeltendeFassung.wxe? Query = Federalstandards&lawnumber = 10002296.

Adams, T. E. *Tacking on Money Laundering Charges to White Collar Crimes: What Did Congress Intend, and What Are the Courts Doing.* 17 Ga. St. U. L. Rev. 531 (2000).

Ai, L. & Tang, J. *Risk-Based Approach for Designing Enterprise-Wide AML Information System Solution.* 18 J. Financ. Crime. 268 (2011).

Albrecht, C., McKay Duffin, K., Hawkins, S. & Morales Rocha, V. M. *The Use of Cryptocurrencies in the Money Laundering Process.* 22 J. Money Laund. Control 210 (2019).

Alexander, K. *The International Anti-money-Laundering Regime: The Role of the Financial Action Task Force.* 4 J. Money Laund. Control 231 (2001).

Alford, D. E. *Anti-money Laundering Regulations: A Burden on Financial Institutions.* 18 NCJ Int'l L. & Com. Reg. 437 (1993).

Alldridge, P. *Money Laundering Law: Forfeiture, Confiscation, Civil Recovery, Criminal Laundering and Taxation of the Proceeds of Crime* (Bloomsbury Publishing 2003).

Alldridge, P. *Money Laundering and Globalization.* 35 J. L. Soc. 437 (2008).

Alomari, K. A. K. *Linking Between E-Government and Money Laundering: The Mediating Role of Compliance Unit.* 10 Int'l J. Acad. Res. Bus. Soc. Sci. 179 (2020).

Amara, I., Khlif, H. & El Ammari, A. *Strengths of Auditing and Reporting Standards, Corruption and Money Laundering: A Cross-Country Investigation.* 35 Manag. Audit. J. 1243 (2020).

Amicelle, A. *When Finance Met Security: Back to the War on Drugs and the Problem of Dirty Money.* 3 Financ. Soc. 106 (2017).

AMLA. *Federal Act on Combating Money Laundering and Terrorist Financing in the Financial Sector* (2015). https://www.admin.ch/opc/de/classified-compilation/19970427/index.html.

Argentiero, A., Bagella, M. & Busato, F. *Money Laundering in a Two-Sector Model: Using Theory for Measurement.* 26 Eur. J. L. Econ. 341 (2008).

Armney, L. E. & Melese, F. *Minimizing Public Sector Corruption: The Economics of Crime, Identity Economics, and Money Laundering.* 29 Def. Peace Econ. 1 (2017).

Arzt, G. *Tax Offences as Predicate Offences – Is the Fight Against Money Laundering Becoming a Pretext? Criticism from Academia?* 4 Der Schweizer Treuhänder 268 (2011).

Arzt, G., Weber, U., Heinrich, B. & Hilgendorf, E. *Criminal Law, Special Part: Textbook* (Gieseking 2009).

Badal-Valero, E., Alvarez-Jareño, J. A. & Pavía, J. M. *Combining Benford's Law and Machine Learning to Detect Money Laundering. An Actual Spanish Court Case.* 282 Forensic Sci. Int'l 24 (2018).

Bagella, M., Busato, F. & Argentiero, A. *Money Laundering in a Microfounded Dynamic Model: Simulations for the US and the EU-15 Economies.* 5 Rev. L. Econ. 879 (2009).

Bahar, R. *Something Old, Something New: The Supervision of Financial Institutions under the Federal Act on Financial Institutions – FinIA Cleared for Takeoff.* CapLaw. 57 (2019).

Bartlett, B. *The Negative Effects of Money Laundering on Economic Development.* Asian Development Bank Regional Technical Assistance Project No. 5967 (2002).

Bello, A. & Harvey, J. *From a Risk-Based to an Uncertainty-Based Approach to Anti-money Laundering Compliance.* 30 Secur. J. 24 (2017).

Benson, K. *Money Laundering, Anti-money Laundering and the Legal Profession,* in The Palgrave Handbook of Criminal and Terrorism Financing Law 109 (C. King et al., eds, Palgrave Macmillan 2018).

Blum, J. A., Levi, M., Naylor, R. T. & Williams, P. *Financial Havens, Banking Secrecy and Money-Laundering* (United Nations Digital Library 1998).

Bogner, A., Littig, B. & Menz, W. *Interviews with Experts: A Practice-Oriented Introduction* (Springer-Verlag 2014).

Boles, J. R. *Anti-money Laundering Initiatives for the South African Real Estate Market.* 1 J. Comp. Urb. L. a. Pol., 197 (2017).

Bryans, D. *Bitcoin and Money Laundering: Mining for an Effective Solution.* 89 Ind. L. J. 441 (2014).

Buchanan, B. *Money Laundering – A Global Obstacle.* 18 Res. Int'l Bus. Finance. 115 (2004).

Campbell-Verduyn, M. *Bitcoin, Crypto-Coins, and Global Anti-money Laundering Governance.* 69 Crime, L. Soc. Chang. 283 (2018).

Canhoto, A. I. *Leveraging Machine Learning in the Global Fight Against Money Laundering and Terrorism Financing: An Affordances Perspective.* J. Bus. Res. (2020). https://doi.org/10.1016/j.jbusres.2020.10.012.

Carlin, A. & Lokanan, M. E. *Ritualisation and Money Laundering in the Swiss Banking Sector.* 21 J. Money Laund. Control 89 (2018).

Cash, D. Sigma Ratings: *Adapting the Credit Rating Agency Model for the Anti-money Laundering World.* 23 J. Money Laund. Control 1 (2019).

Cassella, S. D. *Reverse Money Laundering.* 7 J. Money Laund. Control 92 (2003).

Cassella, S. D. *Toward a New Model of Money Laundering: Is the 'Placement, Layering, Integration' Model Obsolete?* 21 J. Money Laund. Control 494 (2018).

Chaikin, D. & Sharman, J. C. *Corruption and Money Laundering* (Palgrave Macmillan 2009).

Cindori, S. *The Significance of Assessing Money Laundering Risks As a Part of Auditing Operations.* AJBE (2018). https://www.econbiz.de/ppn/1010636774.

Clarke, A. E. *Is There a Commendable Regime for Combatting Money Laundering in International Business Transactions?* J. Money Laund. Control (2020). https://doi.org/10.1108/JMLC-05-2020-0057.

Crawford, J. & Guan, Y. *Knowing Your Bitcoin Customer: Money Laundering in the Bitcoin Economy.* 1 IEEE 38 (2020).

Cuéllar, M. F. *The Tenuous Relationship Between the Fight Against Money Laundering and the Disruption of Criminal Finance.* 93 J. Crim. L. Criminol. 311 (2003).

Custers, B., Oerlemans, J. J. & Pool, R. *Laundering the Profits of Ransomware: Money Laundering Methods for Vouchers and Cryptocurrencies.* 28 Eur. J. Crime Crim. L. Crim. Justice 121 (2020).

Dagirmanjian, A. *Laundering the Art Market: A Proposal for Regulating Money Laundering Through Art in the United States.* 29 Fordham Intell. Prop. Media & Ent. L. J. (2019).

Danwerth, C. *The Regulation of Bitcoin and Other Virtual Currencies under Japanese Law in Comparative Perspective.* 2 Zeitschr. vergl. Rechtswiss. 117 (2018).

De Boyrie, M. E., Pak, S. J. & Zdanowicz, J. S. *The Impact of Switzerland's Money Laundering Law on Capital Flows Through Abnormal Pricing in International Trade.* 15 Appl. Financial Econ. 217 (2005).

De Koker, L. *Money Laundering Control: The South African Model.* 6 J. Money Laund. Control 166 (2003).

De Koker, L. *Money Laundering Control and Suppression of Financing of Terrorism: Some Thoughts on the Impact of Customer Due Diligence Measures on Financial Exclusion.* 13 J. Financ. Crime 26 (2006).

Deleanu, I. S. *Do Countries Consistently Engage in Misinforming the International Community About Their Efforts to Combat Money Laundering? Evidence Using Bendford's Law.* 12 PLoS ONE (2017). https://doi.org/10.1371/journal.pone.0169632.

Del Mundo, C. F. S. *How Countries Seek to Strengthen Anti-money Laundering Laws in Response to the Panama Papers, and the Ethical Implications of Incentivizing Whistleblowers.* 40 Northwest. J. Int'l. L. Bus. 87 (2019).

Demetis, D. S. *Fighting Money Laundering with Technology: A Case Study of Bank X in the UK.* 105 Decis. Support Syst. 96 (2018).

De Vos Burchart, F. *Trustees in Switzerland: The Office of Trustee under the (Draft) Financial Institutions Act.* 3 GesKR 281 (2017).

Dietzi, H. *Combating Money Laundering: Model Case Switzerland?* (Helbing & Lichtenhahn 1992).

Dionysios, S. D. & Angell, I. O. *The Risk-Based Approach to AML: Representation, Paradox and the 3rd Directive.* 10 J. Money Laund. Control 412 (2007).

Dobrowolski, Z. & Sulkowski, L. *Implementing a Sustainable Model for Anti-money Laundering in the United Nations Development Goals.* 12 Sustainability 1 (2019). https://doi.org/10.1038/s41598-020-75653-x.

Donatsch, A., Heimgartner, S. & Simonek, M. *International Mutual Legal Assistance: Including Administrative Assistance in Tax Law* (Schulthess 2011).

Doyle, T. *Cleaning up Anti-money Laundering Strategies: Current FATF Tactics Needlessly Violate International Law.* 24 Hous. J. Int'l L. 279 (2001).

Dupuis, D. & Gleason, K. *Money Laundering with Cryptocurrency: Open Doors and the Regulatory Dialect.* 28 J. Financ. Crime 60 (2020). https://doi.org/10.1108/JFC-06-2020-0113.

Dyntu, V. & Dykyl. O. *Cryptocurrency in the System of Money Laundering.* 4 Balt. J. Econ. Stud. 75 (2018).

Eifrem, E. *How Graph Technology Can Map Patterns to Mitigate Money-Laundering Risks.* 10 Comput. Fraud. Secur. 6 (2019).

ElYacoubi, D. *Challenges in Customer Due Diligence for Banks in the UAE.* 23 J. Money Laund. Control 527 (2020).

Farfán-Méndez, C. *The Structure of Drug Trafficking Organizations and Money Laundering Practices: A Risk Appetite Hypothesis.* 1 JIED 294 (2019).

Favarel-Garrigues, G., Godefroy, T. & Lascoumes, P. *Sentinels in the Banking Industry Private Actors and the Fight Against Money Laundering in France.* 48 Br. J. Criminol. 1 (2008).

Ferwerda, J., Deleanu, I. S. & Unger, B. *Strategies to Avoid Blacklisting: The Case of Statistics on Money Laundering.* 14 PLoS ONE 1 (2019). https://doi.org/10.1371/journal.pone.0218532.

Ferwerda, J. & Kleemans, E. R. *Estimating Money Laundering Risks: An Application to Business Sectors in the Netherlands.* 25 Eur. J. Crim. Policy Res. 45 (2019).

Ferwerda, J. & Reuter, P. *Learning from Money Laundering National Risk Assessments: The Case of Italy and Switzerland.* 25 Eur. J. Crim. Policy Res. 5 (2018).

Ferwerda, J., van Saase, A., Unger, B. & Getzner, M. *Estimating Money Laundering Flows with a Gravity Model-based Simulation.* 10 Sci. Rep. 1 (2020). https://doi.org/10.1038/s41598-020-75653-x.

Fletcher, E., Larkin, C. & Corbet, S. *Countering Money Laundering and Terrorist Financing: A Case for Bitcoin.* 56 Res. Int'l Bus. Finance (2021). https://doi.org/10.1016/j.ribaf.2021.101387.

Florea, I. O. & Nitu, M. *Money Laundering Through Cryptocurrencies.* 23 Rom. Econ. Bus. Rev. 66 (2020).

Flühmann, D. & Bahar, R. *FINMA Grants Banking Licenses to New Swiss Crypto Banks, Introduces New Strict AML Rules Regarding Payments on Blockchain.* 42 CapLaw (2019).

Flühmann, D., Hsu, P. & Ender, T. *Regulation of Electronic Payment Service Providers in Switzerland.* 1 GesKR 5 (2017).

Force, F. A. T. *Money Laundering* (Report on Money Laundering 1999).

Freij, A. *Using Technology to Support Financial Services Regulatory Compliance: Current Applications and Future Prospects of Regtech.* 21 J. Invest. Compliance 181 (2020).

Frick, T. A. *Virtual and Cryptocurrencies: Regulatory and Anti-money Laundering Approaches in the European Union and Switzerland.* 20 ERA Forum (2019).

Friedrich, C. & Quick, R. *An Analysis of Anti-money Laundering in the German Non-financial Sector.* 23 J. Manag. Gov. 1099 (2019).

Froschauer, U. & Lueger, M. *The Qualitative Interview* (WUV 1992).

Gaetke, E. R. & Welling, S. N. *Money Laundering and Lawyers.* 43 Syracuse L. Rev. 1165 (1992).

Gambarov, H. D. *Regional Anti-money Laundering Cooperation in the African Union.* 3 B - 126 (2018).

Gao, S. & Xu, D. *Conceptual Modeling and Development of an Intelligent Agent-Assisted Decision Support System for Anti-money Laundering.* 36 Expert Syst. Appl. 1493 (2009).

Gao, Z. & Ye, M. *A Framework for Data Mining-based Anti-money Laundering Research.* 10 J. Money Laund. Control 170 (2007).

GCC. *Criminal Code in the Version Promulgated on 13 November 1998 (Federal Law Gazette I p. 3322), as Amended by Article 1 of the Act of 12 June 2015 (Federal Law Gazette I p. 926)* (2015). http://www.gesetze-im-internet.de/bundesrecht/stgb/gesamt.pdf.

Geiger, H. & Wuensch, O. *The Fight Against Money Laundering: An Economic Analysis of a Cost-Benefit Paradoxon.* 10 J. Money Laund. Control 91 (2007).

Gichuki, N. E. *The Conflict Between Anti-money Laundering Reporting Obligations and the Doctrine of Confidentiality for Legal Practitioners in Kenya.* J. Money Laund. Control (2020). https://doi.org/10.1108/JMLC-05-2020-0055.

Gill, M. & Taylor, G. *Preventing Money Laundering or Obstructing Business? Financial Companies' Perspectives on 'Know Your Customer' Procedures.* 44 Br. J. Criminol. 582 (2004).

Gilmore, W. C. *International Efforts to Combat Money Laundering.* 18 Commonw. L. Bull. 1129 (1992).

Gläser, J. & Laudel, G. *Expert Interviews and Qualitative Content Analysis* (VS Verlag 2010).

Go, L. & Benarkah, N. *Quo Vadis Legal Profession Participation in Anti-money Laundering.* 22 J. Money Laund. Control 764 (2019).

Godinho Silva, P. *Recent Developments in EU Legislation on Anti-money Laundering and Terrorist Financing.* 10 New J. Eur. Crim. L. 57 (2019).

Gordon, J. E. *Prosecutors Who Seize Too Much and the Theories They Love: Money Laundering, Facilitation, and Forfeiture.* 44 Duke L. J. 744 (1995).

Gouvin, E. J. *Bringing Out the Big Guns: The USA Patriot Act, Money Laundering, and the War on Terrorism.* 55 Baylor L. Rev. 955 (2003).

Graber, C. *Geldwäscherei: ein Kommentar zu Art. 305bis und 305ter StGB* (Stämpfli 1990).

Graber, C. *Das neue GwG: Gesetzesausgabe mit englischer Übersetzung, Ausführungserlassen und Anmerkungen* (Schulthess 2009).

Grosse, R. E. *Drugs and Money: Laundering Latin America's Cocaine Dollars* (Greenwood Publishing Group 2001).

Gurule, J. *Money Laundering Control Act of 1986: Creating a New Federal Offense or Merely Affording Federal Prosecutors an Alternative Means of Punishing Specified Unlawful Activity.* 32 Am. Crim. L. Rev. 823 (1994).

Haffke, L., Fromberger, M. & Zimmermann, P. *Cryptocurrencies and Anti-money Laundering: The Shortcomings of the Fifth AML Directive (EU) and How to Address Them.* 21 J. Bank. Regul. 125 (2020).

Hall, M. R. *An Emerging Duty to Report Criminal Conduct: Banks, Money Laundering, and the Suspicious Activity Report.* 84 Ky. L. J. 643 (1995).

Hameed, T. M. *The Role of Electronic Currencies in Money Laundering.* 14 JMCMS 326 (2019).

Hampton, M. P. & Levi, M. *Fast Spinning into Oblivion? Recent Developments in Money-Laundering Policies and Offshore Finance Centres.* 20 Third World Q. 645 (1999).

Harmon Jr, J. D. *United States Money Laundering Laws: International Implications.* 9 N.Y.L. Sch. J. Int'l & Comp. L. 1 (1988).

Hartman, B. R. *Coercing Cooperation from Offshore Financial Centers: Identity and Coincidence of International Obligations Against Money Laundering and Harmful Tax Competition.* 24 BC Int'l & Comp. L. Rev. 253 (2000).

Harvey, J. *Compliance and Reporting Issues Arising for Financial Institutions from Money Laundering Regulations: A Preliminary Cost Benefit Study.* 7 J. Money Laund. Control 333 (2004).

Harvey, J. *An Evaluation of Money Laundering Policies.* 8 J. Money Laund. Control 339 (2005).

He, P. *A Typological Study on Money Laundering.* 13 J. Money Laund. Control 15 (2010).

Hernandez, B. E. *RIP to IRP-Money Laundering and Drug Trafficking Controls Score a Knockout Victory Over Bank Secrecy.* 18 NCJ Int'l L. & Com. Reg. 235 (1992).

Hinterseer, K. *Criminal Finance: The Political Economy of Money Laundering in a Comparative Legal Context* (Vol. 15, Kluwer Law International 2002).

Holder, W. E. *The International Monetary Fund's Involvement in Combating Money Laundering and the Financing of Terrorism.* 6 J. Money Laund. Control 383 (2003).

Hugel, P. & Kelly, J. *Internet Gambling, Credit Cards and Money Laundering.* 6 J. Money Laund. Control 57 (2003).

Hughes, S. J. *Policing Money Laundering Through Funds Transfers: A Critique of Regulation Under the Bank Secrecy Act.* 67 Ind. L. J. 283 (1991).

Hülsse, R. *Creating Demand for Global Governance: The Making of a Global Money-laundering Problem.* 21 Glob. Soc. 155 (2007).

Hülsse, R. & Kerwer, D. *Global Standards in Action: Insights from Anti-money Laundering Regulation.* 14 Organ. 625 (2007).

Imanpour, M., Rosenkranz, S., Westbrock, B. & Unger, B. *A Microeconomic Foundation for Optimal Money Laundering Policies.* 60 Int'l Rev. L. Econ. (2019). https://doi.org/10.1016/j.irle.2019.105856.

Isa, Y. M., Sanusi, Z. M., Haniff, M. N. & Barnes, P. A. *Money Laundering Risk: From the Bankers' and Regulators Perspectives.* 28 Procedia Econom. Financ. 7 (2015).

Jansics, D. *Shell Companies and Government Corruption*, in Global Encyclopedia of Public Administration, Public Policy, and Governance (A. Farazmand, ed., Springer International Publishing AG 2018).

Jayasekara, S. D. *How Effective Are the Current Global Standards in Combating Money Laundering and Terrorist Financing?* J. Money Laund. Control (2020). https://doi.org/10.1108/JMLC-05-2020-0047.

Jayasuriya, D. *Money Laundering and Terrorist Financing: The Role of Capital Market Regulators.* 10 J. Financ. Crime 30 (2003).

Hunter, T. *Handbook of Safety Hazards* (Springer Fachmedien Wiesbaden 2015).

Johnson, J. *11th September, 2001: Will It Make a Difference to the Global Anti-money Laundering Movement?* 6 J. Money Laund. Control 9 (2003).

Johnson, J. & Desmond Lim, Y. C. *Money Laundering: Has the Financial Action Task Force Made a Difference?* 10 J. Financ. Crime 7 (2003).

Jositsch, D. *Das Schweizerische Korruptionsstrafrecht: Art. 322terbis Art. 322octies StGB* (Schulthess 2004).

Jost, P. M., & Sandhu, H. S. *The Hawala Alternative Remittance System and Its Role in Money Laundering* (Interpol 2003).

Jourová, V. *Strengthened EU Rules to Prevent Money Laundering and Terrorism Financing* (European Commission Fact Sheet 9 July 2018).

Kersten, A. *Financing of Terrorism – A Predicate Offence to Money Laundering?* in *Financing Terrorism* 49 (M. Pieth, ed., Springer Netherlands 2002).

Killias, M. *Grundriss des Allgemeinen Teils des Schweizerischen Strafgesetzbuches* (Stämpfli 2009).

Killias, M. *Grundriss der Kriminologie: eine europäische Perspektive* (2nd ed., Stämpfli 2011).

Killias, M. *Why Fight Money Laundering? Eleven Thought Splinters* (Killias Research and Consulting 2015).

Kingdon, J. *AI Fights Money Laundering.* 3 IEEE Intell. Syst. 87 (2004).

Kirschenbaum, J. & Verón, N. *A Better European Union Architecture to Fight Money Laundering.* Bruegel Policy Contribution, No. 2018/9 (Bruegel 2018). http://hdl.handle.net/10419/208028.

Klimova, S. & Grigoryan, A. *IT-Solutions in Money Laundering/Counter Terrorism Financing Risk Assessment in Commercial Banks*, in Brain-Inspired Cognitive Architectures for Artificial Intelligence: BICA*AI 2020. BICA 2020. Advances in Intelligent Systems and Computing (Vol. 1310, A. V. Samsonovich, R. R. Gudwin & A. S. Simões, eds, Springer 2020).

Klimova. S., Zhampeiis, N. & Grigoryan, A. *Contemporary Approaches to Money Laundering/Terrorism Financing Risk Assessment and Methods of Its Automation in Commercial Banks.* 169 Procedia Comput. Sci. 380 (2020).

Kobryn, K. M. *Seizure and Confiscation of Assets 'Laundered' in Switzerland from a Purely Foreign Predicate Offence.* 4 Forumpoenale 234 (2017).

Koh, J. M. *Suppressing Terrorist Financing and Money Laundering* (Springer Science & Business Media 2006).

Kordik, M. & Kurilovska, L. *Protection of the National Financial System from the Money Laundering and Terrorism Financing.* 5 Entrepreneurship Sustain. Issues 243 (2017).

Koster, H. *Toward Better Implementation of the European Union's Anti-money Laundering and Countering the Financing of Terrorism Framework.* 23 J. Money Laund. Control 379 (2020).

Krambia-Kapardis, M., Dimitriou, S. & Stylianu, I. *Disentangling the Expectation Gap for Compliance Officers.* Financ. Compliance 205 (2019).

Kruisbergen, E. W., Leukfeldt, E. R., Kleemans, E. R. & Roks, R. A. *Money Talks Money Laundering Choices of Organized Crime Offenders in the Digital Age.* 42 J. Crim. Justice 569 (2019).

Kurum, E. *RegTech Solutions and AML Compliance: What Future for Financial Crime?* J. Financ. Crime (2020). https://doi.org/10.1108/JFC-04-2020-0051.

Lacey, K. A. & George, B. C. *Crackdown on Money Laundering: A Comparative Analysis of the Feasibility and Effectiveness of Domestic and Multilateral Policy Reforms.* 23 Nw. J. Int'l L. & Bus. 263 (2002).

Lawlor-Forsyth, E. & Gallant, M. M. *Financial Institutions and Money Laundering: A Threatening Relationship?* 19 J. Bank. Regul. 131 (2018).

Leonov, S., Yarovenko, H., Boiko, A. & Dotsenko, T. *Prototyping of Information System for Monitoring Banking Transactions Related to Money Laundering.* 65 SHS Web Conf. (2019). https://doi.org/10.1051/shsconf/20196504013.

Levi, M. *Regulating Money Laundering – The Death of Bank Secrecy in the UK.* 31 Br. J. Criminol. 109 (1991).

Levi, M. *Money Laundering and Its Regulation.* 582 Ann. Am. Acad. Political Soc. Sci. 181 (2002).

Levi, M. *Evaluating Control of Money Laundering and Its Underlying Offences: The Search for Meaningful Data.* 15 Asian J. Criminol. 301 (2020a).

Levi, M. *Making Sense of Professional Enablers' Involvement in Laundering Organized Crime Proceeds and Their Regulation.* 24 Trends Organ. Crime 96 (2021). https://doi.org/10.1007/s12117-020-09401-y.

Levi, M. & Gilmore, W. *Terrorist Finance, Money Laundering and the Rise and Rise of Mutual Evaluation: A New Paradigm for Crime Control?* in Financing Terrorism 87 (M. Pieth ed., Springer Netherlands 2002).

Levi, M. & Reuter, P. *Money Laundering.* 34 Crime Justice 289 (2006).

Levi, M., Reuter, P. & Halliday, T. *Can the AML System Be Evaluated Without Better Data?* 69 Crime L. Soc. Change 307 (2017).

Levi, M. & Soudijn, M. *Understanding the Laundering of Organized Crime Money.* 49 Crime Justice 579 (2020).

Lilley, P. *Dirty Dealing: The Untold Truth About Global Money Laundering, International Crime and Terrorism* (Kogan Page Publishers 2003).

Loayza, N., Villa, E. & Misas, M. *Illicit Activity and Money Laundering from an Economic Growth Perspective: A Model and an Application to Colombia.* 159 J. Econ. Behav. Organ. 442 (2019).

Lord, N. J., Campbell, L. J. & van Wingerde, K. *Other People's Dirty Money: Professional Intermediaries, Market Dynamics and the Finances of White-Collar, Corporate and Organized Crimes.* 59 Br. J. Criminol. 1217 (2019).

Lowe, R. J. *Anti-money Laundering – The Need for Intelligence.* 24 J. Financ. Crime 472 (2017).

Lutz, P. & Kern, M. *Geldwäscherei und das qualifizierte Steuervergehen von Art. 305bis Ziff. 1 bis StGB.* 113 SJZ 97 (2017).

Lutz, P. & Kern, M. Anwälte im GwG-Schleppnetz – Berufsgeheimnis als Beifang. Lawyers' Review 435 (2019).

Lyden, G. A. *International Money Laundering Abatement and Anti-terrorist Financing Act of 2001: Congress Wears a Blindfold While Giving Money Laundering Legislation a Facelift.* 8 Fordham J. Corp. & Fin. L. 201 (2003).

Lyeonov, S., Kuzmenko, O., Yarovenko, H. & Dotsenko, T. *The Innovative Approach to Increasing Cybersecurity of Transactions Through Counteraction to Money Laundering.* 3 Market. Manag. Innov. 308 (2019).

Mabunda, S. *Cryptocurrency: The New Face of Cyber Money Laundering.* 2018 International Conference on Advances in Big Data, Computing and Data Communication Systems. Durban, South Africa (2018). http://dx.doi.org/10.1109/ICABCD.2018.8465467.

Madinger, J. *Money Laundering: A Guide for Criminal Investigators* (CRC Press 2011).

Masciandaro, D. *Money Laundering Regulation: The Micro Economics.* 2 J. Money Laund. Control 49 (1998).

Masciandaro, D. *Money Laundering: The Economics of Regulation.* 7 Eur. J. L. Econ. 225 (1999).

Masciandaro, D. *False and Reluctant Friends? National Money Laundering Regulation, International Compliance and Non-cooperative Countries.* 20 Eur. J. L. Econ. 17 (2005).

Masciandaro, D. & Filotto, U. *Money Laundering Regulation and Bank Compliance Costs: What Do Your customers Know? Economics and the Italian Experience.* 5 J. Money Laund. Control 133 (2001).

Mayring, P. *Qualitative Content Analysis: Basics and Techniques* (Beltz 2010).

McCusker, R. *Underground Banking: Legitimate Remittance Network or Money Laundering System?* (Australian Institute of Criminology 2005).

McDowell, J. & Novis, G. *The Consequences of Money Laundering and Financial Crime.* 6 Econ. Perspect. 6 (2001).

Mekpor, E. S. *Anti-money Laundering and Combating the Financing of Terrorism Compliance: Are FATF Member States Just Scratching the Surface?* 22 J. Money Laund. Control 451 (2019).

Mekpor, E. S., Aboagye, A. & Welbeck, J. *The Determinants of Anti-money Laundering Compliance Among the Financial Action Task Force (FATF) Member States.* 26 J. Financ. Regul. Compliance 442 (2018).

Mitchell, A., Sikka, P. & Willmott, H. *Sweeping It Under the Carpet: The Role of Accountancy Firms in Money Laundering.* 23 Account. Organ. Soc. 589 (1998).

Mitchell, D. J. *US Government Agencies Confirm that Low-Tax Jurisdictions Are Not Money-Laundering Havens.* 11 J. Financ. Crime 127 (2004).

Mitsch, W. *Strafrecht Besonderer Teil 2* (Springer Berlin Heidelberg 2015).

Mitsilegas, V. & Gilmore, B. *The EU Legislative Framework Against Money Laundering and Terrorist Finance: A Critical Analysis in the Light of Evolving Global Standards.* 56 Int'l Comp. L. Q. 119 (2007).

Molo, G. & Drzalic, J. *Können Kryptowährungen compliant sein?* 1 AJP 40 (2019).

Morris-Cotterill, N. *Money Laundering.* 124 Foreign Policy 16 (2001).

Moser, M. *Switzerland: New Exceptions to Bank Secrecy Laws Aimed at Money Laundering and Organized Crime.* 27 Case W. Res. J. Int'l L. 321 (1995).

Mugarura, N. & Ssali, E. *Intricacies of Anti-money Laundering and Cyber-Crimes Regulation in a Fluid Global System.* 24 J. Money Laund. Control 10 (2020). https://doi.org/10.1108/JMLC-11-2019-0092.

Muller, W. H., Kalin, C. H. & Goldsworth, J. G. (Eds). *Anti-money Laundering: International Law and Practice* (John Wiley & Sons 2007).

Müller. L., Reutlinger, M. & Kaiser, J. A. *Entwicklungen in der Regulierung von virtuellen Währungen in der Schweiz und der Europäischen Union.* 3 EUZ 80 (2018).

Murrar, F. & Barakat, K. *Role of FATF in Spearheading AML and CFT.* 24 J. Money Laund. Control 77 (2020). https://doi.org/10.1108/JMLC-01-2020-0010.

Nagel, T. *Soll das Aufbewahren von Vermögenswerten künftig dem Geldwäschereigesetz unterstellt werden?* 1 GesKR 113 (2020).

Naheem, M. A. *Regulating Virtual Currencies – The Challenges of Applying Fiat Currency Laws to Digital Technology Services.* 25 J. Financ. Crime 562 (2018).

Naheem, M. A. *The Agency Dilemma in Anti-money Laundering Regulation.* 23 J. Money Laund. Control 26 (2020).

Nguyen, C. L. *Preventing the Use of Financial Institutions for Money Laundering and the Implications for Financial Privacy.* 21 J. Money Laund. Control 47 (2018).

Nichols, L. T. *Social Problems as Landmark Narratives: Bank of Boston, Mass Media and 'Money Laundering'.* 44 Soc. Probl. 324 (1997).

Norton, S. D. *Suspicion of Money Laundering Reporting Obligations: Auditor Compliance, or Skeptical Failure to Engage?* 50 Crit. Perspect. Account. 56 (2018).

Nougayrède, D. *Anti-money Laundering and Lawyer Regulation: The Response of the Professions.* 43 Fordham Int'l L. J. 321 (2019).

Ozkan, O. *Money-Laundering Activities of the PKK,* in Eradicating Terrorism in the Middle East 315(A. R. Dawoody, ed., Springer International Publishing 2016).

Passas, N. *Informal Value Transfer Systems, Terrorism and Money Laundering.* Report to the National Institute of Justice (Northeastern University 2003).

Passas, N. *Report on the Debate Regarding EU Cash Payment Limitations.* 25 J. Financ. Crime 5 (2018).

Pavlidis, G. *Financial Information in the Context of Anti-money Laundering: Broadening the Access of Law Enforcement and Facilitating Information Exchanges.* 23 J. Money Laund. Control 369 (2020).

Perkel, W. *Money Laundering and Terrorism: Informal Value Transfer Systems.* 41 Am. Crim. L. Rev. 183 (2004).

Peyer, M. & Winter, G. *Swiss Financial Market Supervisory Authority Publishes New Guidelines for 'Stable Coins'.* 4 CapLaw 25 (2019).

Philippsohn, S. *Money Laundering on the Internet.* 20 Comp. Secur. 485 (2001).

Pieth, M. *Criminal Law History* (Helbing Lichtenhahn Verlag 2015).

Pieth, M. & Aiolfi, G. *A Comparative Guide to Anti-money Laundering* (Edward Elgar 2004).

Pieth, M. & Ivory, R. *Corporate Criminal Liability: Emergence, Convergence, and Risk* (Vol. 9, Springer Science & Business Media 2011).

Plombeck, C. T. *Confidentiality and Disclosure: The Money Laundering Control Act of 1986 and Banking Secrecy.* 22 Int'l Lawyer, 69 (1988).

Pol, R. F. *Anti-money Laundering Effectiveness: Assessing Outcomes or Ticking Boxes?* 21 J. Money Laund. Control 215 (2018).

Pol, R. F. *Anti-money Laundering: The World's Least Effective Policy Experiment? Together, We Can Fix It.* 3 PDP (2020). https://doi.org/10.1080/25741292.2020.1725366.

Quirk, P. J. *Macroeconomic Implications of Money Laundering.* 2 Trends Organ. Crime 10 (1997a).

Quirk, P. J. *Money Laundering: Muddying the Macroeconomy.* 34 Finance Dev. 7 (1997b).

Ravenda, D., Valencia-Silva, M. M., Argiles-Bosch, J. M. & Garcia-Blandon, J. *Accrual Management as an Indication of Money Laundering Through Legally Registered Mafia Firms in Italy.* 31 Account. Audit. Account. J. 286 (2018).

Ravenda, D., Valencia-Silva, M. M., Argiles-Bosch, J. M. & Garcia-Blandon, J. *Money Laundering Through the Strategic Management of Accounting Transactions.* 60 Crit. Perspect. Account. 65 (2019).

Razzano, F. C. *American Money Laundering Statutes: The Case for a Worldwide System of Banking Compliance Programs.* 3 J. Int'l L. & Prac. 277 (1994).

Reuter, P. *Chasing Dirty Money: The Fight Against Money Laundering* (Peterson Institute 2004).

Riccardi, M. & Levi, M. *Cash, Crime and Anti-money Laundering,* in The Palgrave Handbook of Criminal and Terrorism Financing Law 135 (J. Gurulé, C. King, & C. H. Walker, eds, Palgrave Macmillan 2018).

Richards, J. R. *Transnational Criminal Organizations, Cybercrime, and Money Laundering: A Handbook for Law Enforcement Officers, Auditors, and Financial Investigators* (CRC Press 1998).

Robinson, J. *The Laundrymen: Inside Money Laundering, the World's Third-Largest Business* (Arcade Publishing 1996).

Ronc, P. & Schuppli, B. *Cryptocurrencies in Light of Swiss Money Laundering Legislation.* 6 Forumpoenale 529 (2018).

Ross, S. & Hannan, M. *Money Laundering Regulation and Risk-based Decision-Making.* 10 J. Money Laund. Control 106 (2007).

Rusanov, G. & Pudovochkin, Y. *Money Laundering in the Modern Crime System.* J. Money Laund. Control (2020). https://doi.org/10.1108/JMLC-08-2020-0085.

Salehi, A., Ghazanfari, M. & Fathian, M. *Data Mining Techniques for Anti-money Laundering.* 12 Int'l J. Appl. Eng. Res. 10084 (2017).

Savona, E. U. *Responding to Money Laundering: International Perspectives* (Psychology Press 2000).

Savona, E. U. & Riccardi, M. *Assessing the Risk of Money Laundering: Research Challenges and Implications for Practitioners.* 25 Eur. J. Crim. Policy Res. 1 (2019).

SCC. *Swiss Criminal Code of 21 December 1937 (as of 1 January 2015)* (2015c). https://www.admin.ch/opc/en/classified-compilation/19370083/.

Schleiffer, P. & von Riedmatten, R. *Supervision of Portfolio Managers and Trustees*. 58 CapLaw (2019).

Schmidt, E. *Handbook Compliance International. Law and Practice of Corruption Prevention* (Erich Schmidt 2015).

Schneider, F. *Money Laundering and Financial Means of Organised Crime: Some Preliminary Empirical Findings*. 10 Glob. Bus. Econ. Rev. 309 (2008).

Schneider, F. *Turnover of Organized Crime and Money Laundering: Some Preliminary Empirical Findings*. 144 Public Choice 473 (2010).

Schneider, F. & Windischbauer, U. *Money Laundering: Some Facts*. 26 Eur. J. L. Econ. 387 (2008).

Schneider, S. *Organized Crime, Money Laundering, and the Real Estate Market in Canada*. 21 J. Prop. Res. 99 (2004).

Schopper, M. D. *Internet Gambling, Electronic Cash & Money Laundering: The Unintended Consequences of a Monetary Control Scheme*. 5 Chap. L. Rev. 303 (2002).

Schott, P. A. *Reference Guide to Anti-money Laundering and Combating the Financing of Terrorism* (World Bank Publications 2006).

Schroeder, W. R. *Money Laundering*. 70 FBI L. Enforc. Bull. 1 (2001).

Senator, T. E., Goldberg, H. G., Wooton, J., Cottini, M. A., Khan, A. U., Klinger, C. D., et al. *Financial Crimes Enforcement Network AI System (FAIS) Identifying Potential Money Laundering from Reports of Large Cash Transactions*. 16 AI Mag. 21 (1995).

Shaikh, A. K. & Nazir, A. *A Model for Identifying Relationships of Suspicious Customers in Money Laundering Using Network Functions*. 1 Proceedings of the World Congress on Engineering, London (4–6 July 2018).

Sharman, J. C. *Power and Discourse in Policy Diffusion: Anti-money Laundering in Developing States*. 52 Int'l Stud. Q. 635 (2008).

Sharman, J. C. & Chaikin, D. *Corruption and Anti-money-laundering Systems: Putting a Luxury Good to Work*. 22 Governance 27 (2009).

Simanjuntak, E. L., Naili, Y. T. & Samekto, F. A. *Free Movement of Judgements in Cross-Border Money Laundering Crimes: A Legal Stance Toward the ASEAN Legal Integration*. 12 J. East Asia Int'l L. 373 (2019).

Simmons, B. *International Efforts Against Money Laundering*. Commitment and Compliance: The Role of Non-binding Norms in the International Legal System, 244 (D. Shelton, ed., Oxford University Press 2000).

Simonova, A. *The Risk-Based Approach to Anti-money Laundering Problems and Solutions*. 14 J. Money Laund. Control 346 (2011).

Singh, K. & Best, P. *Anti-money Laundering: Using Data Visualization to Identify Suspicious Activity*. 34 Int'l J. Account. Inf. Syst. (2019). https://doi.org/10.1016/j.accinf.2019.06.001.

Sittlington, S. & Harvey, J. *Prevention of Money Laundering and the Role of Asset Recovery*. 70 Crime L. Soc. Change 421 (2018).

Sobreira Leite, G., Bessa Albuquerque, A. & Rogerio Pinheiro, P. *Application of Technological Solutions in the Fight Against Money Laundering – A Systematic*

Literature Review. 9 Appl. Sci. 4800 (2019). https://doi.org/10.3390/app9224800.

Stacchezzini, R., Rossignoli, F. & Corbella, S. *Corporate Governance in Practice: The Role of Practitioners' Understanding in Implementing Compliance Programs.* 33 Account. Audit. Account. J. 887 (2020).

Stack, G. *Money Laundering in Ukraine: Tax Evasion, Embezzlement, Illicit International Flows and State Capture.* 18 J. Money Laund. Control 382 (2015).

Steblianko, A.V., Chernadchuk, T.O., Kravchenko, I.O., Andriichenko, N.S. & Rudanetska, O.S. *International Law Enforcement Cooperation Against Money Laundering.* 37 Cuestiones Políticas 217 (2020).

Stessens, G. *Money Laundering: A New International Law Enforcement Model* (Vol. 15, Cambridge University Press 2000).

Stratenwerth, G. *Schweizerisches Strafrecht, Besonderer Teil II* (Stämpflis Juristische Lehrbücher 1984).

Straub, J. P. *Prevention of E-money Laundering: Tracking the Elusive Audit Trail.* 25 Suffolk Transnat'l L. Rev. 515 (2001).

Sultzer, S. *Money Laundering: The Scope of the Problem and Attempts to Combat It.* 63 Tenn. L. Rev. 143 (1995).

Suter, C., Remund, C. & Lumengo Paka, N. *Steuervortaten zur Geldwäschereit.* 4 GCCR 522 (2019).

Svedberg Helgesson, K. & Mörth, U. *Client Privilege, Compliance and the Rule of Law: Swedish Lawyers and Money Laundering Prevention.* 69 Crime L. Soc. Change 227 (2018).

Svenonius, O. & Mörth, U. *Avocat, Rechtsanwalt or Agent of the State? Anti-Money Laundering Compliance Strategies of French and German Lawyers.* 23 J. Money Laund. Control 849 (2020).

Takáts, E. *A Theory of 'Crying Wolf': The Economics of Money Laundering Enforcement* (No. 7-81, International Monetary Fund 2007).

Teichmann, F. *How Sensible Is the Abolition of Cash to Combat Money Laundering and Terrorist Financing?* 6 ius.full 154 (2016a).

Teichmann, F. *Money Laundering in Switzerland.* 4 ZRFC 163 (2016b).

Teichmann, F. *Anti-bribery Control and Incentives as Agency Theory Approaches.* 3 J. Bus. Adm. L. Soc. Sci. 116 (2017a).

Teichmann, F. *Bribery and Corruption – Challenges and Potential Solutions in Multinational Corporations.* 2 SEER 100 (2017b).

Teichmann, F. *Combating Terrorist Financing – A Hopeless Path?* 3 ius.full 77 (2017c).

Teichmann, F. *Financing Terrorism via Swiss Banks – Concrete Procedures.* 12 Kriminalistik 757 (2017d).

Teichmann, F. *Money Laundering in the Real Estate Industry.* 3 Kriminalistik 194 (2017e).

Teichmann, F. *Money Transfer Service Providers – A Dream for Money Launderers and Terrorist Financiers?* 6 ZRFC 264 (2017f).

Teichmann, F. *Suitability and Detection Risks of Terrorist Financing via Swiss Banks.* 12 Kriminalistik 762 (2017g).

Teichmann, F. *Twelve Methods of Money Laundering.* 20 J. Money Laund. Control 130 (2017h).

Teichmann, F. *Whistleblowing Incentives – A Way to Fight Bribery?* 3 J. Bus. Adm. L. Soc. Sci. 116 (2017i).

Teichmann, F. *Geldwäsche und Terrorismusfinanzierung – Ein Blick auf das Bankensystem in Deutschland, Österreich, Liechtenstein und der Schweiz.* 1 ZWF 55 (2018a).

Teichmann, F. *Real Estate Money Laundering in Austria, Germany, Liechtenstein and Switzerland.* 21 J. Money Laund. Control 370 (2018b).

Teichmann, F. *Bribery – An Obstacle to International Development.* 26 J. Financ. Crime 746 (2019a).

Teichmann, F. *Recent Trends in Money Laundering and Terrorism Financing.* 27 J. Financ. Regul. Compliance 2 (2019b).

Teichmann, F. *Current Developments in Money Laundering and Terrorism Financing.* J. Money Laund. Control (2020a). https://doi.org/10.1108/JMLC-05-2019-0043.

Teichmann, F. *How Useful Are Anti-money Laundering Mechanisms in Combating Bribery?* 23 J. Money Laund. Control 309 (2020b). https://doi.org/10.1108/JMLC-03-2018-0025.

Teichmann, F. *Money Laundering and Terrorist Financing – Unsolved Issues.* 23 J. Money Laund. Control 90 (2020c).

Teichmann, F. *Money Laundering in the Jewellery Business.* 23 J. Money Laund. Control 691 (2020d).

Teichmann, F. & Camprubi, M. *Money Laundering Through Consulting Firms.* 5 CEJ 60 (2019).

Teichmann, F. & Falker, M. C. *Can the Issue of Corruption Be Solved? An Analysis of Corruption in the Balkans and Potential Solutions.* 23 SEER 91 (2020a).

Teichmann, F. & Falker, M. C. *Cryptocurrencies and Financial Crime: Solutions from Liechtenstein.* J. Money Laund. Control (2020b). https://doi.org/10.1108/JMLC-05-2020-0060.

Teichmann, F. & Falker, M. C. *Money Laundering in the Real Estate Industry Using the Example of Switzerland.* 3 Compliance Berater 54 (2020c).

Teichmann, F. & Falker, M. C. *Money Laundering Through Banks in Dubai.* 28 J. Financ. Regul. Compliance 337 (2020d).

Teichmann, F. & Falker, M. C. *Money Laundering Through Consulting Companies.* 28 J. Financ. Regul. Compliance 485 (2020e). https://doi.org/10.1108/JFRC-07-2019-0091.

Teichmann, F. & Falker, M. C. *Money Laundering Through Deposit Boxes.* 23 J. Money Laund. Control 805 (2020f).

Teichmann, F. & Falker, M. C. *Money Laundering, the Gold Method.* J. Money Laund. Control (2020g). https://doi.org/10.1108/JMLC-07-2019-0060.

Teichmann, F. & Falker, M. C. *Money Laundering Through Exchange Offices.* 28 J. Money Laund. Control (2020h). https://doi.org/10.1108/JMLC-07-2019-0059.

Teichmann, F. & Falker, M. C. *Money Laundering Through Raw Diamonds.* J. Money Laund. Control (2020i). https://doi.org/10.1108/JMLC-07-2019-0057.

Teichmann, F. & Falker, M. C. *Money Laundering via Cryptocurrencies – Potential Solutions from Liechtenstein.* 24 J. Money Laund. Control 91 (2020j). https://doi.org/10.1108/JMLC-04-2020-0041.

Teichmann, F. & Falker, M. C. *Money Laundering via Underground Currency Exchange Networks.* 29 J. Financ. Regul. Compliance 1 (2020k). https://doi.org/10.1108/JFRC-01-2020-0003.

Teichmann, F., Falker, M. C. & Sergi, B. S. *Gaming Environmental Governance? Bribery, Abuse of Subsidies, and Corruption in European Union Programs.* 66 Energy Res. Soc. Sci. (2020). https://doi.org/10.1016/j.erss.2020.101481.

Teichmann, F. & Hürlimann, C. *Money Laundering and Terrorist Financing: Unsolved Problems.* 5 ZRFC 215 (2019).

Teichmann, F. & Köb, A. *Money Laundering and Terrorist Financing in the Antiques Trade – How Criminals in Europe Conduct Money Laundering and Terrorist Financing in the Disguise of the Antiques Trade.* 4 ZWF 217 (2018).

Teichmann, F. & Park, E. *Geldwäscherei und Terrorismusfinanzierung im Diamantenhandel.* 5/6 Compliance Berater 183 (2018a).

Teichmann, F. & Park, E. *Money Laundering and Terrorist Financing in the Trade of Jewellery and Antiques.* 3 ZRFC 119 (2018b).

Teichmann, F. & Park, E. Geldwäscherei und Terroismusfinanzierung über Beratungsunternehmen. 13 ZRFC 66 (2018c).

Thony, J. F. *Processing Financial Information in Money Laundering Matters: The Financial Intelligence Units.* 4 Eur. J. Crime Crim. L. & Crim. Just. 257 (1996).

Trautmann, K. & Kissler, M. *Kryptowerte: Hinweise und Besonderheiten betreffend die Prävention von Geldwäsche und Terrorismusfinanzierung.* 11 Compliance Berater 418 (2020).

Trechsel, S. *Money Laundering: Prevention and Measures to Combat It* (Schulthess Polygraphischer Verlag 1997).

Tsingou, E. *Global Financial Governance and the Developing Anti-money Laundering Regime: What Lessons for International Political Economy?* 47 International Politics 617 (2010).

Tsingou, E. *New Governors on the Block: The Rise of Anti-money Laundering Professionals.* 69 Crime L. Soc. Change 191 (2018).

Unger, B. *Money Laundering – A Newly Emerging Topic on the International Agenda.* 5 Rev. L. Econ. 807 (2009).

Unger, B. & Busuioc, E. M. *The Scale and Impacts of Money Laundering* (Edward Elgar Publishing 2007).

Unger, B., Siegel, M., Ferwerda, J., de Kruijf, W., Busuioic, M., Wokke, K. & Rawlings, G. *The Amounts and Effects of Money Laundering* (Ministry of Finance 2006).

Vaithilingam, S. & Nair, M. *Factors Affecting Money Laundering: Lesson for Developing Countries.* 10 J. Money Laund. Control 352 (2007).

Van Duyne, P. C. *Money-Laundering: Estimates in Fog.* 2 J. Financ. Crime 58 (1994).

Van Duyne, P. C. *Money-Laundering: Pavlov's Dog and Beyond.* 37 Howard J. Crim. Justice 359 (1998).

Van Duyne, P. C. *Money Laundering Policy – Fears and Facts.* Criminal Finances and Organising Crime in Europe 67 (P.C. Van Duyne, K. von Lampe & J.L. Newell, eds, Wolf Legal Publishers 2003).

Van Duyne, P. C., Groenhuijsen, M. S. & Schudelaro, A. A. P. *Balancing Financial Threats and Legal Interests in Money-Laundering Policy.* 43 Crime L. Soc. Change 117 (2005).

Van Duyne, P. C., Harvey, J. H. & Gelemerova, L. Y. *Money-Laundering: A Global Issue and Scarce Knowledge,* in The Critical Handbook of Money Laundering: Policy, Analysis and Myths 1 (P. C. Van Duyne, J. H. Harvey & L. Y. Gelemerova, eds, Palgrave Macmillan 2018).

Van Fossen, A. B. *Money Laundering, Global Financial Instability, and Tax Havens in the Pacific Islands.* 15 Contemp. Pac. 237 (2003).

Verhage, A. *Between the Hammer and the Anvil? The Anti-money Laundering-Complex and Its Interactions with the Compliance Industry.* 52 Crime L. Soc. Change 9 (2009).

Verhage, A. *Great Expectations but Little Evidence: Policing Money Laundering.* 37 Int'l J. Sociol. Soc. Policy 477 (2016).

Vlcek, W. *A Leviathan Rejuvenated: Surveillance, Money Laundering, and the War on Terror.* 20 Int'l J. Politics Cult. Soc. 21 (2008).

Vnukova, N., Kavun, S., Kolodiziev, O., Achkasova, S. & Hontar, D. *Determining the Level of Bank Connectivity for Combating Money Laundering, Terrorist Financing and Proliferation of Weapons of Mass Destruction.* 14 Banks Bank Syst. 42 (2019).

Walker, J. *How Big Is Global Money Laundering?* 3 J. Money Laund. Control 25 (1999).

Walker, J. & Unger, B. *Measuring Global Money Laundering: 'The Walker Gravity Model'.* 5 Rev. L. Econ. 821 (2009).

Watkins, R. C., Reynolds, K. M., Demara, R., Georgiopoulos, M., Gonzalez, A. & Eaglin, R. *Tracking Dirty Proceeds: Exploring Data Mining Technologies as Tools to Investigate Money Laundering.* 4 Police Pract. Res. 163 (2003).

Weber, J. & Kruisbergen, E. W. *Criminal Markets: The Dark Web, Money Laundering and Counterstrategies – An Overview of the 10th Research Conference on Organized Crime.* 22 Trends Organ. Crime 346 (2019). https://doi.org/10.1007/s12117-019-09365-8.

Welling, S. N. *Smurfs, Money Laundering, and the Federal Criminal Law: The Crime of Structuring Transactions.* 41 Fla. L. Rev. 287 (1989).

Williams, P. *Crime, Illicit Markets, and Money Laundering.* Managing Global Issues: Lessons Learned, 106 (P.J. Simmons & C. de Jonge Oudraat, eds, Carnegie Endowment for Int'l Peace 2001).

Wohlers, W. *BVerfG, 30. 3. 2004-2 BvR 1520/01. Geldwäsche durch Annehmen des Strafverteidigerhonorars?* 59 JuristenZeitung 670 (2004).

Wohlers, W. & Kudlich, H. *Wirtschaftsstrafrecht – Insbesondere Kapitalmarktstrafrecht, Insolvenzstrafrecht, Korruptionsstrafrecht, Glücksspiel und Geldwäsche.* 122 Zeitschrift für die gesamte Strafrechtswissenschaft 627 (2010).

Yeoh, P. *Banks' Vulnerabilities to Money Laundering Activities.* 23 J. Money Laund. Control 122 (2019).

Zagaris, B. *Merging of the Anti-money Laundering and Counter-terrorism Financial Enforcement Regimes After September 11, 2001.* 22 Berkeley J. Int'l L. 123 (2004).

Zagaris, B. & Castilla, S. M. *Constructing an International Financial Enforcement Subregime: The Implementation of Anti-money-laundering Policy.* 19 Brook. J. Int'l L. 871 (1993).

Zagaris, B. & MacDonald, S. B. *Money Laundering, Financial Fraud, and Technology: The Perils of an Instantaneous Economy.* 26 Geo. Wash. J. Int'l L. & Econ. 61 (1992).

Zali, M. & Maulidi, A. *Fighting Against Money Laundering.* 5 Brics L. J. 40 (2018).

Zdanowicz, J. S. *Money Laundering AND Terrorist Financing.* 47 Commun. ACM 53 (2004).

Zdanowicz, J. S. *Trade-Based Money Laundering and Terrorist Financing.* 5 Rev. L. Econ. 855 (2009).

Zhang, Z. M., Salerno, J. J. & Yu, P. S. *Applying Data Mining in Investigating Money Laundering Crimes.* Proceedings of the Ninth ACM SIGKDD International Conference on Knowledge Discovery and Data Mining 747 (2003).

Zolkaflil, S., Omar, N. & Nazri, S. N. F. S. M. *Implementation Evaluation: A Future Direction in Money Laundering Investigation.* 22 J. Money Laund. Control 318 (2019).

Internet Sources

3sat. *Art Washes Whiter – Of Art Trade, Corruption, Money Laundering* (2014). http://www.3sat.de/page/?source=/kulturzeit/themen/177518/index.html.

Aargauer Zeitung. *The Last Secret Is to Fall: Politicians Take Aim at the Bank Safe.* Aargauer Zeitung (11 August 2013). https://www.aargauerzeitung.ch/wirtschaft/das-letzte-geheimnis-soll-fallen-politiker-nehmen-den-bank-safe-ins-visier-ld.1783029.

Arnold, T. *UAE Strengthens Enforcement Against Money Laundering.* The National (1 May 2014). http://www.thenational.ae/business/industry-insights/finance/uae-strengthens-enforcement-against-money-laundering.

Bankers Academy. *Anti Money Laundering (AML) in the United Arab Emirates (UAE)* (2015). http://bankersacademy.com/resources/free-tutorials/57-ba-free-tutorials/608-aml-uae-sp-875.

Barone, R., Delle Side, D. & Masciandaro, D. *Drug Trafficking, Money Laundering and the Business Cycle: Does Secular Stagnation Include Crime?* BAFFI CAREFIN Centre Research Paper Series No. 47 (2017). http://ssrn.com/abstract=2896012.

Barone, R. & Masciandaro, D. *Cryptocurrency or Usury? Crime and Alternative Money Laundering Techniques.* Bocconi Working Paper No. 101 (2018). http://ssrn.com/abstract=3303871.

Bartz, T. *Suspicion of Money Laundering Worth Millions at Deutsche Bank.* Manager Magazin, Banken (20 May 2015). http://www. manager-magazin.de/companies/banken/verdacht-auf-millionenschwere-geldwaesche-in-der-deutschen-bank-a-1034618.html.

Buomberger, T. *Money Laundering: Luxurious Loopholes for Dirty Money.* Observer (17 January 2012). http://www.beobachter.ch/justiz-behoerde/gesetze-recht/artikel/geldwaescherei_luxurioese-schlupfloecher-fuer-schmutziges-geld/.

Buomberger, T. *Geldwäsche im Kunsthandel ist einfach.* Handelszeitung, Politics (12 May 2015). http://www.handelszeitung.ch/politik/geldwaesche-im-kunsthandel-ist-einfach-782327.

Breslow, S., Hagstroem, M., Mikkelsen, D. & Robu, K. *The New Frontier in Anti-money Laundering: New Analytical Tools and Surgical Automation Can Help Banks Take the Fight to Fraudsters* (2017). https://www.mckinsey.de/~/media/McKinsey/Business%20Functions/Risk/Our%20Insights/The%20new%20frontier%20in%20anti%20money%20laundering/The-new-frontier-in-anti-money-laundering.pdf.

Corriere del Mezzogiorno. *Money Laundering, 34 Arrests: In Handcuffs also Professor Lapis and a Regional Official.* Corriere del Mezzogiorno, Palermo (16 March 2013). https://corrieredelmezzogiorno.corriere.it/palermo/notizie/cronaca/2013/16-maggio-2013/riciclaggio-34-arresti-ci-sono-anche-due-carabinieri-magistrato-tar-lazio-2121164204352.shtml.

Deloitte. *About the Need of Forensic and Anti-money Laundering Services for Art Market Professionals* (2014). http://www2.deloitte.com/content/dam/Deloitte/lu/Documents/risk/lu-forensic-aml-art-market.pdf.

Der Spiegel. *Belgium: Little Paradise.* Der Spiegel (11 August 1997). http://www.spiegel.de/spiegel/print/d-8757970.html.

Die Welt. *EU Cracks Down on Money Laundering.* Die Welt, Economy (5 February 2013a). http://www.welt.de/newsticker/dpa_nt/infoline_nt/wirtschaft_nt/article113396670/EU-geht-gegen-Geldwaesche-vor.html.

Die Welt. *Money Laundering: A Playboy, a Gangster and a Swiss Account.* Die Welt, Money (19 April 2013b). http://www.welt.de/finanzen/article115432878/Ein-Playboy-ein-Gangster-und-ein-Schweizer-Konto.html.

Fahmi, M. *Interview: 'The Real Estate Sector Is Vulnerable to Money Laundering'.* Tagesanzeiger (29 October 2010). http://www.tagesanzeiger.ch/schweiz/standard/Der-Immobiliensektor-ist-anfaellig-fuer-Geldwaescherei/story/14106128.

Financial Times. *UAE Updates Money Laundering Regulations* (2008). http://www.ft.com/intl/cms/s/0/25d75988-4098-11dd-bd48-0000779fd2ac.html#axzz3gkCszcYk.

Financial Times. *Law Firms Scrutinized in Anti-money Laundering Push* (2014). http://www.ft.com/intl/cms/s/0/0edb6ed4-3521-11e4-a2c2-00144feabdc0.html#axzz3gkCszcYk.

Finews. *Money Laundering: Need for Action in Switzerland* (28 January 2021). https://www.finews.ch/news/finanzplatz/44794-transparency-international-schweiz-korruptionsbekaempfung-geldwaescherei.

Focus. *Economy: Panama Cracks Down on Money Laundering.* Focus, News (28 April 2015). http://www.focus.de/finanzen/news/wirtschaftsticker/konjunktur-panama-geht-gegen-geldwaesche-vor_id_4643268.html.

Forgang, G. *Money Laundering Through Cryptocurrencies.* Economic Crime Forensics Capstones, 40 (2019). https://digitalcommons.lasalle.edu/ecf_capstones/40?utm_source=digitalcommons.lasalle.edu%2Fecf_capstones%2F40&utm_medium=PDF&utm_campaign=PDFCoverPages.

Gara, M., Manaresi, F., Marchetti, D. J. & Marinucci, M. *The Impact of Anti-money Laundering Oversight on Banks' Suspicious Transaction Reporting: Evidence from Italy.* Banca d'Italia Occasional Papers No. 491 (2019). https://www.bancaditalia.it/pubblicazioni/qef/2019-0491/QEF_491_19.pdf.

Giuffrida, A. *Dubai Labors under Money-Laundering Image*. New York Times (1 December 2010). http://www.nytimes.com/2010/12/02/business/global/02iht-m02blaunder.html?_r = 0.

Goldhill, O. *Colombia Investigates Gold Trades for Suspected Cocaine Money-laundering*. The Telegraph (26 May 2014). http://www. telegraph.co.uk/finance/financial-crime/10857780/Colombia-investigates-gold-trades-for-suspected-cocaine-money-laundering.html.

Handelszeitung. *Ausbleibende Miete überführt Geldwäscher*. Handelszeitung, Politics (14 May 2013). http://www.handelszeitung.ch/politik/ausbleibende-miete-ueberfuehrt-geldwaescher.

Handelszeitung. *Schweiz bleibt attraktiv für Geldwäsche*. Handelszeitung, Money (19 June 2015). http://www.handelszeitung.ch/invest/schweiz-bleibt-attraktiv-fuer-geldwaesche-800688.

Hunter, L. *Is the Federal Reserve Using Money-Laundering Techniques to Cleanse Banks' Balance Sheets?* Forbes (29 October 2012). http://www.forbes.com/sites/lawrencehunter/2012/10/29/are-federal-reserve-regulated-banks-laundering-dirty-money/.

International Monetary Fund. *Anti-money Laundering/Combating the Financing of Terrorism (ALM/CFT). Reference Materials, Research and Publications* (2015). http://www. imf.org/external/np/leg/amlcft/eng/aml4.htm.

Jahn, J. *After OECD Rebuke: Federal Government Takes Tougher Action Against Money Laundering*. Frankfurter Allgemeine Zeitung, Economy (2012). http://www.faz.net/aktuell/wirtschaft/nach-oecd-ruege-bundesregierung-geht-schaerfer-gegen-geldwaesche-vor-12912495.html.

Mair, S. *Geldwäsche mit Kunst: Härtere Regeln nicht gefragt*. Handelszeitung, Company (12 June 2013a). https://www.handelszeitung.ch/unternehmen/geldwaesche-mit-kunst-haertere-regeln-nicht-gefragt.

Mair, S. *Warnung vor Geldwäsche im Kunsthandel*. Handelszeitung, Politics (12 June 2013b). https://www.handelszeitung.ch/politik/warnung-vor-geldwaesche-im-kunsthandel.

Meldestelle für Geldwäscherei, Jahresbericht 2018 (April 2019). https://www.google.com/url?sa = t&rct = j&q = &esrc = s&source = web&cd = &ved = 2ahUKEwjc-4mqn93xAhXE_rsIHfLNAIEQFjABegQICRAD&url = https%3A%2F%2Fwww.fedpol.admin.ch%2Fdam%2Ffedpol%2Fde%2Fdata%2Fkriminalitaet%2Fgeldwaescherei%2Fjabe%2Fjb-mros-2018-d.pdf.download.pdf%2Fjb-mros-2018-d.pdf&usg = AOvVaw0g0P4iiDcuUPIFrq7d7q-u.

Müller, S.C. *Mafia-Like Structures: Criminals Use Spain As a Money Laundering Paradise*. Wirtschaftswoche, Politics (2015). http://www.wiwo.de/politik/europa/mafioese-structures-criminals-use-spain-as-money-laundering-paradise/11542094.html.

Neue Zürcher Zeitung. *Control of Bureaux de Change: New British Steps Against Money Laundering*. Neue Zürcher Zeitung (16 October 2001). http://www.nzz.ch/article7Q67J-1.487589.

Neue Zürcher Zeitung. *Possible Concealment of the Criminal Origin of Cash: Art Trade Vulnerable to Money Laundering.* Neue Zürcher Zeitung (30 June 2009). http://www.nzz.ch/kunsthandel-geldwaesche-1.2852770.

Neue Zürcher Zeitung. *EU Tightens Fight Against Money Laundering.* Neue Zürcher Zeitung, Wirtschaft (17 December 2014). http://www. nzz.ch/economy/eu-tightens-fight-against-money-laundering-1.18546054.

Palazzolo, S. *Finance Infiltrator in the Money Laundering Network – Arrested Lapis, Ciancimino's Former Front Man.* Nunzio Spanò (2 December 2011). https://nunziospano.com/2011/12/02/infiltrato-della-finanza-nella-rete-del-riciclaggio-arrestato-lapis-ex-prestanome-di-ciancimino/.

Pipitone, G. *Palermo, Found a Recycling Centre. A Judge and Two Carabinieri in Handcuffs.* Il Fatto Quotidiano, Chronicle (16 March 2011). http://www.ilfattoquotidiano.it/2013/05/16/palermo-trovata-centrale-del-riciclaggio-in-manette-anche-magistrato-del-tar-del/595504/.

Ramthun, C. *Money Laundering: Suspicion of Money Laundering in Luxury Purchases.* Wirtschaftswoche, Finanzen (2012). http://www.wiwo.de/finanzen/steuern-recht/geldwaesche-geldwaescheverdacht-beim-luxuskauf/6215652.html.

Reuters. *EU Parliament Adopts Rules Against Money Laundering and Tax Fraud.* Reuters (2015). http://de.reuters.com/article/worldNews/idDEKBN0O51Q220150520.

Rose-Ackerman, S. *Corruption, Organized Crime, and Money Laundering.* World Bank Roundtable on Institutions, Governance and Corruption. Montevideo (26–27 May 2016). http://www.ridge.uy/wp-content/uploads/2016/05/Rose-Ackerman_Susan.pdf.

Salmen, I. *Berlin 'Bulky Waste Mafia' Cheats Google Out of Half a Million Euros.* Tagesspiegel, Berlin (15 January 2021). https://www.tagesspiegel.de/berlin/polizei-justiz/internet-anzeigen-nicht-bezahlt-berliner-sperrmuellmafia-betruegt-google-um-eine-halbe-million-euro/26822284.html.

Schumacher, P. & Bossard, T. *Banks Again in the Spotlight Despite Stricter Money Laundering Rules.* SRF, News (24 January 2021). https://www.srf.ch/news/schweiz/finanzplatz-schweiz-banken-erneut-im-zwielicht-trotz-schaerferen-geldwascherei-regeln.

Sonntagszeitung. *Swiss Business with the Drug Lords' Gold.* Sonntagszeitung (2014). http://www.sonntagszeitung. ch/read/sz_26_10_2014/focus/Swiss-business-with-the-gold-of-the-drug-bosses-17783.

Spiegel Online. *Deutsche Bank Reports Money Laundering Suspicions in Russia.* Spiegel, Economy (20 May 2015). http://www.spiegel.de/wirtschaft/unternehmen/deutsche-bank-meldet-geldwaesche-verdacht-in-russland-a-1034773.html.

Stefano, R. *Goldraffininerien: Unter dem Radar.* Handelszeitung, Money (2 January 2013). http://www.handelszeitung.ch/invest/goldraffinerien-unter-dem-radar.

Süddeutsche Zeitung. *Geldwäschegesetz – Einmal Barren für 15'000 Euro, bitte.* Süddeutsche Zeitung (2011). http://www.sueddeutsche.de/wirtschaft/geldwaeschegesetz-psst-wollen-sie-nen-barren-kaufen-1.1133077.

Tagesanzeiger. *Safe Deposit Boxes Attract Dirty Money in Ticino.* Tagesanzeiger, Economy (4 December 2014). http://www.tagesanzeiger.ch/wirtschaft/Schliessfaecher-ziehen-im-Tessin-schmutziges-Geld-an/story/25202432.

Tagesschau. *New EU Directive Against Money Laundering: The Death of the Letterbox Company?* Tagesschau (20 May 2015). https://www.tagesschau.de/wirtschaft/eu-geldwaesche-101.html.

Tagesspiegel. *Video: Mafia Launders Money with Gold.* Tagesspiegel (2012). http://www.tagesspiegel.de/wirtschaft/video-mafia-waescht-geld-mit-gold/6972138.html.

The Independent. *The Great British Money Launderette: At Least 19 UK Firms Under Investigation for an Alleged Conspiracy to Make $20bn of Dirty Money Seem Legitimate.* The Independent (2014). http://www.independent.co.uk/news/business/news/the-great-british-money-launderette-at-least-19-uk-firms-under-investigation-for-alleged-conspiracy-to-make-20bn-of-dirty-money-seem-legitimate-9797097.html.

Theurer, M. *London's Property Market Is a Paradise for Money Laundering.* Frankfurter Allgemeine Zeitung, Wirtschaft (2015). http://www. faz.net/aktuell/wirtschaft/immobilien/londons-immobilienmarkt-ist-ein-paradies-fuer-geldwaesche-13463694.html.

Thompson, T. *Drug Gangs Go to London's Diamond Dealers for Cash.* The Guardian (9 March 2003). https://www.theguardian.com/uk/2003/mar/09/drugsandalcohol.ukcrime.

Zeit Online. *Money Laundering: The New Law Cannot Put a Stop to Organised Criminals: 'Always One Step Ahead'.* Zeit Online, Economy (1994). http://www.zeit.de/1994/46/immer-einen-schritt-voraus/seite-2.

Trade Arabia. *Dubai Police in New Drive to Combat Money Laundering.* Trade Arabia, Finance & Capital Market (7 March 2015). http://www.tradearabia.com/news/BANK_277005.html.

Transparency International. *Corruption, Money Laundering and Compliance in International Business Transactions – A Stocktaking* (2014). https://www.transparency.de/fileadmin/pdfs/Further_Dates/Events-Archive/Hammacher_Petersberger_Schiedsgerichtstage_Tagungsunterlage.pdf.

Trettmann, N. *Black Money: London's Properties Are True Money Laundering Wonders.* Die Welt, Wirtschaft (6 August 2014). http://www.welt.de/wirtschaft/article130919720/Londons-Immobilien-sind-wahre-Geldwaesche-Wunder.html.

Ungerman, J. *The IRS Targets Jewelers for Compliance with Anti-money Laundering Rules.* Forbes (21 March 2011). http://www.forbes.com/sites/irswatch/2011/03/21/the-irs-targets-jewelers-for-compliance-with-anti-money-laundering-rules/.

United Nations Office on Drugs and Crime. *United Nations Instruments and International Standards* (2015). https://www.unodc.org/unodc/en/money-laundering/Instruments-Standards.html.

Wirtschaftsblatt, *Fine in the Millions: Deutsche Bank Loses Face in Dubai.* Wirtschaftsblatt (2015). http://wirtschaftsblatt.at/home/boerse/europa/4709042/MillionenStrafe_Deutsche-Bank-mit-Gesichtsverlust-in-Dubai.

Index

C